Managing Human Resources
in Africa

As rival economies such as Asia mature, attention is now shifting to new frontiers
like Africa. But academic debate too often neglects the complexities and diversity
of this continent, and the challenges faced by both multinational companies working
across Africa and domestic African companies, particularly in the human resource
(HR) field.

Managing Human Resources in Africa is a refreshing new book that boldly tackles the
HR challenges in countries right across the African continent, examining the impact of
contextual factors on the development of HR practices in Africa.

Taking a regional approach to the subject, and featuring chapters on South Africa,
Botswana, Zambia, Mauritius, Tanzania, Kenya, Ethiopia, Ghana, Ivory Coast, Tunisia,
and Libya, this comprehensive study is written and edited by those with the knowledge
and experience of the complexities of the continent. It offers a fresh perspective on
a growing subject area, and shows readers not only how to develop techniques and
practices that reflect the real needs of workers in Africa, but also provides a more
balanced analysis of the area than they might usually expect.

Valuable to not only students and researchers in international management, human
resources, organization theory and cross-cultural management, this topical and
much-needed study is also critical reading for managers of multinational companies
and domestic managers in Africa.

Ken N. Kamoche is Associate Professor at City University of Hong Kong.
Yaw A. Debrah is Reader at Brunel University, UK. **Frank M. Horwitz** is Professor
at the University of Cape Town, South Africa. **Gerry Nkombo Muuka** is Associate
Professor at Murray State University, USA.

Routledge Global Human Resource Management Series

Edited by Randall S. Schuler, Susan E. Jackson, Paul Sparrow and Michael Poole

Routledge Global Human Resource Management is an important new series that examines human resources in its global context. The series is organized into three strands: content and issues in global Human Resource Management (HRM); specific HR functions in a global context; and comparative HRM. Authored by some of the world's leading authorities on HRM, each book in the series aims to give readers comprehensive, indepth and accessible texts that combine essential theory and best practice. Topics covered include cross-border alliances, global leadership, global relations and global staffing.

Managing Human Resources in Cross-Border Alliances
Randall S. Schuler, Susan E. Jackson and Yadong Luo

Managing Human Resources in Africa
Edited by Ken N. Kamoche, Yaw A. Debrah, Frank M. Horwitz, and Gerry Nkombo Muuka

Managing Human Resources in Africa

Edited by Ken N. Kamoche, Yaw A. Debrah, Frank M. Horwitz, and Gerry Nkombo Muuka

Routledge
Taylor & Francis Group

LONDON AND NEW YORK

First published 2004 by
Routledge 11 New Fetter Lane, London EC4P 4EE

Simultaneously published in the USA and Canada by
Routledge 29 West 35th Street, New York, NY 10001

Routledge is an imprint of the Taylor & Francis Group

Typeset in Times New Roman by
Keystroke, Jacaranda Lodge, Wolverhampton
Printed and bound in Great Britain by
TJ International Ltd, Padstow, Cornwall

British Library Cataloguing in Publication Data
A catalogue record for this book is available from the British Library

Library of Congress Cataloging in Publication Data
    Managing human resources in Africa / edited by Ken N. Kamoche . . . [*et al.*].—1st ed.
       p. cm. — (Routledge global human resource management series; 2)
    Includes bibliography references and indexes.
    1. Personnel management—Africa.   2. International business
enterprises—Personnel management. I. Kamoche, Ken N. II. Series.

    HF5549.2.A35M36 2003
    658.3′00967—dc21   2003008118

ISBN 0–415–36948–7 (hbk)
ISBN 0–415–36949–5 (pbk)

For Anna, Mum and the memory of Dad

Ken

Kwadwo Debrah and Afua Fofie

Yaw

To Dianne

Frank

To Mum and Dad: Mary Mutinta Muuka and Cornerious Mufundisi Muuka, back in Monze, Zambia

Gerry

Contents

Illustrations

Figure

Tables

Contributors

Abdoulhakem Almhdie is a faculty member at Sabha University, Libya, Faculty of Economics. He is currently completing a Ph.D. at Northumbria University, Newcastle upon Tyne.

Samuel Aryee is a Professor of Human Resource Management and Organizational Behavior at Hong Kong Baptist University. He obtained his Ph.D. from McMaster University, Ontario.

Constant D. Beugré is an Associate Professor at Delaware State University. He holds Ph.D.s from Rensselaer Polytechnic Institute, Troy, New York, and from the Université Paris X, Nanterre.

Yaw A. Debrah is Reader in Management and International Business at Brunel University, West London. He holds a Ph.D. from Warwick University.

Frank M. Horwitz is Professor in Business Administration, University of Cape Town. He obtained his Ph.D. from the University of the Witwatersrand.

Ken N. Kamoche is Associate Professor in Management at City University of Hong Kong. He obtained his D.Phil. from Oxford University as a Rhodes scholar.

Aminu Mamman is a Senior Lecturer at the Institute for Development Policy and Management, University of Manchester. He received his Ph.D. from Cardiff Business School.

Semaw Mekonnen is Human Resource and Administration Director of Food for the Hungry International/Ethiopia. He holds an M.Sc. degree from the University of Manchester.

Dorothy Mpabanga is a lecturer at the University of Botswana. She is currently a Doctoral Researcher at the University of Strathclyde in Glasgow.

Munyae M. Mulinge is a Senior Lecturer of Sociology at the University of Botswana at Gaborone. He obtained his Ph.D. from the University of Iowa.

Gerry Nkombo Muuka is an Associate Professor of Business Strategy at Murray State University, Kentucky. He obtained his Ph.D. from Edinburgh University.

Kenneth Kaoma Mwenda, a Rhodes scholar, is presently with the World Bank, Washington DC.
He earned his Ph.D. at the University of Warwick.

Stella M. Nkomo is the Bateman Professor of Business Leadership at the University of South Africa. She received her Ph.D. from the University of Massachusetts at Amherst.

Stephen M. Nyambegera is a Senior Lecturer at Daystar University, Nairobi. He received his Ph.D. from the University of Sheffield.

Mahamed Rajah is Associate Professor at the University of South Africa.

Anita Ramgutty-Wong is Senior Lecturer in Human Resource Management at the University of Mauritius.

Mahmoud Yagoubi is an Associate Professor at the University of René Descartes, Paris 5. He is currently a Ph.D. student at the University of Panthéon-Sorbonne.

Foreword

Global HRM is a series of books edited and authored by some of the best and most well-known researchers in the field of human resource management. This series is aimed at offering students and practitioners accessible, coordinated, and comprehensive books in global HRM. To be used individually or together, these books cover the main bases of comparative and international HRM. Taking an expert look at an increasingly important and complex area of global business, this is a groundbreaking new series that answers a real need for serious textbooks on global HRM.

Several books in this series, Global HRM, are devoted to human resource management policies and practices in multinational enterprises. Some books focus on specific areas of HRM policies and practices, such as global leadership, global compensation, global staffing, and global labor relations. Other books address special topics that arise in multinational enterprises such as managing HR in cross-border alliances, the role of the HR profession, and the role of HR in multinational enterprises.

In addition to books on HRM in multinational enterprises, several other books in the series will adopt a comparative approach to understanding HRM. These books on comparative human resource management describe the HRM policies and practices found at the local level in selected countries in several regions of the world. The comparative books utilize a common framework that makes it easier for the reader to systematically understand the rationale for the HRM practices in different countries. This book, *Managing HR in Africa*, edited by Ken Kamoche, Yaw Debrah, Frank Horwitz, and Gerry Muuka, is the first of these comparative HR books. Featuring contributions from the experts, this book is organized by country and includes full chapters on countries across the length and breadth of Africa, from Tunisia and Libya in the north to South Africa and Botswana in the south; from Kenya and Tanzania in the east to Ivory Coast and Ghana in the west. This is the first book to tackle HRM across Africa on such a scale. We are optimistic that you will be as impressed as we are with this book.

This Routledge series, Global HRM, is intended to serve the growing market of scholars and practitioners who are seeking a deeper and broader understanding of the role and importance of human resource management in companies as they operate throughout the world. With this in mind, all books in the series provide a thorough review of existing research and numerous examples of companies around the world. Mini-company stories and examples are found throughout the chapters. In addition, many of the books in the series include at least one detailed case description that serves as a convenient practical illustrations of topics discussed in the book.

Because a significant number of scholars and practitioners throughout the world are involved in researching and practicing the topics examined in this series of books, the authorship of the books and the experiences of companies cited in them reflect a vast global representation. The authors in the series bring with them exceptional knowledge of the HRM topics they address. In many cases the authors have been the pioneers for their topics, so we feel fortunate to have the involvement of such a distinguished group of academics in this series.

The publisher and editor also have played a major role in making this series possible. Routledge has provided its global production, marketing, and reputation to make this series feasible and affordable to academics and practitioners throughout the world. In addition, Routledge has provided its own highly qualified professionals to make this series a reality. In particular we want to indicate our deep appreciation for the work of our series editor, Francesca Poynter. She, and her predecessor Catriona King, have been behind the series from the very beginning and have been invaluable in providing the needed support and encouragement to us and to the many authors in the series. She, along with her staff, has helped make the process of completing this series an enjoyable one. For everything they have done, we thank them all.

Randall S. Schuler, Rutgers University/GSBA Zurich
Paul Sparrow, Manchester University
Susan E. Jackson, Rutgers University/GSBA Zurich
Michael Poole, Cardiff University

Preface

KEN N. KAMOCHE, GERRY NKOMBO MUUKA,
FRANK M. HORWITZ, AND YAW A. DEBRAH

An introductory background

The terrain of management in Africa remains largely unexplored as researchers
continue to set their sights on the West and the East. The debate on management in
Africa has remained in limbo somewhere between these two geographical spaces.
There has been an enormous amount of work on economic development, trade, and
foreign aid. This particular emphasis signals some of the more significant priorities for
Africa: those revolving around economic development and the eradication of poverty.
In the majority of cases, the State still plays a predominant role in driving industrial and
economic development through a wide range of mechanisms, including investing through
parastatal organizations, soliciting foreign aid, and employment creation. When most
African countries were gaining independence, particularly in the 1960s and 1970s,
these measures proved particularly critical because colonial administrations of the
time had failed to engender a broad-based and thriving private sector.

Managing Human Resources in Africa is a book inspired by the need to not only
examine management practices in Africa, but also to highlight the realities and
challenges faced by both local and foreign companies as they confront human resource
management concerns on the continent. As the various contributors to this volume point
out, economic and industrial development in Africa has been hampered by a number
of factors, both internal and external to the continent. Among these are the harsh global
economic realities which directly impact Africa, economic mismanagement, political
ineptitude, and corruption. In spite of impressive advances in education and training,
Africa is experiencing a serious brain drain as many pursue greener pastures in other
countries in Africa or overseas. Factors that drive Africans away from home range
from the more extreme life-threatening ones (such as civil wars) to socio-economic
concerns such as a lack of employment opportunities occasioned by stagnant economies
and declining opportunities for personal growth, particularly among professionals.
When professionals educated at huge public expense depart to pursue their careers
elsewhere, African countries are deprived of a great opportunity to generate and
sustain the human capital on whose shoulders lies the urgent search for solutions to
the continent's multifaceted development challenge.

Foreign firms can play a vital role in Africa by developing human capital, investing in leadership capital, and diffusing knowledge; while recognizing that the vast opportunities available to them in Africa go beyond merely "exploiting" cheap resources (Harvey *et al.*, 2002). They have a responsibility to act responsibly, responding to the needs of their African partners and employees, and being sensitive to the local cultures and environment. Apart from the traditional approach of investing in factories, training local workers, and transferring managerial expertise and technology, multinational firms need to formulate new mechanisms for knowledge diffusion which recognize that knowledge-diffusion is a two-way symbiotic process. Research in these activities also needs to progress from the overwhelming concern with cultural differences to a consideration of concepts like "timescapes," which recognize that knowledge transfer and international competition involve critical temporal dimensions, a time-oriented mindset, and organizational agility (Harvey and Kamoche, 2003). As African economies are drawn increasingly within the hypercompetitive business world through the forces of globalization, the capacity to achieve some degree of synchronicity with international collaborators and competitors becomes a critical determining factor in how to leverage knowledge. This is currently difficult to achieve because of the brain drain, and the fact that Africa is yet to take full advantage of the opportunities available through technological advancement and the emergence of the knowledge economy.

The challenge of managing people

While sandwiched uneasily between the two larger domains of the East and West, human resource management (HRM) problems and challenges in Africa have not been addressed critically in the mainstream literature. Contributions to a 2002 special issue on HRM in Africa in the *International Journal of Human Resource Management*, edited by Ken Kamoche, noted that much work remains to be done to strengthen the theoretical underpinnings of HRM and to bring about more effective management practices. Human resource issues that have been identified in the emergent literature include the inappropriate use of foreign concepts, a reliance on particularistic practices driven by local institutional and legislative regimes and nepotistic considerations, lack of transparency in often highly politiciced decision making, and a concern with procedural and transactional HRM rather than strategic issues.

These issues reflect important concerns about the way people are managed in Africa. They also represent the kinds of impediments that managers have to overcome before HRM can come of age. Contemporary ideas are gradually being introduced by multinational firms as well as by local managers taking MBA degrees locally and abroad. They, too, are just as concerned about the contribution of HRM to organizational performance as are researchers in the mainstream literature debating the contribution of HRM to competitive advantage (Schuler and Jackson, 1999). Given the nature of African society which is characterized by extended family, patriarchal, and often collective decision-making considerations, HRM cannot simply be viewed as a set of practices expected to contribute to the achievement of organizationally defined objectives. Managers often have to satisfy many stakeholders, some of whom represent institutional interests that contribute little to organizational strategic issues but impact profoundly on the organization's very existence. This might happen when instructions are received "from above" to hire or promote particular people, or when training activities are undertaken for political rather than developmental ends. These realities suggest that the prescription and, more importantly, the application of standard management tools cannot always be expected to work.

In parastatal organizations (the term commonly given to the public sector in Africa), where there is typically insufficient procedural discipline, the challenge of managing people according to well-known precepts can easily become a futile activity. This is not to argue that so-called modern management practices have no place in the African workplace. On the contrary, managers in Africa fully recognize the need to apply mechanisms, tools, and practices that are effective, developmental, and appropriate. The point to note is that the adoption of HR practices does not exist in a vacuum. It is important to understand the particular contextual circumstances within which managers operate, the sort of challenges they face, and how they respond to those challenges. This is important if we are to develop appropriate theory and practice of HRM in developing countries or emergent economies (see also, Budhwar and Debrah, 2001; Kamoche, 2000).

One recent effort to formulate a paradigm for managing in Africa is the concept of "ubuntu"—the notion that "I exist because of others" (Mbigi and Maree, 1995). Ubuntu is said to signify an indigenous African philosophy of management which captures the complex social relations between people and the idea of caring for others as though they were members of one's own family. The emergence of such world views clearly signifies the need for researchers to take a more critical look at the challenges of managing people and how HR approaches might be better informed by prevailing socio-philosophical developments.

Many observers tend to make sweeping generalizations about the "African management context" while ignoring the very unique features exemplified in each country. The diversity of Africa cuts across many dimensions: ethnically, with some 2,000 different ethno-cultural communities; historically, with effects going back to whether the country is a former colony of Britain, France, and Portugal for example; politically, with (military) dictatorships alongside democracies; economically, with several high-income countries amidst a poverty-stricken majority, and various shades of socialism/capitalism. It is also erroneous to assume homogeneity within specific countries since many African countries are a loose collection of diverse ethno-cultural communities struggling to establish an identity as a nation-state.

It is impossible to do justice to the entirety of African countries in one volume. However, by including a wide range of countries that span the length and breadth of the continent, we aim to present the reader with as rich a flavor as is possible within the space constraints of the diversity of the challenges, opportunities, and complexities that lie beneath the rather amorphous landscape of the "African management context." These chapters will hopefully highlight the important trends and patterns that have been emerging on the continent and how the extant HR practices and policies have been shaped by industrial, socio-cultural, legal-political, and institutional factors.

In countries like Zambia and Ghana that have undertaken extensive privatization of state-owned enterprises (SOEs), the HRM landscape has been reshaped in many significant and lasting ways. Many Zambian SOEs, for instance, have been bought by South African companies, whose managers have brought their own HRM practices to bear on employment practices in Zambia. As a number of contributors have shown, the Southern African region (in particular Botswana and South Africa) has emerged as a catchment area for talent from other parts of Africa, in particular East and Central Africa. With regard to South Africa, this brain drain in part reflects the neglect of education and training during the apartheid years.

Much has been written about labor relations in Africa, and there has also been a substantial body of knowledge on the challenges and difficulties of transferring technology to the continent, as well as the strategies for rejuvenating African economies. Foreign investors tend to rely heavily on this corpus of knowledge in deciding whether to invest in Africa or not. What is lacking is knowledge at the level of the organization, in particular how to apply HR techniques which are not only suitable for the context in question but which are effective in improving organizational performance.

In the absence of reliable knowledge on the HR situation in Africa, investors and expatriate managers are likely to make inappropriate decisions and to ignore the unique features of the African context as they import their thinking and practices. Asia offers some useful lessons. Back in the early to mid-1980s, when the West first became fascinated by Japanese management practices and sought to emulate the success of Japanese firms, there was an explosion of literature dedicated to understanding Japanese culture and business practices. A decade later, interest shifted to China, where scholars have been grappling with elusive concepts like *guanxi* (networking) and "face." This region is seen as offering the kind of business opportunities that may be absent in Africa today. However, it is evident that scholars and management practitioners alike have made efforts to learn about the respective cultures of Asian countries, if for no other reason than to avoid embarrassing faux pas while conducting business negotiations. As Africa seeks to attract foreign investors, and as the latter begin looking more closely at African markets as the Asian ones begin to mature, there is a real need for both interested parties to devise ways to learn more effectively from each other.

There are many challenges facing workers as well as managers in Africa today. Forced to open their markets as part of World Bank and IMF structural adjustment programs (SAPs), and finding many foreign markets closed to their products, organizations have borne the brunt of globalization, resulting in plant closures and high unemployment. In the worst case scenarios, countries like the Democratic Republic of Congo and Somali have been so ravaged by war that they have no real economy to speak of, while ceasing or almost ceasing to function as modern nation-states. There have also been some success stories, and these need to be acknowledged and studied so that useful lessons can be drawn not merely at the level of economic transformation and democratization but also in the development and use of appropriate and effective human resource practices.

A summary of the contributions

Our intellectual journey across Africa begins from the south and proceeds through the east, central, and west, and ends in the north. In Chapter 1, Frank M. Horwitz, Stella M. Nkomo, and Mahamed Rajah highlight the need to address the discriminatory legacy of apartheid and adversarial relationships. They argue that HR strategies should be formulated at both the national and organizational levels. Legislative requirements to enhance racial and gender diversity also require systemic change in HR practices and transformation of organizational cultures. They evaluate the dual challenges of achieving both employment equity, necessary to redress past unfair discrimination, and achieving high performance, necessary for competitive advantage.

In Chapter 2, Dorothy Mpabanga details how, over a three-decade period, Botswana rose from one of the poorest nations in the world to one of the fastest growing economies and an African economic success story. These macro-economic advances have not, however, been matched by effective strategies in the management of people, particularly in the public sector. This is now a major challenge for Botswana, including how to grapple with problems like high unemployment, poverty, and HIV/AIDS.

In Chapter 3, Gerry Nkombo Muuka and Kenneth Kaoma Mwenda trace the HRM landscape in Zambia with a review of past practices, present realities, and what they see as future HRM challenges in the country. They consider the impact of issues like privatization and unemployment on HRM practices, as well as HRM challenges that have continent-wide implications, such as the HIV and AIDS crisis, Africa's huge informal sector, and the likely beneficial role of electronic human resources management (e-HRM).

Chapter 4 takes us to the Indian Ocean island of Mauritius. Anita Ramgutty-Wong discusses how factors like adaptability in international trade, long-term strategic thinking, a commitment to training and education, and so forth, have combined to make Mauritius one of Africa's most impressive economies. The pressures of globalization are now forcing Mauritian managers to rethink their strategies for developing sound management and cultivating a high quality and competent workforce against a backdrop of entrenched nepotism.

In Chapter 5, Yaw A. Debrah analyzes the first East African country, Tanzania. He examines how a history of socialism meant to ensure self-reliance and equitable distribution of income ultimately ground the economy to a halt, subsequently necessitating unprecedented reforms. A series of reforms have brought about some measure of economic recovery and the country is now embarking on efforts to bring about an improvement in the creation and utilization of human resource stocks, particularly in the public sector. The challenge is to ensure that the private sector follows suit and that the reforms do not alienate those they are supposed to benefit: the workers.

In Chapter 6, Ken N. Kamoche, Stephen M. Nyambegera, and Munyae M. Mulinge analyze the HR challenges in Kenya. They argue that after independence Kenya started off on a promising note and was seen as an engine of growth for East Africa. Unfortunately, these dreams were not fulfilled as political ineptitude, economic mismanagement, and endemic corruption plunged the economy into a spiral of decline and stagnation. As in Botswana and South Africa, human resource stocks are also under threat from AIDS and a serious case of brain drain. With the installation of a new democratic government in early 2003, there is hope now that some of these problems can be resolved, with the ultimate objective of improving the plight of ordinary people.

Chapter 7 takes a look at Ethiopia. Semaw Mekonnen and Aminu Mamman note that, against the backdrop of a chequered political past, Ethiopia has lagged behind in the education, training, and development of her people. Crucially, education and training seem to be at odds with the needs of the economy. This problem has further been exacerbated by a brain drain as Ethiopians pursue a better quality of life abroad. The authors recommend the introduction of modern management practices while recognizing the limitations imposed by factors like governmental interference, nepotism, and various cultural factors.

In Chapter 8, Samuel Aryee analyzes HRM in Ghana. He notes that Ghana started off at independence on a very promising economic and political note but, in a familiar theme, was derailed through economic mismanagement and political ineptitude. This context has subsequently had a significant impact on the generation of human resource stocks and the use of appropriate human resource practices. The author proposes some approaches for addressing these weaknesses and helping organizations adopt more effective human resource practices.

In Chapter 9, Constant D. Beugré examines Ivory Coast, a country which has enjoyed relative economic success and serves as an economic powerhouse for francophone Africa. The analysis proceeds to identify the role of culture on management practices and proposes how the introduction of new management practices and information technology might contribute to the better utilization of human resources.

In our first of two chapters on the Maghreb, Mahmoud Yagoubi analyzes HRM in Tunisia. He considers various cultural, political, and economic factors that have shaped the practice of HRM over the decades, and how these practices have struggled to gain acceptance in the Tunisian business environment. Thus, while substantial progress has been made in education, employee selection, and training, there still remain concerns about managerial competence, especially amongst HR managers. The author finds that this is a matter of concern as the subsequent leadership styles result in high absenteeism and high turnover.

Abdoulhakem Almhdie and Stephen M. Nyambegera take a look at Libya in Chapter 11. They examine the origins and effects of the country's revolutionary political ideology which combines socialism and Islam. In the earlier days, this ideology sought to combat bureaucratic inefficiency and political apathy, among other things, and to create a sense of participation in government and economic activity amongst the people. The authors analyze the various challenges and achievements over the years in the management of people and identify the need to address current shortages in skilled labor.

While the rest of the book explores the HRM terrain and examines the diverse HRM practices in Africa, the final chapter takes a different path. Here, the editors turn their attention to the key themes emerging from the chapters. The identified themes discussed in this chapter are those that we believe are likely to spawn future research, contribute meaningfully to the debates in the field, and have the potential to enhance our understanding of HRM policies and practices in Africa. To this end, the emergent themes and issues discussed provide not only food for thought but also a research agenda for rigorous and empirical academic research in HRM in Africa.

Concluding remarks

Managing Human Resources in Africa combines features that are both rare and unique among HRM texts. It is one of very few books that employ a multi-country approach to management in Africa, offering a teaching, research, and practical perspective. In this regard, it has important lessons for a variety of stakeholders including policy makers in and outside Africa, graduate and undergraduate management students, as well as consultants and researchers interested in a multidimensional perspective of human resources management. The contributors to this volume were selected on account of their intimate knowledge of the respective countries they are writing about and their ability to bring a revelatory perspective to their analysis. Virtually all were either born or partly educated in Africa, and continue to engage in research, consultancy, and teaching on the continent. Spread across institutions around the world, the editors and authors bring their collective cross-cultural knowledge to bear on one of the most important challenges of our times: the need to educate the rest of the world about the wider management landscape in Africa. For a continent whose development challenge is as complex as it is multifaceted, *Managing Human Resources in Africa* provides a fresh and refreshing reminder that in the twenty-first century it is no longer HRM as usual.

References

Budhwar, S.P. and Debrah, Y.A. (eds.) (2001) *Human resource management in developing countries*, London: Routledge.

Harvey, M. and Kamoche, K. (2003) "Managing knowledge, learning, and time in relationships between Western and African organizations," *Journal of African Business* 3(2).

Harvey, M., Myers, M., and Novicevic, M.M. (2002) "The role of MNCs in balancing the human capital 'books' between African and developed countries," *International Journal of Human Resource Management* 13: 1060–1076.

Kamoche, K. (2000) *Sociological paradigms and human resources: An African context*, Aldershot: Ashgate.

Mbigi, L. and Maree, J. (1995) *Ubuntu: The spirit of African transformational management*, Rannburg, South Africa: Knowledge Resources.

Schuler, R.S. and Jackson, S.E. (eds.) (1999) *Strategic human resource management*, Oxford: Blackwell.

Frontispiece: Map of Africa showing the countries covered by this book.

1 HRM in South Africa

FRANK M. HORWITZ, STELLA M. NKOMO, AND
MAHAMED RAJAH

Introduction

Any discussion of human resource management in South Africa (SA) must consider
both global and local context. Much work has occurred on the promulgation of labor
legislation to redress historical workplace discrimination in SA. Whilst local institutional
context in labor relations and particularism in HRM practices remain important, the
influence of convergent forces such as globalization, information technology, and
increased competition have become much more prominent in post-apartheid SA.
We explore the complex context influencing the management of human resources in
SA and its impact on human resource practices in organizations.

South Africa has a total population of 45.31 million and a GDP per head of R21,889
(US$2,230) (Statistics SA, 2002). Its GDP is R243.22 billion (US$23.65 billion).
GDP growth for the past three years has been around 3 percent, slightly above the
global average. Inflation has been below 10 percent for the past six years, but moved
above this in 2002–2003 (11.6 percent). Formal sector employment is approximately 15
million. Over 500,000 jobs have, however, been lost in this sector due to retrenchments
following organizational restructuring and downsizing since 1994. There is a rapidly
growing informal and casual worker sector. Historically, the economy was dependent on
the mining industry, including gold, coal, and other minerals. Over the past decade the
GDP contribution of these sectors declined to under 35 percent as industrial and export
strategies in the auto assembly, manufacturing, and agriculture sectors were aggressively
pursued. Although SA has made a relatively successful transition from a resource-based
economy to a manufacturing and export oriented model, it has not created significant
formal employment (Fraser, 2002), although the post-apartheid open economy saw
significant growth in the tourism and hospitality industries. Whilst the economic
fundamentals of macro-economic policy appear sound, high unemployment persists,
estimated at 29 percent (Statistics SA, 2002). Crime and an HIV/AIDS epidemic are
pressing social problems for policy choices. Estimated shrinkage from year 2002 to
2015 of real GDP owing to AIDS ranges from 2.8 to 9.6 percent (ABSA Bank and ING
Barings, 2002).

South Africa is an ethnically diverse society. English, Xhosa, Zulu, Sotho, and Afrikaans are the most widely spoken languages. Black people (Africans, colored people, and Indians) comprise over 75 per cent of the population. Since its establishment as a trading post by the Dutch East India Company in 1652, SA had colonial governments from Britain and the Dutch (Afrikaaner) settlers. Racial discrimination and wars for control over territories and land were a feature of SA's history for over two centuries. Apartheid was formally instituted as a political system by the Nationalist Party in 1948, and abandoned in 1994 with the country's first democratic election, after decades of a continuing political struggle by the African majority and its representative parties such as the African National Congress. The latter and other opposition groups had been banned from the 1960s until the release from prison of Nelson Mandela and other political prisoners in 1990.

The industrialization of SA began with the discovery of gold and diamonds at the end of the nineteenth century. Preference for skilled and managerial work was given to white workers, who were given trade union and collective bargaining rights by the Industrial Conciliation Act (1924). African workers were excluded from these rights until 1980. Access to training and skilled work was denied to Africans. The legacy of institutionalized workplace discrimination has meant that organizations in the "new South Africa" now have to develop a skilled and productive workforce, which was previously under-utilized, poorly trained, and alienated from performance improvement and competitiveness goals. This is a vital challenge for human resource management today.

Major stakeholders in HRM and labor relations are represented in the tripartite National Economic Development and Labor Council (NEDLAC). Employers may belong to employer organizations represented nationally by bodies such as the SA Chamber of Business. Trade unions belong to union federations such as the Congress of South African Trade Unions (COSATU), with some 3 million members in its affiliates. NEDLAC is an important statutory body aiming to foster a social partnership amongst organized business, labor, and the State, through joint consensus seeking on national labor market policy issues and proposed labor legislation such as skills development, employment equity, and labor relations laws. NEDLAC also has a chamber where small business can be represented as an interest group.

Many human resource practitioners are members of a professional association, the Institute for People Management (IPM), which, together with the SA Board for Personnel Practice (SABPP), seeks to enhance the professional standing of the HR profession by providing professional accreditation and standards of ethical and professional conduct. The IPM provides an educational function, running seminars, diploma and advanced programs, and disseminating relevant information through newsletters to members. The SABPP is accredited with the national skills and qualification authority and has played a key role in the formation of this body. The IPM has its own HR magazine, *People Dynamics*, aimed at practitioners. It hosts a large annual conference, with local and international experts as speakers. Many industrial relations specialists belong to the

Industrial Relations Association of SA (IRASA), an affiliate of the International Industrial Relations Association (IIRA) based at the ILO in Geneva.

Strategic human resource imperatives

Two imperatives reflect the critical relevance of a strategic approach to HR in SA. First, to address the discriminatory legacy of apartheid in removing unfair discrimination in the workplace and enhancing organizational representation of Africans, colored people, Indians, and women. Apartheid education and skills legislation created a relatively unique basis for skills and earnings inequalities. African access to trades and skilled work was legislatively prohibited by job reservation in favor of white employees in the then Industrial Conciliation Act (1956) and the Mines and Works Act. These were repealed in 1980—some twenty years ago, yet African progress into skilled and managerial work has been slow. A new culture of learning and integration rather than reliance only on "access and legitimacy and discrimination and fairness" perspectives has become necessary to ensure cohesive and productive work group relations in diverse settings (Ely and Thomas, 2001).

The second strategic imperative is formulating HR strategies at both national and organizational levels to enhance competitiveness and performance improvement. South Africa's re-entry into competitive global markets in the 1990s created new managerial challenges. Human resource practitioners in SA see the most important workplace challenges as performance improvement, employment equity, training and development, and managing trade union expectations (Templer and Hofmeyr, 1989). It is essential that South African organizations spend between 0.5 to 1.5 percent of the payroll on training compared to 5 percent in Europe and the USA and 8 percent in Japan. The apartheid legacy in SA created a racial segmentation of the labor market in respect of access to higher level technological skills (Barker, 1999; Isaacs, 1997; Standing et al., 1996). Training and development are seen by both managers and frontline employees in the services industry in SA as vital in addressing the skills gap and developing the capacity to meet competitive demands (Browning, 2000). Although not yet viewed by a majority of South African firms as a strategic issue, the rate of HIV/AIDS in the labor force is viewed by some as having the potential to erode productivity gains made through skill development efforts. According to the Medical Research Council of South Africa, about 12–15 percent of the population is HIV-infected. AIDS has become the single biggest cause of death (Dorrington et al., 2001). Firms in the mining industry are expected to be hit particularly hard because of the legacy of migrant labor. Some large firms, like AngloGold, have responded by offering employees access to HIV drugs. As the impact of the disease becomes more evident, firms may have no choice but to address it has a strategic human resource management challenge.

Templer et al. (1997: 551–558) found a preference for developing an African model of management, with less reliance on American and Japanese approaches. A comparative study found agreement between human resource practitioners in Canada, SA, and

Zimbabwe on the need for flexible work practices and cost effectiveness, but significant differences in priorities. South African practices under apartheid focused on personnel administration and industrial relations. This has shifted to emphasizing employment equity, performance management, and organizational restructuring, often resulting in downsizing and retrenchments. The twin challenges of redressing labor market inequalities created by apartheid and simultaneously and rapidly creating competitive capabilities are daunting, often competing, but unavoidable HRM challenges. The magnitude of these challenges is best understood within their historical and stakeholder context. African economic empowerment has become a priority for the new government as a strategy to break through the social closure created by past discriminatory policies.

A feature of macro-economic policy is to attract foreign direct investment and multinational firms, often in joint ventures with local empowerment companies. An important question arises whether the influence/power of multinational corporations (MNCs) is so extensive and penetrative as to override local implementation factors such as the regulatory environment, including legislated employment standards and collective bargaining, and cultural factors. Effective diffusion and integration of HR practices will therefore depend on the relative importance of these factors. The stakeholder perspective is relatively well accepted in SA's new democracy. The historical exclusion of key stakeholders under apartheid has been replaced by a new emphasis on consultation and involvement of key groups and individuals, for example in NEDLAC. It includes organized business, labor and government departments in formulating industry, and labor market policies. Arguably, the stronger the stakeholder and pluralist perspectives are institutionalized in a society, the more likely that "crossvergent" or hybrid models of HRM will develop.

The labor market and institutional environment— emergent trends

A structural inequality in the skill profile exists: a shortage of occupationally and managerially skilled employees is contrasted with an oversupply of unskilled labor, ill equipped for a modernizing economy with increasing knowledge and service sector priorities. South Africa has a rapidly growing and large youth population, which is predominantly African, poor, and lacking in education and skills. This presents a huge challenge to the state, public institutions, and private sector. The labor market absorption rate for young entrants, given modest economic growth of 2 to 3.5 percent over the past six years, has been low. Given the lack of relevant skills in market demand fields, coupled with shrinking formal core employment, youth unemployment is high. Socio-economic and labor market issues remain pressing managerial and business challenges in the post-apartheid transitional economy. The government has relaxed legislative provisions on basic conditions of employment to allow greater flexibility for small firms and is encouraging better education and occupationally relevant skills through the Skills Development Act (1998). It aims at encouraging the provision of opportunities for new labor market entrants to develop skills and gain experience for better employment prospects.

Human resource development priorities and policy challenges in achieving organisational change and capacity building in the labor market are critical to enhancing SA's international competitiveness. In SA, a developing economy, skilled jobs are growing and unskilled jobs are declining. Professional, managerial and transport occupations account for an increase of around 2 million jobs since 1970. More skilled employees have been absorbed into service industries, due to a structural shift from the primary sector to growth in services, accompanied by rising capital to labor ratios. Greatest demand is expected for skills in IT and finance (Bhorat, 1999). The labor absorption capacity into higher skill and managerial jobs is being nudged by supply-side measures such as employment equity legislation. Table 1.1 shows that employed Africans, both men and women, tend to be concentrated in lower income levels.

Although changing, with use of unfair discrimination legal action, a "glass ceiling" still remains for designated groups. Research by the University of Cape Town's Breakwater Monitor Project shows that the percentage of Africans in managerial positions increased from 1997 to 2001. White employees still held over 60 percent of management positions and still constituted the majority of managerial promotions (Bowmaker-Falconer 2000). This research also found that 25 percent of managerial promotions were women, with only 6 percent African women. Deloitte and Touche

Table 1.1 Claimed monthly household income by race, 2000

	African (%)	Asian and colored (%)	White	Total population (%)
R1–R499	15.8	1.3	0.3	11.8
R500–R899	26.2	4.4	1.2	20.1
R900–R1399	21.2	6.4	2.9	1`7.1
R1,400–R2,499	17.1	10.2	5.8	15.2
R2,500–R3,999	8.7	12.6	9.7	9.8
R4,000–R6,999	6.8	23.7	24.2	11.5
R7,000–R11,999	3.0	24.5	31.5	9.0
R12,000+	1.1	17.0	24.4	5.6
All (a) (R)	**100.0**	**100.0**	**100.0**	**100.0**
Average (R): 2000 (b)	1,865	7,265	9,108	3,368
Percentage change:				
1999–2000	19.3	3.4	4.2	5.7

Source: South African Advertising Research Foundation (2000) "All Media Products Survey," p. 30.

(2001), in a survey of the transformation of top management positions in South African firms, found that among 44 companies in the chemical, financial services, public service, manufacturing and engineering sectors, that men hold 85 percent of all top management positions. African women fill less than 10 percent of top management positions. The survey also revealed that although 74 percent of the firms claimed employment equity to be one of their top five business priorities, progress was still disappointingly slow.

Employment relations and legislative developments

Employment relations in SA have undergone major changes over the past two decades (Rajah, 2000). An adversarial race-based dualistic system evolved following labor legislation in 1924 which led to trade union rights which excluded Africans. Only in 1980 were unions representing African workers legitimized. Inclusive bargaining councils were fostered through the Labor Relations Act in 1995. African unions grew to over 3 million members in 2001, from less than 10 percent of the formal sector workforce in the late 1970s. The largest unions are affiliated to union federations such as the Congress of South African Trade Unions (COSATU) and the National Council of Unions (NACTU).

The Labor Relations Act (1995) also established labor and labor appeal courts, and the Commission for Conciliation, Mediation and Arbitration (CCMA). The CCMA handles both procedural and distributive or substantive justice in considering the fairness of a matter such as dismissal. The new Act sought to bring employment law in line with the constitution and ratified Conventions of the International Labor Organization. It aims to give effect to constitutional rights permitting employees to form unions, to strike for collective bargaining purposes, and the right to fair labor practices. Employers have the right to form and join employers' organizations and the recourse to lockout for the purpose of collective bargaining. Strike action is protected only if a specified dispute procedure is followed.

Whist centralized industry level and decentralized enterprise or plant bargaining may occur, increased devolution and fragmentation of bargaining has occurred in the past nine years. The number of bargaining councils has declined to less than 80 as employers withdraw from them, favoring plant or enterprise bargaining and increased employment flexibility. This has occurred, for example, in the building and construction industries, as new forms of employment emphasizing flexibility using independent sub-contractors, outsourcing, part-time and temporary work, and increased casualization and informalization of work. These practices are associated with a recent decline in private sector union density and some evidence of deterioration in employment standards in certain sectors. The Basic Conditions of Employment Act (1998), however, provides for establishing minimum standards of employment. These conditions cover areas from the designation of working hours to termination regulations and have been extended to farm and domestic workers.

Work days lost through strike action have also declined since 1994. Whilst under apartheid African unions fought for fair labor practices, worker rights, and better pay and conditions of employment, they also were at the forefront of the struggle for political rights. Once political and labor rights complemented each other in the first democratic elections in 1994, this labor paradox was resolved. This resulted in an intense policy debate within the union movement as to its repositioning in the new SA. The workplace as an arena for political struggle has largely been replaced with an emphasis on measures to try and preserve employment and HR issues such as training and development and employment equity.

The Labor Relations Act seeks to promote employee participation in decision making through workplace forums and employee consultation and joint decision making on certain issues. It provides for simple procedures for the resolution of labor disputes through statutory conciliation and arbitration, and through independent alternative dispute resolution services. Amendments to the Act came into effect on 1 August 2002. New forms of dispute resolution were developed to include pre-dismissal arbitration and one-stop dispute resolution, known as CON-ARB. Both unions and management have the power to request the CCMA to facilitate retrenchment negotiations to achieve constructive outcomes.

A key challenge in employment relations is the need to shift from a legacy of adversarial relationships to work place cooperation to successfully compete in the market place. There is evidence in some sectors such as auto assembly that this is understood by both parties. There is increasingly a blurring of the distinction between employment relations and HRM. The new agenda focuses beyond the traditional collective bargaining items and adversarial dismissal disputes, to organizational transformation, performance improvement, human resource development, and employee benefits. Trade unions have become more willing to engage employers around these issues. Finding a productive balance between equity and workplace justice imperatives on the one hand, and HR and employment relations strategies enhancing competitiveness on the other, is a vital challenge for managers and unions.

Employment equity legislation and human resource practices

Legislative prohibitions against unfair discrimination are intrinsic to SA's Constitution (1996). Chapter 2 (the Bill of Rights) contains an equality clause, which specifies a number of grounds which constitute unfair discrimination. Additionally, Schedule 7 of the Labor Relations Act (1995) considers unfair discrimination either directly or indirectly as a residual unfair labor practice. Grounds include race, gender, ethnic origin, sexual orientation, religion, disability, conscience, belief, language, and culture. The Employment Equity Act (1998) focuses on unfair discrimination in employment and HR practices. Employers are required to take steps to end unfair discrimination in employment policies and practices. It prohibits the unfair discrimination against employees, including job seekers, on any arbitrary grounds including race, gender, pregnancy, marital status, sexual orientation, disability, language, and religion.

The Constitution and prohibitions contained in the Employment Equity Act and other labor legislation sorts pemissible discrimination from impermissible discrimination. All designated employers (these who employ 50 or more people) have to prepare and submit to the Department of Labor an employment equity plan setting out goals, targets, timetables, and measures to be taken to remove discriminatory employment practices and achieve greater workforce representation, especially at managerial and skilled category levels. The Employment Equity Act does not set quotas, but rather enables individual employers to develop their own HR and equity plans. Criteria regarding enhanced representation include national and regional demographic information and special skills supply/availability.

The Employment Equity Act includes provisions against unfair discrimination in selection and recruitment, aptitude testing, HIV/AIDS testing, promotions, and access to training and development opportunities. It is generally accepted that an "apartheid wage gap" saw pay discrimination evolve over some four decades or more. More recent equalization of opportunities has not always led to pay parity for work of equal value. Section 27 of the Employment Equity Act somewhat controversially requires designated employers, as part of a required employment equity plan, to submit to the Department of Labor a statement on the remuneration and benefits received in each occupational category and level of the employer's workforce. Where disproportionate income differentials are reflected in the statement, an employer is required to take measures to progressively reduce such differentials. Measures include collective bargaining, skills formation, compliance with other wage regulating instruments, and benchmarks set by the Employment Conditions Commission.

As part of a required employment equity plan, designated employers have to review employment and HR practices to remove provisions or practices which may have an unfair discriminatory effect. This includes recruitment and selection and remuneration. An applicant for a job is included in the definition of "employee", making illegal unfair discrimination in pre-employment recruitment and selection practices, such as psychometric assessment, interviews, and application form questions which do not pertain directly to the ability of the person to do the job. South African labor law allows discrimination on the basis of inherent job requirements, but the object of an employer's conduct must be fair, and the means rational.

It is in these areas, as well as in the provision of substantive benefits and conditions of employment, that unfair discrimination is most likely. The notions of disproportionate effect and adverse impact are considered in this regard. Once an employee claims discrimination, the evidentiary burden shifts to the employer to show that the discrimination is not unfair. It is nonetheless very difficult for an employee to prove pay discrimination conclusively. In particular, whilst discrimination may occur, an employer may cogently submit that pay and skill differences were not the result of unfair discrimination, but due to factors such as differences in performance, experience, competencies, and service.

Recent court cases show that even in an environment where affirmative action to overcome past discrimination is accepted as an appropriate method to achieve equity, there are continuing differing interpretations about its aims and effects on HR practice. Decisions based on race or gender, unless they related to a genuine skills or occupational requirement, could be found to be arbitrary and unfair labor practices (Van Vuuren (1998) and Liberty Life (1996) cases). Affirmative action, though, is not regarded as unfair discrimination in SA labour law. Both the policy and organizational contexts in which the dispute arise are pertinent. This tends to reflect the limitations of the "discrimination and fairness" as well as "access and equal opportunity" perspectives as legalistic and procedural remedies to race and ethnic relations problems in the workplace. Change management and "soft" HR strategies focusing on relationship building and cultural transformation to integrate diversity as a value in itself for effective work group relations, have been found to be more effective than reliance on procedural justice approaches alone.

Even when employers explicitly espouse these policies, the consequences of years of systematic discrimination continue to skew both internal and external labor markets. Managers' failure to adequately address both skills and pay practices in the service industry in SA has a direct adverse impact on service behavior of frontline employees (Browning, 2000). Human resource policies and remuneration practices do not occur in a "neutral" or unbiased context. The institutional environment remains a powerful influence on HRM in SA, mitigated to an extent by the competitive forces of global competition.

Cultural factors and Human Resource Management

Considerable research has been conducted on the issue of cultural factors in the diffusion of HRM practices (Debrah and Smith, 1999; Jackson, 2000; Kamoche, 1997; 2000). A facet of this research is a focus on integration/divergence of work values cross-culturally. The question of cultural influence on work values and HRM practices is important in assessing the extent and type of hybridization which occurs in adopting HR practices, developed elsewhere, and how culture and labor market institutions influence such adoption.

Cross-cultural variation in the labor market and skills supply for addressing market needs is an important consideration by MNCs in the decision regarding foreign direct investment (FDI). South Africa and its regional economy have an oversupply of manual, relatively unskilled workers and, as in many emergent economies, a shortage of technology, financial, and managerial skills. The Skills Development and Employment Equity Acts have sought to put policy emphasis on human resource development, with levy and grant incentives.

A theme in the literature on developing countries is the appropriateness of Western management principles and practices. Many authors have challenged the tendency by MNCs as well as local managers to adopt practices with little consideration of the suitability and relevance of such practices. Some have identified the limitations of concepts formulated in the West (Kamoche, 1993; 1997a; Nzelibe, 1986), while others have offered empirical evidence on the nature of extant practices, pointing to their appropriateness or lack thereof (Kamoche, 2000). The importance of family and community are seen in the network of interrelationships, extended family, and mutual obligations. This results in a sense of communalism (Nzelibe, 1986).

Some advocate African "ubuntu" as a basis for fostering an Afrocentric managerial culture with regiocentic HRM practices (Mbigi, 2000). The notion of "ubuntu" literally translated, means "I am who I am through others." This in contrast to the Western tenet of "cogito ergo sum"—"I think therefore I am." It is this contrasting of a form of communal humanism with individualism and instrumentalism which has a normative appeal for advocates of an African economic and cultural renaissance, and is posited as having the potential to build competitive advantage (Jackson, 2000; Mangaliso, 2001). But a desired future vision may be confused with current empirical reality. The socio-economic context of management in SA reflects high unemployment, poverty, and illiteracy. At the same time there is a high need to develop people and provide a globally competitive economy (Kamoche, 1997b).

However, macro-cultural comparative analyses (Hofstede, 1991; Trompenaars, 1993) may have adequate face validity, but often neglect deeper consideration of diversity within certain contexts and the power of organizational culture in MNCs. The latter may act as rival causal factors in the propensity to successfully adopt HR practices cross-culturally. This is particularly relevant in SA, with its diverse cultural and ethnic fabric, and where research on cross-cultural diversity in organizational contexts is embryonic. Hofstede's original study in 1980 included SA. With its sample of only one firm—IBM in SA, which was at the time predominantly white in its staffing composition—the study failed to discern the multidimensional nature of even his own model. Additionally, the longitudinal changes in the employment and staffing structure of SA organizations have become more diverse and multicultural at all levels, especially since 1994. It is likely therefore that constructs such as individualism/collectivism, risk-taking and avoidance, may show quite varied patterns today.

Booysen (1999) investigated perceptions of national culture among retail banking managers from three of the largest banks in South Africa. She found significant differences between African and white racial groups on seven of the eight dimensions of national culture examined. The cultural constellation of the white management group reflected a Eurocentric or Western orientation that emphasizes individual self-sufficiency, competition and work orientation, and structure and planning. In contrast, the cultural constellation of African managers reflected high levels of collective solidarity, group significance, valuing of harmonious interpersonal and group relations, consensual decision making, building of trust and reciprocity, nurturing and coaching (Mangaliso,

2001), and below average levels of assertiveness (Booysen, 1999). These latter attributes reflect cultural values congruent with Afrocentric management systems.

In contrast, Thomas and Bendixen (2000) found little significant difference among the 586 managers they sampled using Hofstede's dimensions of national culture model. Their sample included 20 different race/ethnic and group groups representing the dominant categories of the South African population (e.g. white Afrikaans-speaking males and females, Zulu-speaking males and females, and Asian males and females). The groups were similar on power distance, individualism, and long-term orientation. Thomas and Bendixen concluded that, at the managerial level, there appears to be a common national culture among South Africans. The results of their study indicate a cultural gap between management and lower level employees. Neither study specifically addressed the impact of national culture on HRM practices. Nor have there been studies within South African organizations to examine whether or not a strong organizational culture can mitigate the effects of national culture. Combined, this limited research suggests that a continuing challenge for the development of high performance HRM practices in South Africa is how to embrace the reality of the duality of both Western and African cultural identities among the workforce. One sobering conclusion is that there may not be universally applicable HRM practices for all employee groups.

Human resource practices in a country are not only products of national culture and environment, but organizational culture, strategy, and structure; which in turn influence design, content, and implementation of performance oriented HRM practices such as staffing, compensation, HR planning, and training/development. The debate regarding convergence/divergence perspectives in the cross-cultural diffusion of HRM practices is a somewhat simplistic one. Convergent similarity of HRM practices exists largely at the nominal level, hence, the need to explain the hybridization of HRM practices, for which the notion of hybridization or "crossvergence" seems apt, especially in a culturally diverse society such as SA. Contextual factors including national and corporate culture may have a determining effect on design and implementation of HR practices (Jackson, 2000; Mbigi, 2000). In SA, the nature of the domestic labor market is important, including the degree of voluntarism or regulation of employment practices such as fair/unfair labor practices, recruitment and selection, pay determination, union influence, human resource development policy, and dismissal law.

Trends in functional dimensions of Human Resource Management

We have earlier evaluated trends dealing with human resource development, skills training, employment equity, and employment relations. Recruitment and selection have become important focal points for both seeking to attract talent and address equity imperatives. Methods for recruitment and selection have come under scrutiny in respect of fair and non-discriminatory practices. Chapter 2 of the Employment Equity Act (1998) makes important provisions regarding the use of psychometric and HIV testing, which are free of any cultural or ethnic bias. Whilst it is good professional practice anyway, this Act requires an employer to conduct a review of recruitment and selection practices and promotion policies to ensure they do not unfairly discriminate. This has resulted in a more professional approach to recruitment and selection. Recruitment agencies are also required to ensure compliance with the non-discriminatory provisions of legislation. An applicant for a job is included in the definition of "employee" in employment equity and other labor laws. This means that a job candidate cannot be discriminated against unfairly on grounds of factors such as race or gender.

Remuneration policy and practice have become an important function for an employer to leverage performance improvement (Horwitz, 2000). Especially at executive level, SA firms are increasingly applying and adapting best pay practices largely from the USA. There is a trend towards performance-based pay, with an increased variable component of pay. Basic pay for executives is declining as a proportion of total package, with more use of share options, profit sharing, and variable and flexible pay measures. At operational levels, and often in negotiation with trade unions, skill-based pay has been introduced. Examples include auto assembly, clothing and textiles, and various engineering and manufacturing firms. But in sectors such as building and construction, increased labor sub-contracting has resulted in a deterioration of conditions of employment for increasing numbers of workers. Rising earning differentials are owed in part to these factors and the legacy of an "apartheid pay gap." It has been difficult to prove that pay differences are exclusively due to racial discrimination and not other factors such as performance, length of service, and relevant experience, even though there is a reverse onus of proof in claims of unfair discrimination. Human resource departments are concerned with both pay administration and measures to improve performance management through pay incentives. Increasingly, the former is being outsourced and/or replaced with technology as IT, and new software packages are designed to do pay administration. For more progressive organizations, this will allow HR functions to concentrate on aligning HR policy and measures with organizational strategy to optimize performance.

The use of job evaluation by HR departments in medium and large organizations is common practice for establishing the relative worth of jobs and ranking jobs as a basis for designing a grading structure. Job evaluation systems were introduced in the mining and beer brewing industries in the early 1970s. Job evaluation systems such as Hay, Peromnes (a widely used, locally developed system), Paterson, and others are variously used in agri-business, engineering, government, insurance and financial services, manufacturing, mining, and tertiary educational institutions such as universities. As organizations restructure and de-layer hierarchies, job evaluation systems have to adapt to deal with processes such as broad-banding and multi-skilling.

Job analysis and work process redesign are increasingly important facets of HR work in SA. Research shows that, although Western HRM practices have prevailed for decades in African countries, there is an increase in South African firms adopting Japanese and east Asian practices (Horwitz, 2002; Faull, 2000). This is particularly evident in the use of lean manufacturing, just-in-time methods, and other operations management measures to reduce product defects, stock holdings, inventory, and waste. These measures have also increased in the manufacturing sector, where firms have introduced kaizen, kanban methods, Nissan-type green areas, Japanese Total Quality Management (TQM) and production systems, and quality improvement teams. However, the adoption of east Asian work practices is seen by many as unworkable. Many firms believe that Japanese work philosophies are rooted in a different cultural context and cannot therefore be copied in African countries (Keenan, 2000: 26). There is case study evidence of forms of functional flexibility in firms such as Pick 'n Pay Retailers, SA Nylon Spinners and Sun International Hotels (Horwitz and Townshend, 1993). However, these practices are less common (under 10 percent) in relation to use of numerical flexibility such as downsizing and outsourcing, and temporal flexibility types such as part-time, temporary and casual, short-term work (Allen *et al.*, 2001). Use of flexible work practices, including functional forms of flexibility such as multi-skilling and performance-based pay, is more common in multinationals in SA than local firms (Horwitz and Smith, 1998: 590–606). South African organizations tend to emphasize collective and procedural relations, whereas foreign-owned firms in SA have more distinctive, often MNC diffused, HRM practices based on individual relations.

Empirical work in SA on the concept of "effectiveness" in HRM and industrial relations practices has attempted to determine the relationship between these factors and performance measures such as service (Browning, 1998; Horwitz and Neville, 1996; Templer and Cattaneo, 1991; Owens and van der Merwe, 1993). Mediating contextual factors in adoption of HRM have been found in other African countries (Kamoche, 1992). Kamoche (1993) offers a provisional model of HRM in Africa. Considering the notion of "effectiveness" in HRM and industrial relations, a critical challenge is that of moving from discriminatory practices, adversarial industrial relations, and an under-skilled workforce, towards a fair HRM regime with high performance practices. Consequently, managing diversity, job design, training and development, and performance management seem to be dominant HRM functional areas driving the agendas of South African organizations.

Managing diversity and changing managerial styles

While many organizations around the world have implemented managing diversity initiatives in response to the growing heterogeneity of the workforce (Nkomo and Cox, 1996), South African organizations generally lag in the adoption of such practices. In a study of the diversity management in a sample of South African companies, Strydom and Erwee (1998) found at the time that the majority were best classified as monolithic companies, wherein blacks were expected to adopt the culture of the white dominant group. Hence, most South African organizations are still using what Ely and Thomas (2001) describe as the discrimination and fairness paradigm in managing diversity. Organizations that look at diversity through this lens focus on recruitment and selection of African, colored people, Indians, and women employees and compliance with provisions of the Employment Equity Act. Such an approach may be justifiable given the mandate of employment equity legislation, union demands, and the historical exclusion of Africans and women from certain occupations. The fairly slow progress in achieving employment equity is due to management's emphasis on numerical goals and not enough attention to creating organizational cultures and workplaces that value diversity as key to competitive advantage. The Report on Employment Equity Registry, issued by the Department of Labor in 2000, cited corporate culture as one of the major barriers to employment equity (Department of Labor, 2000). Nevertheless, the specific strategies adopted by South African firms to value and manage diversity will have to take into consideration the specificity of the local and historical context. An example of such an approach is the one taken by First National Bank. Their unique approach was designed to address the dual challenges of low employee morale due to perceptions of racism among black employees and feelings of reverse discrimination among white employees and a business need to increase checking account revenues from the growing black urban population. In addition to cultural diversity awareness training, the program required all managers to spend two days in an African township to better understand customer needs. Additionally, the bank institutionalized ongoing staff gatherings and the use of collective decision making in branches (*Sunday Times*, 2002).

Managerial styles reflect organizational and national cultural patterns. In SA, whilst achievement is valued, group and organization conformity is also important. Whilst there is a paucity of empirical research on managerial culture in SA firms, a masculine dominance is evident across ethnic groups (Horwitz, 2002: 215–217), underlined by individualist values and a relatively large power distance between groups based on historical racial and ethnic disparities. However, an emergent African middle class has begun to occupy decision-making roles. Class mobility is likely to have an impact on managerial culture and inform strategic choices about appropriate organizational culture, business, and HRM practices in SA. Organization and national culture reflect considerable diversity and pluralism. Managerial styles in SA reflect both Western values based on individualism and meritocracy, and an authoritarian legacy of apartheid. These are often rooted in highly masculine cultures (Hofstede, 1991). However, indigenous models struggle to assert themselves in the face of a converging global business orthodoxy (Mbigi, 2000).

Conclusions and implications

Hybrid forms of HR practice may occur in nomenclature, design, content, and implementation processes. There is some evidence of reverse diffusion. SAB Miller's (South African Breweries owns the US beer company) jointly owned breweries in Poland have successfully implemented best operating practices and management know-how on systems, processes, and technology based on Japanese practices and its experience in emergent economies. A balance will need to be struck between indigenous responses to past discrimination and the clear need for high performance practices.

Although progress has been made to enhance racial and gender diversity, this is an incremental process that has to be supported by coherent human resource development priorities and changes in organizational culture. This is vital at both public policy and organizational levels. Rising income inequalities are beginning to cut across racial and ethnic lines. This could create a new fault line of inequality. An increased earnings gap has an adverse impact on mainly African people; this, in spite of increasing diversity and the multi-racial character of a growing middle class. The biggest priority must be human resource development and education in skills and competencies needed in a transitional society. Several sectors need both high and low level skills. The former are in the information economy and high value-adding occupations, while the latter are in service sectors such as hospitality.

Given the ethnic demography of South African society, most of this underclass is African. Arguably this is a bigger policy and practical challenge than managerial and executive employment equity, where the focus seems to lie. Skills formation and entrepreneurial development are vital, especially in a country with huge transitional challenges. These can be summed up in one word—"development." Economic empowerment and employment equity are not possible without human resource development and education as a fundamental national priority. Large scale labor absorption into a shrinking formal labor market is unlikely, given the shift of employment to service and informal non-core work mainly outside the ambit of employment equity legislation. The priority of practical policy initiatives by government, private sector firms, labor market institutions such as sector training authorities, and bargaining councils must be large scale initiatives to train and retrain for enhancing employability in the changing labor market.

South African managers live in a society rich in diversity. Organizations will need to shift from compliance to a commitment model that has an organizational culture reflecting the notion of ubuntu and capacity building as vital for both competitiveness and equity in the workplace. South Africa faces a double transitional challenge: to redress the historical inequalities by building a democracy based on human rights and tolerance; and to simultaneously and speedily develop its human capital capacity to compete in a harsh global economy. It is a daunting challenge.

References

ABSA Bank and ING Barings (2002) *Special reports on HIV/AIDS in Southern Africa*, 1–12.
Allen, C., Brosnan, P., Horwitz, F.M., and Walsh, P. (2001) "From standard to non-standard employment," *International Journal of Manpower* 22 (8): 748–763.
Barker, F. (1999) *The South African labour market*, Pretoria: J.L. van Schaik, pp. 23–25.
Bhorat, H. (1999) [Quoted in] *Quarterly Trends—National Business Initiative Publication* December: 3.
Booysen, L. (2001) "The duality of South African leadership: Afrocentric or Eorocentric?" *South African Journal of Labour Relations*, Summer: 36–60.

Bowmaker-Falconer, A. (ed.) (2000) *Breakwater Monitor Report on Employment Equity*, University of Cape Town, pp. 1–80.

Browning, V. (1998) "Creating service excellence through human resource practices," *South African Journal of Business Management* 29 (4): 125–141.

Browning, V. (2000) "Human resource management practices and service-oriented behavior in South African organizations," Invited paper presented at the Eric Langeard International Research Seminar in Service Management, Toulon France, 5–8 June: 1–16.

Debrah, Y.A. and Smith, I.G. (1999) "Globalization, employment and the workplace: Responses for the millennium," Employment Research Unit Annual Conference, Cardiff Business School, University of Wales, 8–9 September: 1–8.

Deloitte and Touche (2001) *Employment equity and transformation survey*, 1–12.

Dorrington, R., Bourne, D., Bradshaw, D., Laubsher, R., and Timaeus, I. (2001) *The impact of HIV/AIDS on adult mortality in South Africa*, Tygerberg: South African Medical Research Council.

Ely, R.J., and Thomas, D.A. (2001) "Cultural diversity at work: The effects of diversity perspectives on work group processes and outcomes," *Administrative Sciences Quarterly* 46: 229–273.

Faull, N. (2000) *The Manufacturing Round Table Project*, Graduate School of Business, University of Cape Town.

Fraser, J. (2002) "Economic transition in SA fails to create jobs," *Business Day*, October 28: 1.

George vs. Liberty Life Association of Africa Ltd. (1996) *Industrial Labour Journal* 17 (3): 571–601.

Hofstede, G. (1991) *Cultures and organizations: Software of the mind*, London: McGraw-Hill.

Horwitz, F.M. (2002) "Whither South African management," in M. Warner, and P. Joynt (eds.) *Managing across cultures*, London: Thomson Learning: 215–220.

Horwitz, F.M. and Neville, M. (1996) "Organisation design for service excellence," *Human Resource Management* 35 (4): 471–492.

Horwitz, F.M. and Smith, D.A. (1998) "Flexible work practices and human resource management: A comparison of South African and foreign-owned companies," *International Journal of Human Resource Management* 9 (4): 690–607.

Horwitz, F.M. and Townshend, M. (1993) "Elements in participation, teamwork and flexibility," *International Journal of Human Resource Management* 4 (4): 17–30.

Horwitz, F.M., Kamoche, K., and Chew Keng-Howe, I. (2002) "Looking east: diffusing high performance work practices in the southern Afro-Asian context," *International Journal of Human Resource Management* 13 (7): 1019–1041.

Isaacs, S. (1997) *South Africa in the global economy*, Durban: Trade Union Research Project (TURP).

Jackson, T. (2000) "Management in Africa: Developing a cross-cultural research agenda," International Academy of African Business and Development Conference. Atlantic City, New Jersey, April.

Kamoche, K. (1992) "Human resource management: An assessment of the Kenyan case," *International Journal of Human Resource Management* 3 (3): 497–519.

Kamoche, K. (1993) "Toward a model of HRM in Africa," *Personnel and Human Resources Management*, Suppl. (3): 259–278.

Kamoche, K. (1997a) "Managing human resources in Africa: Strategic, organizational and epistemological issues," *International Business Review* 6: 537–558.

Kamoche, K. (1997b) "Competence creation in the African public sector," *International Journal of Public Sector Management* 10 (4): 268–278.

Kamoche, K. (2000) *Sociological paradigms and human resources: An African context*, Aldershot: Ashgate.

Keenan, T. (2000) "You can never be too rich or too lean," *Finance Week*, October: 26–27.

Mangaliso, M.P. (2001) "Building competitive advantage from ubuntu: Management lessons from South Africa," *Academy of Management Executive* 15 (3): 23–32.

Mbigi, L. (2000) "Making the African renaissance globally competitive," *People Dynamics* 18 (11): 16–21.

Nkomo, S. and Cox, T.H. (1996) "Diverse identities in organizations," in S. Clegg, C. Hardy, and W. Nord (eds.) *Handbook of organization studies*, London: Sage, pp. 338–356.

Nzelibe, C.O. (1986) "The evolution of African management thought," *International Studies of Management and Organization* 16 (2): 6–16.

Owens, J. and van der Merwe, J. (1993) "Perspectives of services provided by the human resource function," *South African Journal of Business Management* 24 (2): 56–63.

Rajah, M. (2000) "The socio-political and work environment as sources of workplace discrimination: Implications for employment equity." *Southern African Business Review* 4 (2): 77–82.

South African Institute of Race Relations (2002) *Fast facts*, 9/10: 3–12.

Standing, G., Sender, J., and Weeks, J. (1996) "Restructuring the labor market: The South African challenge," Geneva: International Labour Office (ILO), 1–11, 185–228.

Statistics SA (2002) Cited in South African Institute of Race Relations, *Fast facts* 9/10.

Strydom, J. and Erwee, R. (1998) "Diversity management in a sample of South African companies," *South African Journal of Business Management* 29 (1): 14–21.

Templer, A. and Cattaneo, J. (1991) "Assessing human resource effectiveness," *South African Journal of Labour Relations* 15 (4): 23–30.

Templer, A. and Hofmeyr, K. (1989) "A national investigation of the correlation between perceptions of human resource practices and organizational effectiveness," *South African Journal of Business Management* 20 (1): 7–11.

Templer, A., Hofmeyr, K., and Rall, J. (1997) "An international comparison of human resource management objectives," *International Journal of Human Resource Management* 8 (4): 550–560.

Thomas, A. and Bendixen, M. (2000) "The management implications of ethnicity in South Africa," *Journal of International Business Studies* 31 (3): 507–519.

Thomas, A. and Robertshaw, D. (1999) *Achieving employment equity*, Randburg: Knowledge Resources, pp. 1–13.

Thomas, A. and Schonken, J. (1998) "Culture-specific management and the African management movement," *South African Journal of Business Management* 29 (2): 53–76.

Thomas, D. and Ely, R. (1996) "Making differences matter: A new paradigm for managing diversity," *Harvard Business Review*, September/October: 79–90.

Trompenaars, F. (1993) *Riding the waves of culture: Understanding cultural diversity in business*, London: Nicholas Brealey.

Van Vuuren vs. Department of Correctional Services (1998) Case No: PA 6/98, Labor Appeal Court.

2 HRM in Botswana[1]

DOROTHY MPABANGA

Introduction

The chapter will first discuss socio-economic developments that have occurred since Botswana gained independence in 1966. The development of public administration from 1966 when the country became independent from the British colonial government will be discussed. The second part will explore different perspectives on HRM, including cross-cultural and crossvergence approaches suggested by various authors when studying HRM practice in Africa (e.g. Jackson, 2002; Kamoche, 2002; Anakwe, 2002). The legislative framework developed in the last 30 years to guide the management of human resource practice in Botswana will be examined. To describe and review human resources management in Botswana requires a focus on HRM policies and practice, including recruitment and selection, rewards, training, performance management, industrial relations, and employee health and safety. These are the core functions of typical HRM departments, sections or units in an organization.

Background on Botswana

Botswana is located in Southern Africa and shares borders with South Africa, Zimbabwe, Zambia, and Namibia. Botswana has a population of approximately 1.7 million (2001 population census) and covers an estimated total area of about 581,730 km^2, about the size of France or Texas. Botswana's population growth rate is estimated at 2.4 percent per annum, which is lower than the 3.4 percent growth rate experienced between 1981 and 1991 (Botswana Government, 2002a). Botswana has special characteristics in Africa; the country has one of the longest surviving democracies and has experienced rapid economic growth in the last 20 years (Molomo, 2000).

Upon gaining independence in 1966, Botswana was listed among the poorest countries in the world, with GDP estimated at P 118 million (Harvey and Lewis, 1990; Salkin *et al.*,

1 I wish to thank my supervisor Dr. Stephen Gibb for his helpful comments.

1997). However, after independence and with the discovery of diamonds in the 1970s, the country was transformed from being one of the poorest countries to one of the fastest developing nations in the world. Between 1966 and 1995, Botswana's per capita gross domestic product grew from about P1,682 to P7,863 (US$2,850) in 1993/94 constant prices. During the same period, employment in the formal sector averaged an annual increase of about 9 percent (Botswana Government, 1997a: 11).

Discovery of diamonds in the 1970s significantly transformed the economy of Botswana. Revenue from the mining sector was invested in developing government structures and social infrastructure. Government established various ministries and departments to implement policies and programs, built health and education centers, and developed transport networks. In addition, mineral revenue was invested in the establishment of public corporations to provide services and facilities not available in the economy, including housing, electricity, telecommunications, and financial services. As the economy of Botswana continued to grow in the 1970s and 1980s, other sectors grew as well. Economic activity increased in the country, resulting in development of various sectors. Major economic activities include mining, government (central and local), financial, manufacturing, telecommunications and electricity, construction, retail and trade, business and services, and tourism.

Since the 1970s, the mining sector has played a significant role in the economy. Botswana is the second largest producer of diamonds (by value) after Russia. Debswana operates the diamond mines. De Beers and the government of Botswana own Debswana in equal shares. In the 1990s, the mining sector contributed about 35 percent to GDP (diamond mining constitutes 91 percent of the mining sector), 41 percent to government revenue and about 5 percent to formal sector employment (Bank of Botswana, 1999). Employment in the mining sector in the 1990s has averaged 3.6 percent of total formal sector employment.

The government plays an important role in the economy in that it is the largest employer and investor. The government's share of formal sector employment was about 36 percent in 1999, employing about 105,200 out of a total of 255,600 employees (Bank of Botswana, 1999: S14). As of March 2001, formal sector employment is estimated at 270,331 people. The government is also the largest investor in the economy through investment in various development projects and programs.

The financial sector has grown in the last ten years, particularly with the relaxation of licensing policies by government to facilitate growth of the financial sector (Bank of Botswana, 1999). With the liberalization of licensing policy, additional banks were established, bringing competition within commercial banks, leading to improvement in service delivery, and an increase in the range of services available to customers—for example, installation of automated teller machines and automated payment systems in order to speed up the payment process and to reduce risk of transporting large sums of money. Regarding financial institutions owned by the government, restructuring was undertaken in order to improve financial performance and service delivery, though there was loss of jobs during the restructuring process. Loss of jobs also occurred in commercial banks, as competition and application of technology into the banking system necessitated reorganization. In the telecommunication industry, use of cellular phones has increased due to deregulation, leading to investment in IT, enabling customers access to, for example, integrated digital networks, and Internet services.

In order to diversify the economy and create employment, the government introduced various policies and incentives to engineer growth in the manufacturing sector. Different policies and assistance programs were introduced to facilitate industrial development. Investors were given financial grants through the financial assistance policy to employ and train workers in return. As a result of financial assistance schemes initiated by government, the manufacturing sector grew by an average of about 8 percent per annum in the 1980s (Bank of Botswana, 1999). However, in the 1990s, growth of the manufacturing sector declined to about 4 percent due to various factors, including the general slowdown of the economy, and the structural adjustment program in Zimbabwe where manufacturing (textiles and clothing) export were mainly destined.

With the increase of economic activity in the country, the construction sector also experienced growth. The construction boom experienced in the 1980s was mainly due to implementation of government projects, including construction of roads and buildings. In addition, an increase in demand for commercial, industrial, and residential buildings boosted construction activity in the country. Employment in the construction sector has been fluctuating over the years. In 1990, the construction sector's share in total employment was about 32 percent. However, with the general slowdown of the economy and completion of major government construction and development projects, employment in construction declined sharply in the early 1990s, recovering slightly in 1996/97, with a growth rate of about 2.7 percent in 1997 (Bank of Botswana, 1999).

Botswana has a cattle farming industry, which constitutes the third principal export after diamonds and copper-nickel. Botswana exports beef to the European Union under the Lome IV Convention through the Botswana Meat Commission. However, the beef industry is susceptible to drought and diseases such as foot and mouth and cattle lung disease. The use of traditional farming methods also impacts on output. The agricultural sector did play a major role in the economy but its significance has declined due to persistent drought affecting the sector and lack of fertile land (two-thirds of Botswana is desert). The contribution of agriculture declined from 45.2 percent of total GDP in 1968 to 3.1 percent in 1998. Employment in the agricultural sector has declined from about 39 percent in 1966 to approximately 16 percent in the 1990s (Bank of Botswana, 1999). Although the majority of households in rural areas depend on the agricultural sector for survival, wages paid are relatively low. Hence, people have very little incentive to seek employment in this sector.

Botswana has wildlife resources and delta that have attracted worldwide attention and interest. The tourism sector is viewed as an opportunity to diversify the economy. A tourism policy was developed in 1998 in order to promote a sustainable and environmentally-sound tourism industry, and to create employment opportunities for the community, especially those living in rural areas. A financial scheme has been developed in order to assist investors interested in tourism. The tourism sector has grown in the last decade, with the number of tourists visiting Botswana increasing by 217 percent between 1986 and 1998.

Botswana has established ties with regional and international organizations including the Southern African Customs Union (SACU) in 1969 and the Southern African Development Community in 1980. Agreement under SACU allows free movement of goods within the union (SACU members are South Africa, Namibia, Lesotho, and Swaziland). Tariffs apply to foreign goods entering the Southern African market. However, SACU is currently under review to address member concerns about revenue sharing and unfair trade practices, as well as to align SACU with WTO obligations. Botswana is also a member of the African Union established in 2002. Botswana has consented to the New Partnership for Africa's Development, which emphasizes principles of African ownership, leadership, and accountability. Botswana is also a member of international organizations such as the World Trade Organization, United Nations, World Bank, International Monetary Fund, and African Caribbean Pacific group of countries.

Regarding Southern Africa, the region is fairly politically stable, particularly after majority rule in South Africa and Namibia and peace negotiations in Angola and Mozambique. Economic recovery in the region is attributed to some reform policies such as privatization and the development of the tourism sector and general infrastructure in an effort to attract foreign investment. For example, in 2000, Southern Africa experienced an aggregate growth rate of about 3.4 percent, with Botswana and Mozambique experiencing the highest growth rate of 8 percent. Zimbabwe recorded a negative growth rate in 2000 (Botswana Government, 2002a). However, recent political developments and land reform policies adopted by the ruling government in Zimbabwe have affected the stability and attractiveness of the region for tourism and investment. Southern Africa is also affected by famine currently existing in Angola, Lesotho, Malawi, Zambia, and Zimbabwe.

The above analysis indicates that Botswana has enjoyed the unique characteristics in Africa of maintaining political stability and sustaining steady economic growth over the last 33 years. These special features were mainly attributed to discovery of diamonds, coupled with prudent macro-economic policies. Growth of the economy and mineral revenue have contributed to large foreign exchange reserves that were US$6.5 billion in January 2001(Botswana Government, 2002b). Botswana has therefore managed the economy in such a way that the country has not experienced any recurring budgetary deficits and unsustainable indebtedness like in other African countries. The rate of inflation has been stable in the last few years; the annual inflation rate was recorded at about 6.6 percent in 2001 compared to 8.5 percent in 2000 (Botswana Government, 2002a). The highest rate of inflation was recorded in 1992, at 16.1 percent (Bank of Botswana, 1999).

The fact that the mineral sector continues to play a significant role in the economy creates dangers associated with dependency on one major commodity. Fluctuations in the global diamond market and prices and the general slowdown in economic growth worldwide affect the mining industry. Botswana has been affected by these factors in the past and they are likely to affect the mining industry in the future. For example, fluctuations in the diamond international market and changes in prices affected government revenue in the 1980s and in 1998, resulting in stockpiling and a decline in government revenue. Furthermore, there is also the possibility that diamond reserves will eventually be depleted. However, the government has taken measures to broaden revenue, including the introduction of value added tax (VAT) in July 2002, at the rate of 10 percent. In addition, structural and legislative reforms are underway to foster sustainable economic growth and development. The government's efforts to diversify the economy are continuing. For instance, the government is attracting investors to venture into tourism and promoting Botswana as the financial services center of Southern Africa. Botswana has received the highest investment ratings in Africa by Moody's Investors Service rating agency, being awarded "A" grade in March 2001, and also by Standard and Poor's Investors Service rating agency in April of the same year (Botswana Government, 2002a). This rating should increase Botswana's attractiveness for foreign investment.

Botswana is faced with problems of unemployment, poverty, and the impact of HIV/AIDS on the economy. In 2000 the rate of unemployment was estimated at 15.8 percent, compared to 21.5 percent in 1996 (Botswana Government, 2002b). There is also the problem of underemployment, particularly of graduates who hold degrees in the social sciences field. Poverty and disparity in income are other problems affecting Botswana. According to the 1993/94 Household, Income, and Expenditure Survey, 38 percent of households were estimated to be living in poverty (Botswana Government, 2002b). The poverty rate is estimated to have declined to about 37 percent in 2001. In an effort to address poverty in female-headed households, the government has introduced programs to increase women's participation in development through policy introduced in 1995. Additional poverty alleviation measures include old age pension scheme, destitute allowance, and drought relief.

The spread of HIV/AIDS is another major challenge facing Botswana. HIV/AIDS is affecting the most productive segments of the population and is depleting the country of limited human and financial resources. The government is addressing the HIV/AIDS problem by developing the necessary infrastructure, including upgrading health facilities, improving access to medication to prevent the spread of AIDS and prolong life, and providing the necessary care and support, as well as increasing public awareness about HIV/AIDS through the media. Efforts to combat the HIV/AIDS pandemic are undertaken in collaboration with organisations such as the Bill and Melinda Gates Foundation.

Development of public administration

Before Botswana became independent, the colonial administration did not have an interest in developing administrative structures and social infrastructure in the then Bechuanaland protectorate, except an interest in maintaining law and order in the country

(Harvey and Lewis, 1990; Hope and Somolekae, 1998). However, once there was change of government from colonial administration to indigenous leaders, the ruling government's priority was to develop administrative structures and social infrastructure in the country, which were non-existent at independence. From 1966 to 1970, government established various ministries and departments, and invested in development projects and programs to provide social services, which were lacking in the country.

After independence in 1966, Botswana inherited administrative systems and practices from the colonial administration, hence the existence of bureaucracy and a hierarchy in Botswana's civil service. In Botswana, bureaucracy and hierarchy thus represent the best model of administration (Sharma, 1998). The public sector bureaucracy conforms to Weber's legal-rational type of authority, which is characterised by job specialisation, authority hierarchy, impersonality, rules and procedures, and recording (Buchanan and Huczynski, 2001: 366). However, there are disadvantages associated with bureaucracy, including delays in decision making, red tape, rigidity, subjectivity, rules and regulation not always followed, and unfairness in application (Beach, 1995; Sharma, 1998).

However, public service management has evolved over time. There has been deregulation, decentralization and devolution in the public services. Computerization has also taken place, aimed at improving management of government employees. The government has, since 1998, invested in computerization of personnel management and an IT system. Computerization should improve the maintenance of accurate documentation, storage, and retrieval of employee data such as age, last promotion, work experience, and recommendation from last performance appraisal. Computerization facilitates prompt decision making relating to promotion, discipline, and transfer of staff, as well as assists managers in carrying out HRM activities. Service delivery should improve in the public services through accurate information storage and access and improved coordination between departments.

Human Resource Management

According to Armstrong (2001), human resources is defined as a strategic and coherent approach to the management of an organisation's assets; while Storey (2001) views HRM as a distinctive approach to employment management which seeks to achieve competitive advantage through the strategic deployment of a highly committed and capable workforce using an array of cultural, structural, and personnel techniques (Storey, 2001: 6). Hendry (1995) considers HRM as an approach that sees people as a valuable resource and focuses on developing and harnessing their contribution and skills for the organization. International HRM emerged as a result of globalization and the demand to effectively manage organizations in diverse and multicultural environments, as well as the need to harmonize HR policies and practices.

The request to manage resources efficiently and effectively is also increasing, including managing human resources. Research has shown that organizations that are characterized by flatter, leaner, more flexible and autonomous structures and systems achieve higher levels of performance (Robbins, 2001). Studies further indicate that organizations that have strategic goals, a clear vision and objectives that are linked to human resource policies perform better (Tyson, 1997). In addition, firms with human resource policies and employment practices that embrace change, diversity, commitment, openness, employee involvement, communicate effectively, and treat people as a valuable resource outperform organizations that have bureaucratic and rigid structures and systems of work (Pfeffer, 1998; Hendry, 1995).

Different firms have used different HRM policies with varying degrees of success. For example, Purcell (1999: 9) notes that "one of the puzzles associated with the best practice model is why it does not spread rapidly to every firm or even within enterprises. . . ." Kochan and Dyer (2001) argue that HR functions within many US corporations remain weak and low in influence relative to managerial functions such as finance, marketing, and manufacturing. Regarding HRM in Africa, Kamoche (2002: 995) asserts that there is a need "to identify the characteristics of HRM in Africa, the diversity and adequacy of approaches currently in use and how these might be affected by the key contextual factors." In her research on HRM practice in organizations in Nigeria, Anakwe (2002) found that human resource practices were a blend of Western or foreign practices and local practices reflecting the significance of local context. Anakwe's findings support a "crossvergence perspective." Regarding HRM in Sub-Saharan Africa, Jackson (2002: 1000) has suggested a model of cross-cultural dynamics and identifies management systems in Sub-Saharan Africa as changing from "post-colonial systems which are control-oriented, post-instrumental systems which are results-oriented, to African Renaissance systems which are people-oriented." Jackson concludes that the "Western view and practice of HRM does not represent a cross-cultural perspective." Furthermore, Jackson suggests that HRM in Africa could be better understood by applying the cross-cultural perspective, and researching on good management practices in Africa based on different management systems.

Regarding management practices in Southern Africa, Horwitz *et al.* (2002) asserts that there is an increase in Southern African firms adopting Japanese and east Asian practices. In Botswana, some organizations, particularly in public services, have adopted Japanese/east Asian/South East Asian practices in addition to Western management practices already in use. For example, in the 1990s, concepts such as Total Quality Management (TQM) and Work Improvement Teams (WITS) were introduced in Botswana following government initiatives to improve productivity and service delivery. The government introduced WITS in the public services, a concept borrowed from Singapore (it originates from Japan). The concept of WITS, among others, was introduced in 1993 to "foster team spirit, teamwork, commitment to work and a mindset that continuously seeks optimum performance" (Directorate of Public Service Management, 1999: 46). The positive aspect of WITS is that it involves employees at all levels and teaches them how to be effective at work through positive relations, continuous learning, and commitment to work. When the government introduced WITS, team leaders, facilitators and team members were sent for training in Singapore where the concept has already been successfully implemented. Officers were also trained at Botswana National Productivity Centre (BNPC) and in local institutions such as Botswana Institute of Administration and Commerce (BIAC). Total Quality Management was introduced through BNPC. BNPC was established in 1993 in order to improve productivity and service delivery; its major function is to facilitate productivity awareness and improvement in the private and public sectors by educating the nation about and sensitizing it to the benefit and importance of high productivity levels in the workplace. BNPC develops and organizes productivity improvement programs, conducts research, and promotes good industrial relations. BNPC is thus meant to improve productivity through, "growth, improvement in quality, lower costs, quicker service delivery, higher output and better service" (Hope, 1998: 129). BNPC also organizes training programs on management techniques such as TQM, quality of working life (QWL) and quality circles (QCs). Other productivity improvement iniatives introduced in the public sector include a policy of employing top civil servants on contract. New Zealand is said to have implemented the policy of contract employment successfully (Christensen and Laegreid, 2002). The policy of weeding out "dead wood" was also implemented in an effort to rid public services of unproductive officers (Botswana Government, 1997b).

However, Horwitz et al. (2002) acknowledge that many see adoption of east Asian work practices as unworkable. In Botswana, problems emerging from management reforms include skepticism, where concepts like TQM and WITS are seen as foreign. Evaluation reports on WITS indicate that the strategy has not been as effective as expected. In his report, Kgosidintsi (1997: 1) observed that, "when WITS was launched, sufficient effort was not made to persuade management to embrace WITS so that they can spearhead by example." The government has, since 1999, decided to integrate WITS into performance management systems (Directorate of Public Service Management, 2002). Regarding the effectiveness of contract employment of top civil servants, the policy has not been as successful as it could be, as the government has acknowledged. Once officers are employed through contract they tend not be as productive as expected, leading to non-renewal of their contract after two years. The government has since revised the policy to reduce costs associated with paying end of contract benefits to officers after two years when their contracts expire (Botswana Government, 1997b).

The role of HR departments and units is changing in some organizations in Botswana. Some organizations seek external assistance with some HR functions; for example, some have requested consulting firms to provide recruitment services, including interviews and recommending best candidates for management positions. Other organizations have engaged HRM consulting firms to review their existing pay structures, as well as provide employee and management development programs. In the public sector, some functions of the Directorate of Public Service Management are decentralized to ministries and departments in an effort to improve decision making in matters relating to recruitment, promotion, discipline, and deployment of staff. Various authors, including Tyson (1995: 146), suggested that the role of HR departments would decline in the future, with devolution of HR responsibilities to line managers and increasing use of consultants by organizations.

HRM regulatory framework

There are laws and regulations to guide personnel management practices in the public and private sectors. These were developed in order to ensure fair employment practices, and "to promote good industrial relations and human relations at the work place" (Botswana Government, 1994). Organizations are expected to conform to these guidelines when designing recruitment, selection, payment, and training structures, as well as when developing industrial relations policies and programs. Employment guidelines and regulations formulated by the government are thus aimed at ensuring that the private sector provides reasonable terms and conditions of work, as well as ensuring health and safety in the workplace. Managers and the business community are guided by policies, regulations, and Acts of Parliament to guide employment practices. The legislative framework designed to guide employment practices includes the Employment Act of 1982, the National Industrial Relations Code of Practice 1994, and the National Policy on Incomes Employment, Prices, and Profits. Employers are also expected to conform to the National Policy on HIV/AIDS and Employment 2001, which is aimed at preventing and minimizing the spread of HIV/AIDS in the workplace.

As indicated in the Industrial Relations Code of Practice 1994, managers should ensure that there are clear structures of communication, that supervisors are properly selected and trained in their roles, and are given reasonable freedom to supervise effectively. Regarding employees, the Industrial Relations Code of Practice advocates that, in exchange for pay, the employees' role should be to work to their best ability (Botswana Government, 1994: 5). Managers should ensure that employees understand the terms and conditions of service to ensure that the two parties work in harmony, with full consultation, respect, and mutual trust. The Employment Act guides employers on the process of recruitment and selection of local and foreign staff into the organization. The Act advocates equal opportunities for qualifying applicants, irrespective of gender, tribe, religion, or political beliefs. The Act stipulates that when a vacancy exists in the government and private sectors, priority should be given to citizens of Botswana and serving officers whenever possible. In the event that there are no qualifying citizen applicants, non-citizens can be selected. The Non-Citizen Employment Act provides guidelines on employment of non-citizens. The National Policy on Incomes, Employment, Prices, and Profits guides salary structures in the government and private sectors. The policy is based on the objective of sustainable economic growth and economic diversification, international competitiveness, equitable income distribution, and wage restraint aims contained in the National Development Plan (NDP). The NDP is produced every five years and Botswana is on its eighth plan, covering 1997–2003 (NDP 8).

HRM practices

Recruitment and selection

As mentioned earlier, recruitment and selection policies and practice are guided by regulations and policies developed by government. Regarding recruitment and selection in the public sector, the Department of Public Service Management (DPSM) is responsible for sourcing staff for government. Human resource management in the public sector is the responsibility of the DPSM, including responsibility to implement, for example, public sector employment policies such as the Public Service Act, Public Service Regulations and Public Service General Orders. Vacancies existing in government ministries and departments are usually filled by promotion within or transfer within, the government. If there are no qualified candidates within the government to fill vacancies, the post is then advertised within and outside the country. When it comes to selection of candidates from a pool of applicants, selection is based on qualifications, work experience, proven merit, and suitability for post. These factors are given more weight than seniority (Botswana Government, 1998a).

The HRM department or section usually carries out recruitment and selection functions in the private and parastatal organizations. Depending on the size of the organization, HR functions can be done by the manager of the organization (for example, a small organization employing less than ten people) or by an HR department/unit in medium to large organizations. HR managers use, for example, the Employment Act and the Industrial Code of Practice to guide the recruitment and selection process. The general procedure is that priority should be given to qualifying candidates within the organization. In the event of unavailability of a qualifying officer within the organization, the post can be advertised to candidates within and outside the country. However, as mentioned earlier, positions requiring technical, scientific, and management staff are normally filled by candidates from outside the country due to their short supply within Botswana. The general shortage of candidates with technical and managerial expertise has resulted in the majority of managerial positions being held by expatriate staff.

Payment systems

Organizations in Botswana use different payment structures and policies to reward employees. For example, the pay structure in the public sector is based on a salary structure, while the private and parastatal sectors apply performance- and competency-based pay structures. The Directorate of Public Service Management administers the payment structure for public officers, based on qualifications and work experience. The government has undertaken several salary reviews to adjust public sector salaries, as well as to attract and retain qualified and experienced staff. Cost of living adjustments are effected on public sector salaries and wages to "ensure that workers' earnings are not substantially eroded by the rate of inflation" (Botswana Government, 1998b: 8).

In the private sector, payment systems differ from those of the government, in that compensation of employees is determined by nature of work, ability to pay, and local labor market forces. There are statutory provisions such as the Incomes Policy and Employment Act, that guide the payment structure in the private sector. In addition, the government has established a minimum wage policy to ensure that low-income earners are not disadvantaged, together with other compensation policies to minimize wage differentials between the public and private sectors. However, organizations in the private sector are free to design their own payment system and policies according to the labor market and what they can afford. Employment policies and codes of conduct encourage organizations in the private and parastatal sectors to establish clear guidelines and inform employees accordingly regarding the payment system, pay periods, overtime, allowances, increments, pay merits, cost of living adjustments, and deductions. Organizations in the private sector use performance-based pay, where employees are awarded salary increases and bonus pay at the end of the year based on their overall performance rating. Salary increases and bonus awards are normally linked to the financial performance of the organization. Non-financial rewards such as certificates, employee of the month awards, with a picture in the company newsletter, and medals are also awarded to employees in some organizations. Other organizations have employee recognition schemes, including gifts such as ornaments and equipment (e.g. gardening and farming tools) to employees to recognize their loyalty to the organization through long service and good conduct. Yet other organizations, including government, offer additional benefits in an effort to attract and retain staff, particularly non-citizen staff. Additional benefits include company housing and company vehicles, as well as payment of travel expenses to and from their home country. According to the Bank of Botswana report (2000: 517), non-citizen employee monthly average earnings are five times higher than citizen staff. The highest employee monthly average earnings are in the financial and business services and the lowest paid are agricultural workers.

Performance management

Performance management is used to manage performance at organizational, departmental, and individual levels. Performance management at the individual level starts when an employee is furnished with job responsibilities and informed about performance standards and output expected from them. The appraisal process entails setting of performance expectations or targets, monitoring of performance, and a formal review of performance at the end of a predetermined period. The immediate supervisor conducts performance reviews using a variety of appraisal methods. In Botswana, organizations use various appraisal techniques to rate employee performance, including rating scale, critical incident, management by objectives, employee competency, and employee comparison. The purposes of performance appraisal include assessment of actual performance against set targets, employee development, guide to job changes, as well as wages and salary increments (Beach, 1995: 314). The appraisal process is associated with various problems though, including the halo effect, leniency or strictness, central tendency, subjectivity, lack of time, and communication problems (Robbins, 2001).

Regarding performance management in the public services in Botswana, the Directorate of Public Service Management is responsible for the administration of government employees. The Directorate furnishes ministries and departments with job descriptions and performance expectations, as well as appraisal instruments. Immediate supervisors at ministerial and departmental level are expected to conduct annual appraisals and make recommendations to the Directorate for follow-up or actions. However, there are delays in acting on appraisals due to the large number of appraisals administered by the Directorate. The appraisal instrument is currently under review to address some of its weaknesses, such as delay in follow-up and decisions on recommendations.

Review of appraisal systems is also carried out to facilitate implementation of Performance Management System (PMS), a strategy that aims to increase productivity through improved individual and organizational performance. Furthermore, the government is developing the use of key performance indicators and key results areas to measure individual and department performance. PMS is a new concept in Botswana; the government introduced it in 1999 in order to improve performance and service delivery in the public sector. The concept of PMS is cascading in organizations in the country; for example the Botswana Telecommunications Corporation and Botswana Housing Corporation are reported to be successfully using this system (Directorate of Public Service Management, 2002). The University of Botswana has also introduced PMS.

Training and development

The government has played a significant role in the training and development of human resources in the last 30 years and continues to do so even today. Training has always been the initiative of the government, mainly because, after independence in 1966, a small number of locals had administrative and technical skills to enable them to take over from the colonial government. This resulted in the government inheriting a bureaucracy staffed with former colonial officers. The goal of government after coming into power was to develop local personnel so that they could take over key decision-making posts occupied by expatriate staff. A training and localization policy was thus developed to achieve localization objectives (Hope, 1998). Regarding training in the private sector, organizations normally develop their own training and development programs in order to train and develop employees. They are guided by government policy, which encourages organizations to train citizen staff in order to develop their technical and management capacity. Organizations are also encouraged to establish career development programs and provide in-service training to employees. Induction courses are also encouraged, including the "induction of new entrants to the labor market so that they develop a positive attitude towards work" (Botswana Government, 1994: 18).

Education and training are seen as vital by the government and the private sector is encouraged to participate in the development of staff, including increasing access to education opportunities and to develop a culture of continuous learning. The government usually provides training grants and scholarships through the Ministry of Education, employers' federations, private, parastatal, and non-governmental organizations. In some organizations, employees are encouraged to initiate training and are reimbursed upon completion.

Despite some achievements in the past three decades in training and developing human resources, Botswana continues to be faced with the problem of an inadequate supply of people qualified in technical and science-related fields. This is mainly because training efforts in the last three decades were not targeted to specific industries. The government and institutions are prioritizing training, with an emphasis on training in areas where there is a critical shortage of human resources. The government, in collaboration with the private sector, endeavours to balance training and development efforts so that they are responsive to industry demands and balance industry needs with employee aspirations.

Employee relations

There are various registered trade unions representing different industries. These include the Botswana Federation of Trade Unions, Botswana Civil Service Association, Botswana Miners Union, Botswana Teachers Union, and Botswana Unified Local Government Service Associations. Organizations have collective agreements with trade unions or employee organizations, and such agreements are in written form. Union representatives in organizations act on behalf of members to consult and negotiate with employers; for example, on issues pertaining to working conditions, unfair dismissal, training, disciplinary action, and pay. Employers are encouraged by employment policies to share as much work-related information as possible, to minimize conflicts and to facilitate collective bargaining processes. Employees are free to join trade unions and staff organizations/associations to protect and represent their interests at work.

To supplement the role of trade unions and to further enhance consultation and communication between the government and its employees, joint ministerial–staff consultative machinery was introduced in 1998. The objectives of the consultative committee are to, amongst others, consider terms and conditions of service, advise on methods to improve general working conditions, and to improve productivity and staff relations. Over the years, there have been conflicts between government and trade unions over issues relating to pay, resulting in strikes. For example, in 2002, there were various strikes in the country, including industrial action by teachers, as well as University of Botswana Non Academic and Academic Staff and Unified Local Government staff unions. Such industrial action prompted the government to appoint a commission in 2002 to review and recommend an appropriate pay structure for all public officers. Trade unions in Botswana are not yet as developed and well organized as those in other countries, and do not have a significant impact on the economy.

Health and safety

Under the Factories Act, employers are expected to provide pleasant and healthy conditions at the workplace. Organizations are expected to provide protective clothing and equipment to protect workers and minimize exposure to hazardous materials and noise. Employers are also encouraged to conduct regular medical examinations for staff members exposed to dangerous materials and working conditions. In addition, organizations are required by legislation to compensate workers injured at the workplace through compensation. Organizations are expected by law to pay terminal benefits to employees dismissed or who die while employed. Employers are also expected to conform to the national policy on HIV/AIDS, which was introduced in 1998 to minimize the spread and impact of HIV/AIDS and infectious diseases at the workplace. The Ministry of Health, through occupational heath units, educates workers through multi-sectoral AIDS committees established throughout the country. Employees are made aware of the importance and benefits of HIV/AIDS testing, treatment, and prevention. Some organizations in the private sector, for example Debswana, are complementing the government's efforts in minimizing the impact of HIV/AIDS at the workplace by providing HIV/AIDS support and care.

Conclusion

The above discussion has captured the socio-economic development of Botswana in the last 33 years, including the development and management of human resources. Botswana has adopted various macro-economic strategies and HRM policies. The macro-economic policies adopted have been successful in maintaining steady economic growth through careful management of resources. However, empirical research to explore and identify HRM practices prevailing should be strengthened in order to enhance effective use of human resources. Researchers, practitioners, and academics in Botswana should persuade organizations to allow HR to play an important role in business strategy. Efforts to minimize environmental and socio-cultural factors that inhibit successful and effective management of human resources should be emphasized through training and development of management and staff.

References

Anekwe, U.P. (2002) "Human resource management in Nigeria: Challenges and insights," *International Journal of Human Resource Management* 13 (7): 1042–1059.

Armstrong, M. (2001) *A handbook of human resource management*, London: Kogan Page.

Bank of Botswana (1999) *Annual report*, Gaborone: Bank of Botswana.

Bank of Botswana (2000) *Annual report*, Gaborone: Bank of Botswana.

Beach, D. (1995) *Personnel: The management of people at work*, New York: Macmillan.

Botswana Government (1984) Employment Act, Chapter 47:01, Gaborone, Government Printer.

Botswana Government (1994) National Industrial Relations: Code of Practice, Ministry of Labour and Home Affairs, Adopted by the National Employment, Manpower and Incomes Council (NEMIC), Gaborone: Government Printer.

Botswana Government (1997a) 'Long Term Vision for Botswana: Towards Prosperity for All', Presidential Task Group for a Long Term Vision for Botswana

Botswana Government (1997b) National Development Plan 8: 1997/98–2002/03, Ministry of Finance and Development Planning, Gaborone: Government Printer.

Botswana Government (1998a) Public Service Regulations Statutory Instrument, No. 69, Supplement C—Botswana Gazette, Gaborone: Government Printer.

Botswana Government (1998b) Report of the Presidential Commission on the Public Service Salaries and Conditions of Service, Gaborone: Government Printer.

Botswana Government (2002a) Budget Speech, delivered by the Minister of Finance and Development Planning to the National Assembly on the 11 February 2002. Online: http://.www.gov.bw (5 December 2002).

Botswana Government (2002b) Draft National Development Plan 9: 2003/04–2008/09: Presentation Speech by the Minister of Finance and Development Planning, Delivered to the National Assembly on the 21 November 2002. Online: http://.www.gov.bw (5 December 2002).

Buchanan, D. and Huczynski, A. (2001) *Organisational behaviour: An introductory text*, London: Prentice Hall.

Christensen, T. and Laegreid, P. (eds.) (2002) *New public management: The transformation of ideas and practice*, England: Ashgate.

Directorate of Public Service Management (1999), "Botswana public service productivity reforms," *Public Service Management Journal* 1 (2): 46–47.

Directorate of Public Service Management (2002) *Botswana Public Service, Implementation of the Performance Management System (PMS)*, the PMS Philosophy Document, Gaborone: Government Printer.

Harvey, L. and Lewis, S.R. (1990) *Policy choice and development performance in Botswana*, London: Macmillan.

Hendry, C. (1995) *Human resource management: A strategic approach to employment*, London: Butterworth Heinman.

Hope, K.R. (1998) "Improving productivity in the public sector," in K.R. Hope and G. Somolekae (eds.) *Public administration in Botswana,* Kenwyn: Juta & Co Ltd.

Hope, K.R. and Somolekae, G. (eds.) (1998) *Public administration and policy in Botswana*, Kenwyn: Juta & Co. Ltd.

Horwitz, F.M., Kamoche, K., and Chew I.K.H. (2002) "Looking east: Diffusing high performance work practices in the Southern Afro-Asian context," *International Journal of Human Resource Management* 13 (7): 1019–1041.

Jackson, T. (2002) "Reframing human resource management in Africa: A cross-cultural perspective," *International Journal of Human Resource Management* 13 (7): 998–1018.

Kamoche, K. (2002) "Human resources in Africa," *International Journal of Human Resource Management* 13 (7): 993–997.

Kgosidintsi, T. (1997) "WITS news: Work improvement teams," *Lessons from a WITS Briefing Tour* 2 (2): 1.

Kochan, T. and Dyer, L. (2001) "HRM: An American view," in J. Storey (ed.) *Human resource management: A critical text*, Sydney: Thompson Learning.

Molomo, G.M. (ed.) (2000) "Elections and democracy in Botswana," *Botswana Journal of African Studies* 14 (1): 1.

Pfeffer, J. (1998) *The human equation: Building profits by putting people first*, Boston, MA: Harvard Business Press.

Presidential Task Group (1997) "Long-term vision for Botswana: Towards prosperity for all," Gaborone: Government Printer.

Purcell, J. (1999) "Best practice and best fit: Chimera or cul-de-sec?" *Human Resource Management Journal* 9: 13. Online: http://www. Proquest.umi.com.

Robbins, S. (2001) *Organisational behavior*, Englewood Cliffs, NJ: Prentice Hall.

Salkin, J., Mpabanga, D., Cowan, D., Selwe, J., and Wright, M. (eds.) (1997) *Aspects of the Botswana economy: Selected papers*, Gaborone: Lentswe la Lesedi.

Sharma, K.C. (1998) "Toward a more ethical and accountable bureaucracy," in K.R. Hope and G. Somolekae (eds.) *Public administration and policy in Botswana,* Kenywn: Juta & Co td.

Storey, J. (ed.) (2001) *Human resource management: A critical text*, Sydney: Thompson Learning.

Tyson, S. (1995) *Human resource strategy*, London: Pitman Publishing.

Tyson, S. (ed.) (1997) *The practice of human resource strategy*, London: Pitman Publishing.

3 HRM in Zambia

GERRY NKOMBO MUUKA AND
KENNETH KAOMA MWENDA

Introduction

Zambia, formerly called Northern Rhodesia, attained independence from Britain
on 24 October 1964, with Kenneth David Kaunda as the first president. The country
has had three presidents since independence. Following Kaunda (24 October 1964
to December 1991), Frederick Titus Jacob Chiluba (December 1991 to December 2001)
was elected, with strong backing from the powerful Zambia Congress of Trade Unions
(ZCTU), which he headed for many years as president. Elections in December 2001
saw the rise to power of the current president, Levy Patrick Mwanawasa. The country
has depended, and still depends, on copper mining for much of its economic activity
and foreign exchange earnings. At independence, copper accounted for roughly
85–90 percent of the country's foreign exchange earnings, and Zambia was the third
largest producer of copper in the world after Chile and then Zaire (now called the
Democratic People's Republic of Congo), respectively. In 2003, the country's
dependence on copper was still significant, accounting for some 60–70 percent
of foreign exchange. Home to one of the seven wonders of the world, the Victoria
Falls on the Zambezi River, the country has an estimated population of some 10
million (Gill *et al.*, 2000: 1; Global Policy Network, 2001), one million of whom live in
the capital city of Lusaka. The country's currency is called the *Kwacha* (K). At 752,612
km^2 (Global Policy Network, 2001: 1), Zambia is larger, in land terms, than the state
of Texas in the U.S.A. It is one of the countries comprising what is commonly known
as Sub-Saharan African. There are some 73 languages and dialects in Zambia, with the
major tribes and languages being Tonga, Bemba, Lozi, Lunda, Luvale, Ngoni, Chewa,
and Kaonde. English is the official language of business and instruction in the entire
educational sector.

Chapter objectives

The discussion on human resources management (HRM) practices and realities in
Zambia covers past practices (so that the reader is aware of where the country has come

from); present realities (necessary in order to appreciate where the country is at); and future challenges (self-evidently necessary in order to provide a glimpse of what the current and emerging realities might mean for the future of HRM in the country). This chapter gives a glimpse of features of the country's labor market prior to 1964. It provides the reader with an appreciation of the changing role of the HRM function in Zambia. There is discussion of Sub-Saharan Africa's adherence to and implementation of World Bank and International Monetary Fund economic reform programs, commonly referred to as Structural Adjustment Programs (SAPs), which have directly impacted the HRM function in Africa. The role and importance of trade unions in Africa, with specific reference to Zambian trade unions, is also discussed, as are some of the emerging HRM issues. These include how AIDS and HIV have impacted the HRM function in Africa in ways that are significantly different from comparable HRM practices in other countries.

Features of the pre-independence Zambian labor market

Managing people at work—more appropriately referred to as Human Resources Management (HRM) in contemporary phraseology—has traditionally involved such functions as recruiting, hiring, training, compensation, appraising, developing employees, as well as matters involving labor relations, health and safety, fairness concerns, and equal employment opportunity (Dessler, 2003: 2). Zambia's pre-independence and post-independence HRM practices are vastly different. Part of the reason is that industrial and formal administrative activity in Zambia during the transition to independence was characterized by insignificant, almost non-existent, indigenous (African) participation (Muuka, 1993). This area was the exclusive preserve of the private, white-settler, "Western" minority who, as Jackson (2002: 999) notes with regard to Africa's colonial period generally, perpetuated a "legacy of under-skilling largely through a concentration on export-led primary production (of copper, in Zambia's case) and low development of consumer economies." Colonial organizations were characterized by a Douglas McGregor conceptualized "Theory X" decision-making orientation. In his "post-colonial" typology of organizational management systems in Africa, Jackson (2002: 1002) typifies a colonial heritage where managers' mistrust of employees manifested itself in autocratic, authoritarian, and rule-bound control of workers, "allowing little worker initiative and rewarding a narrow set of skills simply by financial means."

There are other features of the pre-independence Zambian labor market that are important to understanding post-independence developments. Under a *migrant labor system*, the mines and (white) European-owned farms needed large numbers of able-bodied male African laborers. A principal tool used to ensure a large pool of this cheap labor was the repressive "native tax" system, a mandatory levy on Africans that ensured that they could only go to the distant farms and mines (leaving their wives and families) to work in order to be able to pay tax to the colonial administration

(Posner, 2001: 15). A *color bar system* was also a way of life among the dominant white minority, emphasizing that no African workers could have a white subordinate (Burawoy, 2000). In essence, this prejudicial system stressed that any Africans who were superordinates to other Africans were still subordinate to all whites. In the *education, training and development* arena, colonial powers had very little interest and stake in ensuring that Africans attained the requisite skills for formal employment, beyond basic primary education. As their interest lay primarily in externalizing as much profit out of the country as possible (from copper revenues and primary commodities from industry), long-term training and empowerment of Zambian workers at the time was not considered an investment. An example of this indifference to the education of Africans is that Zambia (with a population of some 3 million people in 1964) had less than 100 university graduates at independence!

Contextual background

Kaunda's first task at independence, after uniting the country behind his leadership under the motto of "One Zambia, One Nation," was to attend urgently to the country's educational needs. The country's first university, the University of Zambia (UNZA) was opened in 1966 in Lusaka, the capital. The government also built primary schools and diploma colleges in towns and rural areas throughout the country. Everyone was entitled to free education up to and including university education. In a bid to indigenize control of Zambia's socio-economic destiny, the Government of the Republic of Zambia (GRZ), in 1968 announced it would acquire a controlling interest (51 percent share holding) and place in state hands (that is, *nationalize*) all vital industries in the country. These came to be known as the 1968/69 Mulungushi/Matero Economic Reforms. The 1968–69 nationalization placed 80 percent of the Zambian economy under government control, thereby creating the country's parastatal (public) sector, largely through the giant Industrial Development Corporation (INDECO). INDECO was formed in 1964, and later placed under a bigger umbrella conglomerate called the Zambia Industrial and Mining Corporation (ZIMCO). ZIMCO was formed in 1970 as the holding company for all of Zambia's state-owned enterprises (SOEs) (Muuka, 1993). Some of the reasons for the nationalization (see, among others, Kaunda 1969; Cunningham, 1985; Stoever, 1985) included the desire by GRZ to control the "commanding heights" of the economy with a view to dictating the pace and direction of development, including investment in new productive capacity. There was a desire to hasten the movement of Zambian citizens into top management and technical positions, commonly referred to as the country's Zambianization Program. There was a need to utilize copper revenues to build up the country's infrastructural network of roads, clinics, and hospitals. Finally, there was concern over the dominance of foreign investors and their lack of interest in re-investing in the economy as manifested by massive repatriation of profits. Kaunda (1969: 51) was particularly concerned with what he described as "our friends who have kept only one foot in Zambia in order to take advantage of the economic boom, the other in South Africa, Europe, India or wherever they come from, ready to jump when they have made enough money, or when they think that the country no longer suits them."

Contemporary practices: post-SAP HRM characteristics

The Bretton Woods Institutions (BWIs, that is the World Bank and the International Monetary Fund) have since the early 1980s played an important role in the economies of many Sub-Saharan African countries using structural adjustment programs (SAPs). The overall objectives of SAPs include the need to increase an economy's outward orientation (or exports, principally through non-traditional exports); to reduce both African rural and urban poverty (both very high) and, ultimately to induce, in a country such as Zambia, a high and sustainable rate of economic growth. Specific measures include adjustment/devaluation of local currencies (the *Kwacha*, in Zambia's case); decontrol of internal price systems as well as external and internal trade flows (trade liberalization); privatization of state enterprises; reforming of banking policy, including interest rate decontrol; and the removal of all consumer subsidies. Under World Bank and International Monetary Fund tutelage, in 1992 the government embarked upon the most far-reaching market-led economic reforms ever seen in Zambia, with privatization of state-owned enterprises (SOEs) taking center stage. Privatization, in general, relates to a range of different policy initiatives designed to alter the balance between the public and private sectors (Cook and Kirkpatrick, 1988: 3), whether it is referred to as de-parastatalization, de-subsidization, de-nationalization, divestiture, or de-monopolization of SOEs. A Privatization Act was passed by the Zambian Parliament in July 1992, paving the way for the eventual privatization or reformation of some 318 SOEs. Although Zambia's privatization program is now coming close to an end—meaning most of the former SOEs have been privatized as of March 2003, with South Africans being the main buyers and beneficiaries—some strategic public utilities are yet to be privatized.

In identifying and discussing contemporary HRM practices, support is given to the view by Jackson (2002: 1009) that, "it may be somewhat idealistic to try to identify a particular African style or even philosophy of management . . . but it is worth pointing to aspects that it may include, so that in empirical studies those aspects may be discerned where they do exist." This is so because, particularly in Zambia, we can conceptualize contemporary management practices and HRM orientations into four distinct categories: public sector, South African, private, foreign-owned, and private indigenous companies.

Public sector cultural orientation

This involves work cultures and management of employees in government and quasi-government ministries and departments, as well as the major public companies

(Zambia Electricity Supply Corporation, Zambia Railways, Zambia Electricity and Supply Corporation, and Zambia National Commercial Bank) that have not yet been privatized under the country's aggressive 1992–2002 privatization program. As a way of redressing some of the colonial imbalances we discussed earlier, and also as a response to other socio-economic realities, many parastatal companies in Zambia have had wider stakeholder expectations extending beyond corporate missions. Jones (1991: 136), writing on Malawi, points out that organizations "tend to be viewed by society as a whole as having a wider mission than is generally understood in the West, being expected to provide socially desirable benefits such as employment, housing, transport, and assistance with important social rituals and ceremonies." Another feature is that managers in SOEs recognize the need to maintain good rapport with governments. This is important because in many cases the managing directors (MDs) or presidents of these companies are government appointees. They therefore have a self-interest in being on the right side of power coalitions and political pressures. As an example of these political pressures, these appointees have often been made to employ more people in their companies than would be considered economically viable. Another public sector feature is that in the event of death of a worker or family member, managers arrange for a coffin and help the deceased's family organize food, drinks, and firewood for the gathering at the funeral.

A troublesome public sector development is the *Wako-ni-Wako employment culture*. This is another name for tribalism, nepotism, and regionalism all rolled into one—that is, the tendency to recruit and promote relatives and people from one's tribe or province. It has been quite pervasive in the parastatal sector. In addition to large power distance and centralized decision-making tendencies, the Wako-ni-Wako culture encourages highly dependent subordinate behavior, as allegiance to superordinates becomes crucial for subordinates to retain and maintain their jobs.

A South African cultural orientation

This reflects the preponderance of South African ownership into Zambia's privatized companies, and how these new owners have brought into the country their own decision-making and HRM practices. South African owners come with their own culture and stereotypes (see the chapter on South Africa in this book), which in many instances may be at variance with Zambian culture. There have been cases of South African managers taken to Zambian courts for use of the "K" word on Zambian workers. In one such case, the Zambian court came down hard on the manager (and rightly so), arguing that there was no place in Zambia (or elsewhere in Africa, for that matter) for derogatory remarks on employees. At the top management level (managing directors, directors of functional areas), the new South African owners recruit parent country nationals (PCNs) from South Africa, while the supervisory and operative levels are predominated by host country nationals (HCNs), that is, Zambians. This *ethnocentric approach to staffing* (where key positions are filled by PCNs, see, among others Dowling *et al.*, 1999: 70) limits promotion opportunities for Zambians. This, coupled with the considerable salary gap between PCNs and HCNs in favor of the former, has in many cases led to frustration and turnover on the part of Zambian middle-level managers.

Private-sector, foreign-owned cultural orientation

There is a sizable private sector that is owned by Zambians of foreign origin, mainly Europeans, Asians (mostly from India), and a growing Lebanese community, especially in the fast foods industry. Depending on their ties to the government, these tend to have employment cultures that are a hybrid of the other three groups.

Private-sector, indigenous Zambian cultural orientation

This describes two types of company: those owned by indigenous Zambians prior to the 1992–2002 privatization, and those owned by indigenous Zambians as a result of the privatization program. Their employment culture tends more towards that of the public sector, with a more pronounced Wako-ni-Wako culture since they are not subject to any government sanction in employment preferences. They are subject only to moral suasion, as well as union pressure. We will discuss unions shortly. Although the four typologies discussed here have distinct characteristics, they do have certain organizational cultural attributes in common. This is particularly true with regard to Hofstede's cultural dimension of *power distance*. In all four types there is high power distance and bureaucratic rule-bound functional structures. A preponderance of companies and organizations in Zambia (and in other African countries, as other chapters in this book show), have highly centralized decision-making styles. Respect for authority and status differences are paramount. Other recruitment, selection, training and development, and union–management relations features in Zambia are discussed next.

Recruitment

What activities are carried out by Zambian companies regarding the identification and attraction of potential employees? Among the recruitment sources in the country are mass media which include *radio* (Zambia National Broadcasting Services, Radio Chikuni, Radio Mazabuka, Radio Maria), *television* (Zambia National Broadcasting Services), and *newspapers* (*Times of Zambia*, *Zambia Daily Mail*, *The Post* and *The Monitor*). Companies also recruit from colleges and at the country's two universities (the University of Zambia in Lusaka and the Copperbelt University in Kitwe). Since the country embarked on trade liberalization and privatization in 1992, new owners of former SOEs have also increasingly recruited expatriates (non-Zambians), Zambian repatriates (those Zambians working in other countries who are attracted back home), as well as third-country nationals (TCNs), such as South Africans recruited to work for German or British subsidiaries in Zambia (e.g. Lever Brothers in Ndola).

Electronic recruiting is also now possible. As Noe *et. al.* (2003: 68) point out, the information superhighway has opened up new avenues for recruiting talent. In the case of Zambia, organizations can now use the national internet provider ZAMNET (http://www.zamnet.zm) to advertise positions.

Selection

How do Zambian organizations identify applicants with the necessary knowledge, skills, and abilities? As in any other country, selection happens mostly after a series of interviews and references, including electronic references. In the South African and private sector, foreign-owned typologies identified earlier, recruitment and selection are usually on merit, as the owners/managers from South Africa (ethnocentric approach to recruitment and selection) do not identify with any local tribe or region for there to be regional or tribal bias in recruitment. On the other hand, the Wako-ni-Wako culture is prevalent, to varying degrees, in the recruitment and selection procedures of private, Zambian-owned organizations. In both cases, of course, there are many exceptions, as there are always people who play or don't play by the rules, whether these are from a moral/stake holder or legal standpoint. In the parastatal sector, attempts have been made to address the Wako-ni-Wako culture in recruitment and selection. One such attempt, in February 1996, involved issuance of the Public Service Management Division (PSMD) Circular No. B5 (see Mataka, 2002). This was aimed at updating or development of clear and results-oriented job descriptions, specifications, and performance standards in some 20 parastatal companies that, at the time, were undergoing restructuring in readiness for privatization. The circular "provided elaborate guidelines on the selection and placement process in the restructured organizations" (Mataka, 2002: 5). The intent, as Mataka points out, was to address the Wako-ni-Wako tendency of the old system, where people were placed in civil service jobs "on a partisan basis or on the basis of political affiliation."

There is little evidence to suggest that the above government selection guidelines made any meaningful headway during the period in question. We do know, of course, that the companies in question have since been privatized, a development that takes this discussion back to selection under the South African and private (foreign-owned, and Zambian) typologies that we have alluded to.

Training and development

In the new post-privatization dispensation, there is unfortunately no government-mandated policy on training, at least not of the type that existed among parastatal companies earlier. Under government control, parastatal companies had a policy of identifying employees at all levels of the corporate hierarchy for further training at local vocational schools, the University of Zambia, and the Copperbelt University, as well as at institutions abroad. Many Zambians acquired undergraduate and graduate degrees, as well as requisite expertise and skills, via this broad, government-led parastatal training policy. The exception to this scenario is in government ministries where, following PSMD Circular No. B5 of February 1996, a Public Service Training Policy was developed to guide government ministries and government agencies in the training and utilization of personnel arising from a training needs identification process (see Mataka, 2002: 5). But, as with all good government intentions under conditions of severe scarcity amid deteriorating economic conditions, this has ended up being a mere "paper" process whose implementation has been difficult, at best.

Training dynamics have changed dramatically in the private sector. Although companies still send employees for training at home and abroad so that they can acquire and share work-related knowledge, skills, and behaviors that are necessary for increased and improved organizational performance, most companies, due to the high incidence of HIV and AIDS, no longer do it with the same keenness as they used to before. Part of the reason, as we shall see later, is that these companies are not sure that the employees that are being trained will live long enough to share their new knowledge and skills.

Unions and labor–management relations

The Industrial Relations Act of 1993 (Amendment) is the main legislation governing employer and employee relations in the country. Not only does the Act provide for the formation of trade unions, it also prescribes conditions under which strikes may be called. As a result, the labor–management relations landscape is replete with unions, both small and large. Most unions in Zambia belong to one umbrella organization, the Zambia Congress of Trade Unions (ZCTU). The contentious issues between unions and management usually center around wages and salary pay rates, cost of living adjustments (COLAs), health care, allowances (housing, overtime, funeral), layoff procedures, leave (sick leave, maternity leave, holidays), training and promotion, pension plans, and disciplinary cases. Personnel management rather than HRM tends to prevail in many companies in the country.

The country has experienced (and is experiencing in 2003) high levels of both unemployment (those who are qualified but cannot find jobs in the formal, above-ground sector) and underemployment (that is, those in formal jobs where they cannot utilize their appropriate skills). It is estimated that the formal sector lost some 61,000 jobs between 1992 and 1995 (Global Policy Network, 2001). According to the country's Central Statistics Office (CSO), Zambia's unemployment rate was estimated at 13 percent of the labor force in 1986, increasing to 22 percent by 1991 (CSO, 1993). We now examine the country's employment and unemployment situations.

It is estimated that about 122,500 young people enter the labor market every year without any hope of finding gainful employment (CSO, 1993). Unemployment is higher among youth and women and is now affecting college as well as University of Zambia and Copperbelt University graduates.

The CSO (2001) and Global Policy Network (2001) say that formal sector employment in the country between 1997 and 2000 stood at 475,161 (1997), 467,193 (1998), 477,508 (1999), and 476,347 in 2000. In the private sector, agriculture is the biggest employer (some 13 percent of the total during this period), followed by trade and distribution. Employment has declined in the key sectors of mining (from 44,498 in 1997 to 35,042 in 2000) and manufacturing. A casual look at these numbers shows that employment levels have, in fact, not changed that much between 1997 and 2000. This cannot be further from the truth. The generation of real jobs in the economy has continued to lag behind the growth in the labor force. In fact, as the Global Policy Network (2001) points out, since the early 1990s the trend in formal sector employment showed a persistent decline up to 1998. In 1997, out of a total labor force estimated at 4.194 million workers, only 11 percent were employed in the formal sector (Global Policy Network, 2001). The remaining 89 percent of the labor force was either unemployed or employed in the informal sector.

An important feature of Zambia's HRM landscape has been the role and strength of the labor movement. The country has been and continues to be highly unionized, with union membership averaging 56 percent over the five-year period 1995–1999. Total union membership has, however, been dropping steadily during the period under review—from a high of 289,322 unionized employees in 1995 to 234,522 in 1999, a total loss of close to 55,000 union members (ZCTU, 1999). During the same period, total formal sector employment declined by some 7,000 employees (from 485,000 in 1995 to 477,508 in 1999, with indications that the trend has been downward in the years since). Job and union membership losses have affected sectors covered by the Airways and Allied Workers Union, the Bankers' Union of Zambia, the powerful Mine Workers Union of Zambia (MUZ), the National Union of Plantation and Agriculture Workers, the National Union of Public Service Workers, and the Zambia National Union of Teachers. Several reasons can be advanced for the decline in both total union membership and its percentage of total formal sector employment. In the case of the Mineworkers' Union of Zambia and the National Union of Public Service Workers, the declining numbers have been largely due to the impact of SOE downsizing and down-scoping as privatization of those SOEs takes root. The new owners of privatized firms have been engaging in "rightsizing," by reducing employment to levels they consider efficient and economically viable. In the financial services sector, two important factors have conjoined to reflect declining employment levels and union membership. First, there have been improvements in technology, especially in banking services, resulting in automated machines replacing human beings. A more serious factor, one that we shall devote considerable space to discussing later, has been the impact of HIV and AIDS in the sector. A glimpse into the problem is provided by the case of AIDS-related deaths at Barclays Bank of Zambia between 1987 and 1992, by age. From a low of six AIDS-related deaths in the bank in 1987, the number had risen to 38 by 1992 (Bollinger and Stover, 1999). The most worrying statistic is the fact that 83 percent of the deaths have occurred among the most productive age group, among employees who are less than 45 years of age. This is a worrying trend for any country.

In the airline industry, after the liquidation of the national carrier (Zambia Airways Limited), the country has no airline of its own and relies, instead, mostly on South African Airways and other international airlines such as British Airways. Many of the country's indigenous travel agencies have closed down as a result, leaving just enough to service foreign airlines. Jobs have been lost as a result, and so has union membership. Another serious problem has been the country's prolonged drought in recent years, which has affected the National Union of Plantation and Agriculture Workers. Their declining numbers have been due to the prolonged drought, especially in the country's major farming regions in southern, central, and eastern provinces. The drought has led to employment cuts in agro-based industries, with resultant knock-on effects in other upstream and downstream industries as well. *Upstream industries* are defined as those in the early part of the value chain (defined as the range of activities involved in the procurement of raw materials, production of goods, and marketing of goods to the ultimate consumers). In this case, upstream industries (synonymous with backward linkages in business strategy phraseology) would be those supplying raw materials in the form of unprocessed agricultural products such as maize (white corn, the staple food in Zambia), tomatoes, tobacco, rice (from any of Zambia's nine provinces), and pineapples (from Mwinilunga in the North-Western Province). *Downstream industries* (synonymous with forward linkages), on the other hand, are found later in the value chain and involve mainly companies in the distribution chain and the marketing and sale of goods to final consumers. Finally, the decline in trade union membership can also be attributed to a lack of capacity by unions to organize in the new and increasingly hostile environment, particularly in the emerging private sector after privatization (Global Policy Network, 2001). The strong union presence has provided needed checks and balances for HRM practices in the four cultural typologies discussed earlier. This has happened in areas such as unfair employment practices (some South African managers in Zambia are known to look down upon Zambian workers and to treat them less than honorably), as well as the whole range of issues from compensation to quality of work life.

Future challenges: emerging HRM issues

HIV and AIDS in Zambia and Africa: no longer HRM as usual

No development in the last ten years has affected the HRM dynamic in Sub-Saharan Africa more than the HIV and AIDS crisis. It is our estimation that HIV and AIDS is by far the biggest HRM challenge facing Africa right now. There is a vicious circle where, if your most educated and productive segment of the population is sick and dying (see the case involving Barclays Bank of Zambia, discussed earlier), the threat to development and security is real, while the impact on economic growth is damaging. In the context of this chapter and this book, there are three relevant questions to be asked, and answered, with regard to HIV and AIDS. How big and widespread is the problem in Africa? How has the crisis affected business—that is, what are the "costs" of AIDS? How has the crisis changed the HRM dynamic?

Magnitude of the HIV and AIDS crisis

The authors of this chapter have had relatives—both close and distant—taken in their prime by what is increasingly becoming the deadliest disease of our generation: Acquired Immune Deficiency Syndrome (AIDS). The AIDS problem in Africa is real. It is massive, and it is no laughing matter. The joint United Nations Program on HIV/AIDS (UNAIDS), in its December 2002 update, reported that a total of 42 million people wordwide were living with HIV and AIDS. Of this total, 29.4 million (or 70 percent) were said to be in Sub-Saharan Africa. Barks-Ruggles *et al.* (2001) observe that since the first HIV/AIDS cases were reported over 20 years ago, nearly 58 million people have been infected and 22 million have died; roughly two-thirds of both numbers occurring in Sub-Saharan Africa. Acknowledging the gravity of the crisis, President George W. Bush of the USA, on 28 January 2003, announced a new $10 billion aid package to help African countries (including Botswana, Namibia, Mozambique, Zambia, Nigeria, Uganda, Kenya, Tanzania, and Ethiopia) and Guyana and Haiti to fight HIV and AIDS. The money is earmarked for drugs, education, doctors, and specialized laboratories.

As Bollinger and Stover (1999) point out, the corporate impact of HIV and AIDS can be assessed in terms of either direct or indirect costs.

Direct costs of HIV and AIDS

These include expenditures for medical care, drugs, and funeral expenses. Firms may experience both an increase in expenditures and a reduction in revenues. Expenditures are increased for health care costs, burial fees, and training and recruitment of replacement employees (Bollinger and Stover, 1999). Revenues may be decreased because of absenteeism due to illness or attendance at funerals and time spent on training. In Zambia, a typical large company will pay workers 90 days of sick leave at full pay, and another 90 days at half pay. The cost of this to a firm, along with annual leave of 30 days for non-unionized workers and 42 days for unionized workers, begins to impact negatively on productivity levels. As Whiteside *et al.* (2000) observe, productivity will fall and costs rise because of:

- *Increased absenteeism*. This will not only be because of the ill health experienced by the employees, but also because they (particularly women) may take time off to care for their families and for funerals.

- *The fact that workers will be less productive at work and may not be able to carry out more demanding physical jobs.* Replacements for AIDS victims may be less skilled and less experienced and require training.

There are also high AIDS-related health issues as a result of costs to cover coffins, transportation for mourners (using company and privately hired buses, minibuses, open lorries), and benefits to survivors, as well as man-hours spent at funerals. Two Zambian firms studied in detail by the AIDSCAP project describe different sets of costs associated with HIV/AIDS: Chilanga Cement in Lusaka Province and Nakambala Sugar Estates in Mazabuka, Southern Province. For Chilanga Cement, the bulk of the costs experienced by the company were increased absenteeism rates, whereas it was increased medical expenses for Nakambala Sugar Company (Bollinger and Stover, 1999). At Chilanga Cement, the hours lost due to illness and funerals increased threefold from 13,380 hours in 1992/93 to 43,370 hours in 1994/95 (Ministry of Health, 1997, as quoted in Kusanthan, 2001).

Indirect costs of HIV and AIDS

Bollinger and Stover (1999) say that indirect costs include lost time due to illness, recruitment and training costs to replace workers, and care of orphans by some companies. There is also increasing *disincentive to train workers*. When people face dramatically shortened life spans, as HIV and AIDS victims do, this raises the opportunity cost of additional training, because few of the costs incurred will be recouped in higher subsequent productivity and earnings. When employers assume that the average productive lifespan of anyone they train will decline, this directly reduces the incentive to support long-term training.

A multi-pronged HRM response: so, what can (should) companies do?

At the macro (national) level, UNAIDS/WHO (2002) point out that 19 African countries have set up national HIV/AIDS councils or commissions at senior levels of government, and local responses are growing in number and vigor. Across the region, 40 countries have completed national strategic AIDS plans aimed at tackling HIV/AIDS as a development issue. Human resource departments, for their part, need to provide policies or guidelines to managers in order to help them respond appropriately to the needs of employees with AIDS or HIV and answer the concerns of co-workers. One sample policy contains the following provisions (see Hickman and Lee, 2001: 102):

- Managers should be sensitive to the special needs of employees and assist them by demonstrating personal support, and referring them to counseling services.

- Co-workers will be expected to continue working relationships with an employee who has AIDS or is HIV-positive.
- An employee with AIDS or HIV is under no obligation to disclose his or her condition to a manager or any other employee.
- An employee with AIDS or HIV is expected to meet the same performance requirements applicable to other employees, with reasonable accommodations if necessary. This may include flexible or part-time work schedules, leave of absence, work restructuring, or job reassignment.

Employee restrictions

Zambia's largest cement company (Chilanga Cement, presented earlier) reported that absenteeism for funerals increased 15-fold between 1992 and 1995 (Whiteside *et al.*, 2000). As a result, the company has restricted employee absenteeism for funerals to only those for a spouse, parent, or child.

Short-term courses

It is also advisable for companies to consider short-term, repeatable training courses that improve worker efficiency and morale to help prevent further declines in productivity (Barks-Ruggles *et al.*, 2001).

The response to HIV/AIDS is therefore not only an individual company's HRM responsibility, it also involves a multi-pronged sectoral, industrial, national, regional, continental, and global approach. In Africa, more than anywhere else, better targeted interventions are not only needed, they are also very urgent. It is clear, from the foregoing discussion on HIV and AIDS, that for countries and companies in Africa, it is no longer "HRM as usual."

The huge informal sector

What happens, and what has happened, to the huge number of employment-eligible Zambians that cannot be absorbed in the formal sector? The point was made and demonstrated earlier that the informal sector is bigger than the formal sector in countries like Zambia. Gill *et al.* (2000: 1) point out, for instance, that in 1993, the country had two million people employed in the informal sector, while only about 600,000 were reported to be in the formal sector.

A plethora of names are used to refer to the informal sector, including second economy, underground economy, the black market, the unobserved economy, and the unreported economy (Feige, 1990). In Zambia, the informal sector typically tends to absorb women, youths, and, increasingly, college and university graduates, who cannot find jobs in the formal sector. Informal activities normally take place in three major places in cities and all small towns (without exception) throughout Zambia: market stalls in the streets (increasingly, to include street vendors or street traders); whenever traffic in town comes to a halt; residential homes; and in unauthorized places, as in the case of illegal mining of precious stones/gemstones. There is a wide range of informal sector activities, among them the sale of second-hand clothes (called *Salaula*, which in many Zambian languages, such as Tonga, literally means "you have a choice" or you can choose). No other informal sector activity was more pronounced than Salaula in the 1990s. Others sell foodstuffs including *nshima*, the country's staple food. There is also illegal mining of precious stones, especially emeralds, malachite, and amethyst, by both Zambians and some foreigners from countries such as Senegal (popularly called Sene-Senes in Zambia). Many illegal mines are found in Ndola Rural and the Luanshya corridor, something of Zambia's "Wild West," where, as Draisma (1997) points out, some private mines were reported to use heavy machinery like bulldozers and pumps.

HRM informal sector characteristics

The informal sector is, despite its huge size, by definition not governed by any formal HRM rules or sanctions. Informal sector activities tend to involve small numbers of owner-managers who operate from makeshift structures. It is not surprising, therefore, that employment usually tends to be of kith and kin, friends, and sons or daughters of neighbors. Longevity in employment can be from a couple of hours in a day (commonly known in Zambia as "piece-work") to a fairly long number of years for the more established activities. There are no formal selection procedures, and job vacancies usually tend to be filled immediately they become open. Training is almost always on the job, hands-on, meant for the trainee to "hit the ground running" and become productive within a very short period of time. Employment security is usually non-existent. "Employees" are not usually assured of any job tenure, neither can they expect to have any formal fringe benefits, let alone health care insurance or pensions/social security benefits. Perhaps more than in the formal sector, the informal sector tends to emphasize a strong linkage between pay and performance. This is not surprising, especially given the fact that without performance the entity might be out of business within a week.

As a conclusion to this section, it has to be argued that the disproportionately large size of the informal sector and associated low pay and inferior conditions of employment limits fair labor standards. This situation is exacerbated by a lack of capacity on the part of the Zambian government to monitor employment trends and practices in the informal sector.

Electronic Human Resources Management (e-HRM)

How technology is affecting the discharge of HRM functions is the final HRM challenge we see emerging in Africa. Large quantities of employee data (including training records, skills, compensation rates, and benefits usage and cost) can easily be stored on personal computers and manipulated using user-friendly spreadsheets or statistical software packages (Noe *et al.*, 2003: 38–39). Although computer usage and connectivity in Africa is not yet at the high levels prevalent in much of the West, the continent's recognition and appreciation of its vital role towards improved work performance is growing. Electronic Human Resource Management (e-HRM) refers to the processing and transmission of digitized information used in HRM, including test, sound, and visual images, from one computer or electronic device to another (Noe *et al.*, 2003: 38–39).

Electronic Human Resource Management has the potential to change the way traditional HRM functions are performed. Noe *et al.* (2003: 39) point out, for instance, that in the analysis and design of work, employees in geographically dispersed locations can work together in virtual teams using video, email, and the Internet. For example, two Zambian employees of National Breweries (producers of the wildly popular local beer called Chibuku) work in two different parts of Zambia: one is at the company's plant in Mbala, in the Northern Province, while the other is at its Choma plant, some 1,000 kilometers away in the Southern Province. They do not necessarily have to meet at the company's plant in Lusaka, the capital, for them to work together. They can use computers to do this. Under the recruitment function, job openings can be posted online, and candidates can apply for jobs online. Online learning can bring training to employees anywhere, anytime (online MBA programs abound, such as those at the University of Phoenix in Arizona and the University of Baltimore in Maryland). On compensation and benefits issues, e-HRM will make it easy for employees to review salary and bonus information and seek information about (and enroll in) benefit plans.

Conclusion

Historical and contemporary practices and policies relating to the management of human resources in Zambia have been examined in this chapter. Much of the discussion centers around contemporary characteristics, realities, and challenges of HRM in the country. Prominent among these are the impact of privatization, unionization, and unemployment on HRM practices. Due recognition is given to some of the emerging HRM challenges facing Africa, especially the continent's huge HIV and AIDS crisis and the large informal sector. Anchoring the chapter is a discussion of e-HRM and how countries like Zambia that need to sell more of their goods and/or services on the global market need to embrace and utilize such emerging technologies.

References

Barks-Ruggles, E., Fantan, T., McPherson, M., and Whiteside, A. (2001) "The economic impact of HIV/AIDS in Southern Africa," The Brookings Institution. Online: http://www.brook.edu/comm/ConferenceReport/cr09.htm

Bollinger, L. and Stover, J. (1999) "The impact of AIDS in Zambia," the Futures Group International, in collaboration with Research Triangle Institute (RTI) and the Center for Development and Population Activities (CEDPA).

Burawoy, M. (2000) "Reaching for the Global," in M. Burawoy *et al.* (eds.), *Global ethnography: Forces, connections, and imaginations in a postmodern world*. Berkeley: University of California Press, pp. 1–40.

Central Statistics Office (1993) *Report*, Lusaka, Zambia.

Central Statistics Office (2001) *Report*, Lusaka, Zambia.

Cook, P. and Kirkpatrick, C. (eds.) (1988) *Privatization in less developed countries*, Sussex: Wheatsheaf Books.

Cunningham, S.J. (1985) "Nationalization and the Zambian copper mining industry," Ph.D. thesis, University of Edinburgh.

Dessler, G. (2003) *Human resource management*, 9th edition, Englewood Cliffs, NJ: Prentice Hall.

Dowling, Peter J., Welch, Denice, E., and Schuler, R.S. (1999). *International human resource management: Managing people in a multinational context*, 3rd edition, Cincinnati, OH: South-Western College Publishing.

Draisma, T. (1997) "Mining and ecological degradation in Zambia: Who bears the brunt when privatization clashes with Rio 1992?" Paper presented at the International Conference on Environmental Justice and Global Ethics for the 21st Century, University of Melbourne, Australia, 1–3 October.

Feige, E.L. (1990) "Defining and estimating underground and informal economies: The new institutional economics approach," *World Development* 18 (7): 989–1002.

Gill, I., Fluitman, F., and Amit, D. (eds.) (2000) "Vocational education and training reform: Matching skills to markets and budgets," a joint study of the World Bank and the ILO, New York: Oxford University Press, pp. 389–400.

Global Policy Network (2001) "Zambia: Socio-economic issues and unionization." Online: http://www.globalpolicynetwork.org

Hickman, G.R. and Lee, D.S. (2001) *Managing human resources in the public sector: A shared responsibility*, Orlando: Harcourt College Publishers.

Jackson, T. (2002) "Reframing human resource management in Africa: A cross-cultural perspective," *International Journal of Human Resource Management* 13 (7): 998–1018

Jones, M.L. (1991) "Management development: An African focus," in M. Mendenhall and G. Oddou (eds) *Readings and cases in international human resource management*, Boston: PWS-Kent, pp. 231–244.

Kaunda, K.D. (1969) "Zambia towards economic independence," speech by the President at the National Council of UNIP at Mulungushi on 19 April 1968, in B.G. Fortman (ed.) *The economics of Zambian humanism after Mulungushi*, Nairobi: East African Publishing House.

Kusanthan, T. (2001) "Zambia HIV/AIDS Business Sector Project: A study of the effectiveness of workplace peer health intervention in Lusaka, Zambia." Online: http://www.enterprise-impact.org.uk/word-files/ZHABS-MTR-Chapter1.doc

Mataka, R. (2002) "Civil Service reform in Zambia." Online: http://www.tanzania.go.tz/psrp/Zambia.html

Muuka, G.N. (1993) "The impact of Zambia's 1983–1993 Structural Adjustment Program on business strategy," PhD Thesis, University of Edinburgh.

Noe, R.A., Hollenbeck, J.R., Gerhart, B., and Wright, P.M. (2003) *Human resource management: Gaining a competitive advantage*, New York: McGraw-Hill Higher Education.

Posner, D.N. (2001) "The colonial origins of ethnic cleavages: The case of linguistic division in Zambia," Conference paper presented at Harvard University, 23–25 March.

Stoever, W.A. (1985) "A business analysis of the partial nationalization of Zambia's copper industry, 1969–1981," *Journal of International Business Studies*, 16 (1): 137–163.

UNAIDS/WHO (2002) *AIDS Epidemic Update 2002*, Joint United Nations Program on HIV/AIDS. Online: http://www.unaids.org/worldaidsday/2002/press/Epiupdate.html

Whiteside, A., O'Grady, M., and Alban, A. (2000) "The economic impact of HIV and AIDS in Southern Africa," AIDS INFORTHEK Magazine. Online: http://www.aidsnet.ch/e/infothek_edition_2_00_020.htm

Zambia Congress of Trade Unions (ZCTU) (1999) "Survey on trade union membership and profile," Lusaka, Zambia.

Zambia Privatization Agency (ZPA) (2001) "Privatization Status Report at 31 December, 2001," Lusaka, Zambia.

4 HRM in Mauritius[1]

ANITA RAMGUTTY-WONG

Introduction

This chapter takes a critical look at the environment and practice of HRM in Mauritius, and examines the evolving context in which HRM has and is taking place in a country which finds itself at a developmental crossroads. Given the dearth of reported research on management philosophies and practices of Mauritian organizations, the focus of this chapter will be the determinants of HRM and indicators of probable future developments or trends in the area.

The special position of Mauritius as a modern economy operating within some typical constraints of developing African nations makes it an interesting case for studying HRM in practice. This is especially so since the island's development defies some propositions about the difficulty of managing in the face of external and internal pressures (Blunt, 1983; Blunt and Jones, 1992; Kiggundu, 1989), although pressures of the internal type in Mauritius are fortunately not of the tragic kind experienced in many other African countries (for example, Botswana and its upward battle against HIV/AIDS, or Zimbabwe and its history of civil strife). One of the most cosmopolitan islands under the sun and Africa's most successful economy (Editorial, 1996), Mauritius is poised to serve as an example of economic success amidst cultural diversity and structural constraints of size and geographical isolation. In giving special attention to the issue of the country's national culture, this chapter will attempt to show the saliency of cultural variables in *any* people management context. Empirical data on HRM in Mauritius is extracted from a nationwide survey of HRM practices, based on interviews of personnel and HR managers, as explained in the section on Methodology.

1 The author wishes to express her gratitude to her students of B.Sc. (Hons) Management and of M.Sc. Human Resource Studies over the years 1999–2002, who contributed with enthusiasm and commitment towards the realization of the survey on the take-off of HRM in Mauritius.

The Mauritian context and determinants of HRM

Mauritius, known as the "Star and Key of the Indian Ocean" since its colonial days, enjoys an interesting geographical position in the southern Indian Ocean. Situated some 800 kilometers east of Madagascar and subsumed under the African continent, Mauritius owes much of its history to the slave era and subsequently to the wave of Indian immigration. With a population of 1.2 million, Mauritius is not only densely populated, but a very ethnically diverse people also. Hindus and Muslims account for 65 percent of the population (48 and 17 percent respectively), followed by the Creole (the euphemistic *general population*) (30 percent); the Chinese (3 percent), and the Franco-Mauritians (2 percent).

For a geographically remote, small-sized country with only its beaches and people as resources, survival is at the price of hard work and relentless effort. Such is the historical, and prevailing, ethic in Mauritius. Successive governments have not challenged the philosophy and ethos put in place since independence from Britain in 1968: the population was politically fortunate, and could be economically so only if its people continued to sweat it out just as their forebears (slaves and indentured laborers) had before them. Thus, just as its finesse in negotiating trade agreements had secured employment and economic stability, so, today, the spectre of a protection-free world economy forces Mauritius to find innovative ways of maintaining its competitive position in world markets. This competitiveness takes the form of top-quality products and services, advanced technology utilization, and flexibility and adaptability in the face of increasingly fickle market and product demands. The government in place has made the "Cyber Island" project its Trojan horse, and is now pressing for concomitant innovations and improvements in skills and knowledge (as it says the country is moving to be a knowledge-economy (k-economy)). In addition, its stance regarding reforms to be brought about in the civil service are encouraging and strong messages that human resource development is a national priority are regularly heard. The recent and "hyped" institution of the National Productivity and Competitiveness Council (NPCC) also reads as government's determination to improve productivity at all levels and integrate all its strategies with the national vision for worldwide global excellence.

What can be said, then, is that the pressures of survival and growth and the national obsession with "success" provide fertile ground for the development of strategic thinking and of HRM-style people management in Mauritius. This is a theory that combines the suggestions of several authors who view the development of HRM as correlating positively with increasing competitive pressures and the related factor of technology adoption (for example, Lado and Wilson (1994) and Kamoche (1996), who refer to factors pushing firms to place importance on sources of sustainable advantage; and Dean and Sussman (1989), who suggest that HRM strategies will be in part determined by firms' anticipation of technological change). Also, the political will to move the island to a k-economy status has spurred a renewed interest in and commitment to training and education, which ought to bode well for the creation of a critical mass of HRM-literate individuals and enterprises.

Methodology

As part of a vision for enriching the teaching and learning environment of HRM classes at the University of Mauritius, this author devised a participatory strategy linking staff, students, and practitioners of HRM in a nationwide survey of the "take-off" of HRM in Mauritius. Due to the existence of the "reluctance factor" prevalent in a large number of private sector organizations that preferred to apply reserve and restrict access rather than imagine the possible benefits of research, no systematic sampling was possible, since we could not pre-select any particular set of organizations. A research strategy was devised to counteract this shortcoming, and is described below.

During the years 1999 and 2000, two cohorts of 45 undergraduate management students were each enlisted to work in groups of two on the empirical project entitled "The take-off of HRM in Mauritius." This yielded a total of 46 companies surveyed for data on HRM. In the years 2000 and 2002, two cohorts of 18 Masters students were also involved in the same survey.

Size of organizations (in workforce terms), although an important variable for consideration in an analysis of HRM "take-off", was not incorporated in the sampling decision, this variable information not being available prior to the start of the project. The average size of respondent organizations emerged as 725 (excluding the largest Mauritius conglomerate), the smallest, 40, and the largest (conglomerate), 10,000.

Data was coded using a scale of 1 to 3, with 1 representing "excellent or good application," 2 representing "moderate or average application," and 3 representing either "poor" or "inexistent" application of various HRM variables (based on the checklist of dimensions of ideal-type HRM from Storey's (1992) study of mainstream British organizations).

National culture and workplace values

With highly differentiated and mostly endogamous population, "the very construction of the social person is based on ethnicity" in Mauritius (Eriksen, 1998: 15). Nepotism on ethnic bases is widespread in the labor market, both in the public and private sectors, and common knowledge has it that public and parastatal sectors are the bulwark of the Indo-Mauritian population, while the private sector, which remains mainly in the hands of a few "Franco-Mauritian" families, caters to the employment needs of the white and Creole communities.

Hofstede (1991) explains differences in national work-related values or cultures in terms of four basic dimensions: power distance, uncertainty avoidance, individualism/collectivism, masculinity/femininity, and a fifth, later dimension, long-term orientation, even though he did not represent Mauritius on his map of national culture indices. Based on two samples of university students, one part-time Masters (in employment) group and one full-time undergraduate group, findings for Mauritian national culture using Hofstede's dimensions reveal that the country is moderately high on power distance and uncertainty avoidance, high on individualism, medium on masculinity, and high on long-term orientation. This can be explained by the disparate psyches of the different ethnic groups present on the island, but also by a strong element of common experience of slavery in its various forms. High power distance is therefore to be expected in a former colony with only a recent history of independence, where status consciousness is probably near the world record, resulting today in an evident achievement culture.

Uncertainty avoidance, similarly, is likely to be on the high side when the majority population has endured abject poverty and has increasingly been averse to risk, but also because this is a population that has, and is still, conditioned by the British and French bureaucratic structures, and so finds reassurance in structure, rules, and standardization. Unlike many developing nations, Mauritius scores low on collectivism (high on individualism), which possibly correlates with the noted achievement orientation. All survey findings report a strong degree of impersonality and even harshness in management philosophy and style. This also serves to comprehend the country's high masculinity score, with the degree of competitiveness in all spheres, and a "hard" approach to human resource management. Storey (1987) explains that HRM can be inclined toward "soft" or "hard" approaches, the former version emphasizing communication, motivation, and leadership, and the latter focusing on the quantitative, business-strategic aspects of managing people as any other economic factor.

The saliency of religion and ethnicity cannot be denied, if only by judging the number of press articles and editorials addressing the subject daily, even if various studies and observations are not in agreement as to the potency of the ethnicity factor. Eriksen (1998) notes a decline, and Carroll and Joypaul (1993) sing the praises of a meritocratic civil service, free of cronyism, while Minogue (1976) long predicted that patronage was here to stay. This has given rise in many quarters to ethnocentric reflexes in the face of otherwise routine human resource decisions and practices. For example, not being recruited would quickly be equated with being struck off the list on grounds of caste or religion. Disciplinary actions would be termed "victimization," and promotion exercises and training sessions are invariably followed by allegations of favoritism and nepotism.

The values and norms present in the corporate landscape of Mauritius thus emerged not directly from those embedded in management theories learnt at university, but from the historical and current political, economic, social, and cultural philosophies and practices of the population. It will come as no surprise to readers that the plural nature of the people, along with the country's political history, are the determinant factors in the formation of work and organizational cultures.

The political economy and HRM

Minogue (1992: 646) has gone so far as to assert that, "Mauritian politics is . . . overwhelmingly the politics of ethnic competition." To be fair, the country is rare among African countries in that it has retained the political system inherited from colonial masters (first French and then British). Twenty-eight years after independence and ten years after attaining republic status, Mauritius' political system is still based on the Westminster model, with few changes to the Constitution. Ethno-politics plagues the system to such an extent that politicians appear to be perpetually in electoral mode, either defending their positions, or endlessly and bitterly attacking the leading party in power, usually with communal[2] weapons.

In essence, it is the hapless blend of politics and ethnicity that gives rise to added complexities in workplace concerns. One must hasten to add that a distinctive feature of corporate Mauritius is the difference in culture between the public and the private sectors. Where politics play a role in private enterprise, inasmuch as political parties are heavily sponsored by private monies, the more overt forms of political interference occur in the public services. Whereas parties finding themselves in government are often led by the nose of their benefactors in a variety of policy matters; on the business front, political interference results in an *ad hoc*, non-strategic, and often incoherent approach to management. Some politicians are also known to adopt a heavy-handed approach to suggesting this recruitment or that promotion. This is widely referred to as the scourge of the public services, with political nominees finding their way to positions high and low, right under the noses of honest and competent civil servants.

Political nomination at high levels is commonest in parastatal organizations, and often in newly (specially?) created such bodies. Strategic thinking is virtually impossible when such nominations arrive in the form of unqualified, inappropriately profiled, and inexperienced (or too nearing retirement) individuals who happen to be "close" to the prevailing regime. At lower levels, political appointees take the form of beefing up manpower in areas already overstaffed, by placing political cronies in positions both in central and local government. Disgust and frustration from legitimately employed staff is the normal consequence, with alienation and lack of commitment showing in customer dealings and interpersonal relationships. Political interference is professed intolerable, yet is tolerated, either for fear of punitive transfer, administrative persecution, or simply because the minister has many supporters. It is well known that the Civil Service employs the best-qualified people in Mauritius, and a large number of professionals work in this sector. Yet, the environment often becomes disabling and stultifying, for lack of clean management, free from party-politic games. "We need a civil service free from politicians, as simple as that," exclaimed one high official during interview. Another respondent to the survey stated, "the public sector simply ignores the need for HRM, whereas the private sector needs quality people."

---

2 *Communalism*: a typically Mauritian term invented to clearly classify ethnic groups.

Economy

As a newly industrialized, middle-income economy, Mauritius has defied Malthusian economic theory and made a successful transition from its monocrop, agricultural activity to a three-pillar economy comprising: tourism, manufacturing, and financial services. The shift from the agricultural to the industrial—and now, increasingly, the "knowledge"—society has deeply impacted on the Mauritian psyche as a whole. Individual and collective expectations now hover around material ease, accomplishment, and increased individualism. Currently, the economic situation of the country is seen as being precarious as a result of the fragile state of the export sector and the necessity for funding large national projects. Although today a middle income economy and posed to be the business hub of the Indian Ocean and a major gateway to Eastern and Southern Africa, and an average growth rate of 5.4 percent over the past 20 years, it is common understanding that the way business has been done so far will have to change, paving the way for a disciplined, skilled, knowledgeable, and IT-enabled new economic landscape.

The fragility of industry characterized by loss of export markets for a variety of reasons has led to several hundreds of workers being laid off, bringing the unemployment level to an unprecedented double-digit figure (estimated at 12 percent) since industrialization. Laid off and voluntarily retired workers are mostly unskilled or too old to start anew in new occupations. At the same time, a shortage of skill is felt in other occupational categories, especially new technology. Fortunately, recent performances indicate that both the tourism and the financial and offshore business services sectors, for their part, may emerge as sure routes to growth. Clearly, one key condition to the development of the services sector is skilled and talented human resources, and this may pose a problem in the short run.

Education and training

Education has probably been the single key factor that has enabled the social mobility of those who came to the island either as immigrants or slaves. Known to be "obsessed with education" (Titmuss and Abel-Smith, 1968), the Mauritian people in general have undergone remarkable sacrifices for the sake of formally educating their children. This, coupled with free access to education, has borne its fruits and been instrumental in the development of a modern and sophisticated economy. However, the educational system has serious drawbacks at the same time, which impact directly on the work ethic, on management style, and on personnel practices. The "school rat race" has produced two sets of problems in relation to skills and knowledge: a large proportion of primary school leavers can hardly read, write, nor count; and currently technical and vocational education opportunities are inadequate. Second, the development of higher-order thinking becomes extremely difficult later in life, this time resulting in a portion of the workforce with impressive academic records but little capability to act as change agents or excellent managers. In terms of human resource professionals as a body of change agents, for example, the critical mass of HRM-trained individuals is not yet reached, such that changes in workplace policies and practices are going to be difficult. Worse, many learners at university, employed at middle management level, explicitly doubt the applicability of academic models, theories, and practices, on the grounds that transfer of such learning is impossible in organizations whose senior managers are unexcited about any such changes, or simply because political and other types of interference block individual initiative with regard to improving personnel practice.

Globalization and the corporate landscape

Eastern and Western, developed and developing, Mauritius is at a crossroads in the management of its enterprises, public and private. Having retained most of the British ways of doing things, including civil service bureaucracy, as well as laws and regulatory institutions, Mauritius is today struggling to find the appropriate mechanisms to cope with a much changed world, and those foresighted management teams that have succeeded in upgrading their technology and have realized that sound management and quality human resources are essential, and are keen to develop a well trained, efficient, and committed workforce (Woo, 2002). However, they are few and far between, with hardly a handful of CEOs and even HR managers considering the challenges of multi-skilling, workforce reduction strategy, retention, career and personal development, motivation and commitment. However, the pressures of globalization for efficiency and quality push Mauritian managements in the direction of the West for "canned" ideas, and solutions, including those of the HRM model type. As Debrah and Budhwar (2002) suggest, globalization also offers possibilities for the shift of people management practices from personnel to HRM. From an academic point of view, however, this carries the well known risk of applying thinking and methods unsuited to the local context; but, as of today, the phenomenon has seemingly not bothered decision makers much, judging by the increasing reliance on management consultants of the Western school.

As mentioned in an earlier section, the middle-range scores of Mauritius on most of Hofstede's dimensions is indicative of the diversity of contributions to the state of organization and management in Mauritius. Culturally and historically attached to ancestral heritage, all the while seeking to emulate the developed societies of the world, this miniscule island, seemingly a dot on the world map, nurtures the fantasy of holding the best of both worlds, but the theory is perhaps deceptive. The managerial system in fact is a combination of entrepreneurial, civil service, and MNC ways, along with the heavy hand of the structural adjustment program that ended in 1985. With most private firms, small and large, living the values of their founders, much of their orientation remains survival and profit, with associated interest in quality, productivity, and competitiveness. Multinationals, for their part, making up some 15 percent of all capital on the island, occupy a current and predictably future role as change agents on the managerial front. They are known to recruit the best and to offer extremely attractive employment packages, as well as operating sound employment practices. Fields *et al.*

(2000) have empirically found this to hold true in the Hong Kong situation, where foreign-owned companies pay more attention to retention of managers and to performance-related pay (PRP), for example.

Structural adjustment brought with it the typical economic liberalization and restructuring that have also exerted an influence on HRM in both public and private firms. However, the Civil Service, employing some 12 percent of the workforce, is characterized by typical bureaucratic management and reputed for its abysmal people management. As more than a few respondents to the HR survey blurted out, HR is simply not possible under bureaucratic structures and nepotistic cultures. So what we see is:

1 Good practice management, information-based HR systems *cohabiting with* other nepotistic and corrupt traditions.
2 Civil servants whiling away the time under archaic administrative systems, *while* the government speaks of a knowledge society and a "cyber island."
3 World-class companies *interacting with* others devoid of any sense of good management.
4 Private-sector employees managed on a performance-based pay system, *while* "Mauritian specificities" are respected through centralized, opaque public recruitment and pay systems.

Drawing from findings of the HRM survey explained in the Methodology section, the following paragraphs provide evidence of the determinants of HRM in Mauritius.

Strategic HRM

The long-term orientation of Mauritians at large[3] might suffice to expect *some* form of strategic management, provided that senior and other managements were adequately educated and trained appropriately. This, however, is nowhere near reality. It is well known that the glass ceiling that exists between middle management and senior levels is largely due to the senior category being the reserve of family members—most Mauritian organizations being family-owned businesses—who do not necessarily feel the need to be educated or trained for management. MBAs mostly cluster in middle management positions, often working for a comfortable employment package, but unable to make much use of their new knowledge. But worse, evidence points to the fact that many top management teams, although aware of good practice in management, and state their recognition of the importance of people, choose not to practice modern strategic HRM in their organizations, lingering with traditional personnel management approaches (specifically, orientated towards welfare and/or administration). In such a context, it is clear that explicit strategic plans are not made. However, typical of the "mixed-mode"

3 Based on a limited survey of educated Mauritians. Popular knowledge suggests that members of the Creole community generally do not share this orientation (Boolell, 2000).

Mauritian scene, evidence is available to support both the presence as well as absence of a strategic approach to HRM (Ramgutty-Wong, 2002). Thus, mostly long-established corporations tend to make use of the stability "slack" to engage in strategic HRM, recruiting highly-educated professionals in the field, placing them in executive positions, and sponsoring best practice approaches. Conversely, two other categories emerge as unremarkable performers in the field: small and medium-sized organizations that have not made the transition from the small family business to the professional firm, and public and para-public enterprises that are plagued with the ills of nepotism, corruption, and political interference.

By and large, the single major culprit of the absence of strategic HRM is lack of top management understanding and/or commitment. Typical statements are:

> "Management abdicates its responsibility for redressing a failing culture, politicking, low morale, disinterest in the customer, and obsession with internal procedures."

> "The HR department is isolated and does not coordinate [its activities] with other departments."

> "HR objectives are set by top management, and do not balance with the challenges from within the organization."

> "In view of the unemployment situation, usually not much is expected from the new employee, who is more concerned about getting a secured job."

Even in the seemingly enlightened conglomerates, the HR managers are quick to explain that, although the HR function has increasingly been given strategic importance, the practice is piecemeal and the HR philosophy is not "total": "a full HRM program involves investment, risk, and culture change, and many organizations are just not willing nor ready to undertake that hassle." And another: "given that organizations [of the private sector] are geared to the export market, they don't implement HRM policies as a whole package, and so make them ineffective."

At a large parastatal organization, known for difficult industrial relations, the HR manager admits that, "jobs have been redesigned, but only to accommodate new technology, not to build in motivation or satisfaction."

Nevertheless, examples of strategic HRM do exist, with over three-quarters of HR managers claiming to have a strategic role in their organizations. Even in the public domain, creative and impressive approaches have been utilized to "get around the system," with examples of established teamworking, quality management, benefits, and line devolution practices that could compete easily with any best practice firm anywhere in the world. Similarly, a few small firms have been found to adopt a totally mainstream HR function, with all activities devolved to line departments, use of sophisticated selection tools, and strong HR philosophy from top management down.

Selection and recruitment

Most organizations in Mauritius use a non-systematic approach to recruitment and selection and rely instead on familiar "procedures" of advertising vacancies in the local press and then conducting interviews. Within this general framework, a diverse mix of approaches is used, ranging from sophisticated recruitment and selection methods, using job analysis, person specifications and job descriptions and structured interviews, batteries of tests, and, timidly but progressively, assessment centers, to the most haphazard, unsystematic "method" of calling a vague shortlist for interviews conducted by intimidating panels with hardly an idea of what kind of person to match to the job. Worse, many such "methods" are known to be "eyewash" techniques to cover up for a predetermined candidate, already chosen for the job through his or her "backing." Now, "backing" may be political or ethnic, but its relevance cannot be denied. Less pejorative is the term *coup de pouce*, denoting the same intervention tactic. This semblance of procedure prevails in both private and public sectors, with obvious consequences for both the quality of the workforce thus recruited, but also for the shortfall in qualified and competent staff simply because, tragically, such a large number of graduates and otherwise qualified people simply cannot get past the sticky floors at the selection stage.

Even in the public service, the Public Service Commission (PSC), the centralized recruiting body, is known for its lack of transparency in its decisions, and the presence of line departments' representatives for their "eyewash" status. As one respondent from a parastatal firm (disguised as X) remarked: "The PSC and the X are two completely different organizations. Although one representative of X is involved, the selection process is dominated by members of the PSC. The final list of [successful] candidates sent to X for employment is completely different from what X's representative had expected [it to be]."

In both sectors, where selection is contracted out to consultant firms, even there practices do not appear any more systematic or sophisticated. Recently, the executive director of a small but very visible parastatal firm had his contract cancelled due to his chronic inability to relate to others in his environment. The board accepted responsibility and stated that they had selected him themselves, and that his record was that of "the ideal candidate on paper."

Among the MNC group, impressive techniques such as application blanks, structured interviews, ability and personality tests, reference checks, and simulations are employed, as well as planned induction programs. In the sugar sector, a diverse life cycle of personnel practices has been noted, with some factories still hanging on to "headhunting for relatives," while one organization claimed to recruit 20 percent of its non-manual workforce through assessment centers.

Much importance is generally placed on formal qualifications on paper, and on the actual interview, in whatever form it is conducted. Also, since a large number of organizations are not innovative and tend to adopt low-risk approaches, fresh graduates without experience have a hard time securing a decent job that matches their expectations. Usually the line manager, if involved, is not skilled in interviewing and has a peripheral role, and other panel members are unsure of how to match the job and the person. Questions are invariably general and predictable and, most often, candidates are not given a chance to ask questions themselves. Few advertisements are seen announcing vacancies for managerial jobs, such that only a low level of regeneration is possible in organizations tenaciously practicing promotion from within.

Performance appraisal and rewards

Here is one function of HRM whose practice is more homogeneous across sectors and organizations. In most cases, performance appraisal either does not exist in Mauritian organizations, or else it remains a purely administrative exercise, whose aim is unclear. Forty-six percent of firms surveyed did claim to have effective performance appraisal systems, while 38 percent said their approach was either ineffective or conducted in an amateur way. A marginal application of PRP systems has been noted, but mostly, wherever it exists, performance appraisal is top-down, non-developmental in orientation, lacks clear purpose, and is probably more of a cost than a benefit. As far as the private sector is concerned, the few enlightened firms that showed some interest in performance appraisal were experiencing difficulties in linking proportionate rewards and/or developmental opportunities to the performance of staff, so dealing a blow to the system. Most other firms simply gave annual increments and production bonuses "across the board," rewarding good as well as bad performance. It would appear that the Mauritian *culture de méfiance* (culture of mistrust) (McCourt and Ramgutty-Wong, forthcoming) limits many managers from setting up appraisal systems in the first place, and from linking assessments with rewards. In the public sector, some effort had been made to introduce a performance appraisal system that would supplant the ancient annual confidential report system (consisting of mysterious "assessment" of staff by often remote superiors, with no input from or feedback to the employee; the annual increment would be given in any case). The initiative failed, and reports of its postmortem are varied and mostly anecdotal: unions had opposed it because it was to be linked to pay, and staff in general resisted it because of the *culture de méfiance* that characterizes staff relationships in multi-ethnic workforces like Mauritius's, but also perhaps because staff are simply so used to the seniority-based system and consequently are apprehensive about performance-based systems. Nevertheless, current efforts are now centering on a more development-oriented approach, in the context of a re-launch of the Reforms program, and only time will tell if this will achieve its objective.

Generally speaking, whether in the private or public sphere, the issue of linking performance to pay is a contentious one, more so because interference, favoritism, and nepotism are likely to seep into the system one way or another. "Backing" continues well beyond the selection stage, and ethnic and political patronage are realities in both sectors, hindering the objectivity so necessary in any performance management system. Also, the complexity of initiating a performance management system is underestimated, with few organizations willing to adopt HRM in its full form, such as through job analysis, systematic selection, and follow-on development from appraisal results. Another common feature is the big pay differentials, with the average income of an executive more than ten or even 20 times that of a worker of the private sector. Proportionately, even in the public service, a permanent secretary's salary is approximately ten times that of a worker in a ministry.

Because social ascension is so related to status in Mauritius, the instrumentality of take-home pay and the attractiveness of perks is a major employment issue. Indeed, many private sector firms offer extremely attractive packages to attract the best, and headhunting and poaching are not uncommon practices. The disparity in take-home pay and other benefits between the private and public enterprises is, of course, one explanation for the state of human resources in general and for the quality of performance and attitude in particular. Indeed, both moonlighting and corrupt behavior are probably direct consequences of the frustration resulting from inadequate rewards packages in the civil service, but the reforms program is yet to propose measures to address this problem. Currently, the Pay Research Bureau (PRB) centrally determines salary scales for each grade of employee and leaves no freedom to line departments in determining the package that would attract the right candidate, nor the increases that would retain performing staff. As it stands, the system makes no difference between a talented employee and a shiftless one, and this is clearly not conducive to HRM at all.

Training and development

The importance of training has grown steadily into a national concern, especially since the setting up of the Industrial and Vocational Training Board (IVTB) in 1988. The IVTB offers, as an incentive to companies, a sizable refund of training costs (referred to as the "levy grant scheme"), which has led over the years to a situation whereby the quantity of training dished out to the workforce has been generally effected in a haphazard manner, with no training needs analyses, no objective selection of trainees, and a low level of learning transfer. Very few companies have an explicit policy of graduate employment, and even fewer have management trainee programs; although a few have training academies (centers) and even training managers. However, a disproportionate interest in cadres' training is noted, especially since the recent mushrooming of business schools offering MBAs and short management courses of all sorts, even by distance learning. In general, private companies do not sponsor many of their executives for university MBAs, but many do provide short *ad hoc* courses usually run by consultants. With one traditional university (The University of Mauritius), one University of Technology, and several private business education providers, opportunities are plentiful for upgrading management knowledge, even though a large number of such learners are self-funded. This also means that such training is not part of a larger, coherent human resource development (HRD) strategy by employing organizations. The IVTB is probably the only institution that reaches a wide net of potential training and responds to the immediate vocational and HRD needs of the country. Under its umbrella is the Hotel School, which has contributed and continues to contribute to the creation of a breed of vocationally-competent workers for the hotel industry. All in all, it is clear that, with limited funds and uncommitted managers, the future of training as a key HRM function is not very bright.

Employee relations

Following the abolition of slavery, Indian workers were brought in in replacement, but the nature of the relationship remained tyrannical. Even today, with economic power predominantly in the hands of the plantation barons' descendants, it would seem that there lies a latent hang-up of colonial employment relations in the psyche of the modern, liberated Mauritian. Alas, there are accounts and facts to support this state of affairs, especially in the private sector: undemocratic work practices, wide wage differentials, domineering management styles, and harsh layoff procedures. The relatively low rate of union membership (12 percent nationally) of the Mauritian workforce is also attributed in many quarters to the intimidating management styles of most employers, such that workers fear being in the "bad books" of their superiors by the simple fact of supporting union activities (where a union exists). The history of the labor movement dates to the plantation days of tyranny, where repression and even execution were the lot of assertive workers, especially in the 1970s. The socio-political environment has much changed since, with the flourishing economy and quasi-full employment lasting two decades since the early 1980s. The Industrial Relations Act and the Trade Unions and Labor Relations Act provide mostly for an interventionist approach, regulating the legal environment within which unions operate. However, this legislation itself has been a bone of contention for decades now, with successive governments promising to review it.

The union scene in Mauritius is characterized as lacking concerted action around essential issues, and falling union density. Another characteristic is the small membership size, with a high proportion of unions with less than 100 members. Union membership is widely spread across sectors, industries, and occupations, although, generally speaking, union activities are not backed by popular support, and their role as political change agents has not so far carried much weight either. Negotiations for annual salary compensations are carried out as tripartites, with the state and the employer groups involved, although the union group is generally not an equal player in the game, being unsophisticated and lacking the preparedness. Also, the fragmentation within the union movement makes it extremely difficult for this stakeholder group to exercise much bargaining power. Thus, although closed shop systems are not legal, the current framework of industrial relations in Mauritius is neither adequately enabling nor particularly repressive.

The fact that wages and conditions remain persistently high on unions' agendas are reflective of an employment situation that is still not quite "right" with the basics. At the same time, although relatively slowed down, the economy has not reached that negative point where worker militancy becomes a *de facto* work value. The new-found materialistic orientation of the working class leaves little room for political ideologies. Let us also not forget the high individualism index of Mauritius, which should not suggest much hope for an upward change in either union membership or involvement in union activities. At company level, two distinct sets of attitudes were noted from our survey. First, HR managers who would rather not have unions, especially in the traditionally union free or anti-union sectors. In the hotel sector, in particular, much anti-union feeling was noted, such as that expressed by one manager of an influential group: "The hotel finds no necessity for trade unions. This is because at the . . . hotel, the maximum is being done to be free of unions. The presence of unions in this sector is detrimental to the hotel as tourists are very sensitive to any factor disturbing their stay." Second, the most commonly occurring response across organizations and sectors was positive towards unions, especially in the larger corporations: "Although unions are becoming weaker, they have their place, since management cannot see and anticipate everything that affects employees," and "Unions are not a problem because here [at this sugar factory] it is seen as an extension of the HR department. Unions help the HR department by showing us what problems may be arising and even by tackling those problems." The highly unionized civil and parastatal services are generally much more tolerant of unions, possibly because the notions of "acquired rights" and meritocracy are ostensibly more entrenched, and possibly because of the purely administrative role of personnel departments in the public services, such that unions play both a welfare and a whistle-blowing role wherever democratic values are perceived to be in peril.

Conclusion

The approach to HRM in Mauritius can be characterized by a few distinctive features. First, the distinction between certain forms of organization. The categories present on the Mauritian scene are: large private sector corporations, medium to small private sector enterprises, the large civil service sector, and the parastatal sector. In the public sector, the centralized and bureaucratic nature of HRM decisions (pay, conditions and promotion, recruitment, training) leaves little room for performance-oriented management and strategic integration of anything at all. The limited research conducted in this area (McCourt and Ramgutty-Wong, forthcoming; Gujadhur-Nowbuth, 2001) has demonstrated the poor take-off of HRM in the public sector, and the extremely limited scope for change in the current practices of people management, at least in the short term. Second, national culture: the pervasiveness of rigid colonial structures and policies inhibits the transition from a personnel management orientation to a more strategic, less piecemeal, approach to people management. Third, the private sector being profit- and market-oriented, is now much more open to business-oriented management approaches, and technological development, with all the direct implications for people management. The efficiency of the public sector is not only a question of reductions in public expenditure, but also of the cost-effective, rational, and ethical utilization of its human assets. In view of the need for public policy to facilitate the emergence of a productivity-based economy, some reforms have taken place and others are in progress.

The state of HRM in Mauritius today is a reflection, inevitably, of the state in which the country finds itself: torn between several worlds, and wishing that things would evolve in a more unidirectional fashion. Mauritian managers do not seem to have given much thought to the indigenous nature of an eventual Mauritian people management style or system, such that some aspects of the HRM they seem to have learnt may be discarded, others retained, and yet others invented. It seems unlikely that Mauritius will turn its back on "evolutions" of the global kind, with its influences, notably from the Western industrialized countries. But it will not seek voluntarily to allow its cultural history and specificity to weaken its hold on national identity. Thus, poised for assimilation into the *cour des grands* and misty-eyed over its cherished history and traditions, the island faces the challenge of integrating the best of all worlds: the traditions and values of the past, the technology and new learning from global contact. Whether the conventional quasi-blind assimilation of knowledge, know-how, and paradigms of the developed West are feasible in the future economic and social landscape of Mauritius really appears to be in the fortune-teller's realm . . .

References

Blunt, P. (1983) *Organizational theory and behaviour: An African perspective*, London: Longman.

Blunt, P. and Jones, M.L. (1992) *Managing organizations in Africa*, Berlin: Walter de Gruyter.

Boolell, S. (2000) *Mauritius through the looking glass*, Cambridge: Pentland Press.

Carroll, B. and Joypaul, S. (1993) "The Mauritian public service since independence: Some lessons for developing and developed nations," *International Review of Administrative Sciences* 59: 423–40.

Dean, J. and Sussman, G. (1989) "Strategic responses to global competition: Advanced technology, organizational design, and human resource practices," in C. Snow (ed.) *Strategy, organizational design, and human resource management*, Greenwich, CT: JAI Press.

Debrah, Y.A. and Budhwar, P.S. (2002) "Conclusion: International competitive pressures and the challenges for HRM in developing countries," in P.S. Budhwar and Y.A. Debrah (eds.) *Human resource management in developing countries*, London: Routledge.

Editorial (1996) "A half-African success story," *The Economist*, 14 December: 45.

Eriksen, T.H. (1998) *Common denominators: Ethnicity, nation-building and compromise in Mauritius*, Oxford: Berg.

Fields, D., Chan, A., and Akshtar, S. (2000) "Organizational context and human resource management strategy: A structural equation analysis of Hong Kong firms," *International Journal of Human Resource Management* 11 (2): 264–277.

Gujadhur-Nowbuth, S.D. (2001) "The applicability of HRM in the public sector with particular reference to the Ministry of Agriculture and Natural Resources," unpublished M.Sc. dissertation, University of Mauritius.

Hofstede, G. (1991) *Culture's consequences: Software of the mind*, London: McGraw-Hill.

Kamoche, K. (1996) "Strategic human resource management within a resource-capability view of the firm," *Journal of Management Studies* 33: 213–234.

Kiggundu, M.N. (1989) *Managing organizations in developing countries*, West Hartford, CT: Kumarian Press.

Lado, A. and Wilson, M. (1994) "Human resource systems and sustained competitive advantage: A competency-based perspective," *Academy of Management Review* 19, 699–727.

McCourt, W. and Ramgutty-Wong, A. (2003) "Limits to strategic HRM: The case of the Mauritian civil service," *International Journal of Human Resource Management* 14 (4): 600–618.

Minogue, M. (1976) "Public administration in Mauritius," *Journal of Administration Overseas* 15 (3): 160–166.

Minogue, M. (1992) "Mauritius: Economic miracle or developmental illusion?" *Journal of International Development* 4: 643–647.

Quinn, J.B. (1980) *Strategies for change: Logical incrementalism*, Homewood, IL: R.D. Irwin.

Ramgutty-Wong, A. (unpublished) "The take-off of HRM in Mauritius: Fact or fiction?" University of Mauritius.

Storey, J. (1987) "Developments in the management of human resources: An interim report," *Warwick Papers in Industrial Relations*, No. 17, IRRV School of Industrial Relations and Business Studies, University of Warwick.

Storey, J. (1992) *Developments in the management of human resources*, Oxford: Blackwell.

Titmuss, R. and Abel-Smith, B. (1968) *Social policies and population growth in Mauritius*, London: Frank Cass.

Woo, F. (2002) "Il y a des employs mais pas de main-d'oeuvre," interview, *L'Express*, 23 June: 4.

HRM in Tanzania

YAW A. DEBRAH

Introduction

Arguably, no Sub-Saharan African country has in recent years undergone more radical transformations in work and employment issues than Tanzania. These transformations have been brought about by the socio-economic and political changes currently underway in the country. The changes focus on the transition from a socialist, one-party state, to multi-party politics and the accompanying development of a free enterprise economy. In many ways, the socio-economic and political "revolution" has necessitated a complete overhaul of people management policies and practices in Tanzania.

The new form of people management is a direct response to the need to develop and enhance the competitiveness of Tanzanian organizations in an era where foreign direct investment (FDI) is actively sought. Until recently, the standard bearer of African socialism, Tanzania has abandoned state-controlled economic policies and is rapidly selling off state-owned enterprises (Turner, 2000: 1). The demise of socialism and the rebirth of free enterprise in Tanzania are inextricably linked to the economic liberalization policies being pursued by the government. These have ushered in a wide range of changes in the society as a whole, in the economy, and in work and employment practices. Indeed, it has been argued that Tanzania is undergoing a transformation that many believe could make it one of Africa's most successful economies within the next decade (*International Herald Tribune*, 1997: 12).

As regards the economic transformation and its consequent social, political changes, and workplace restructuring, it appears the government's efforts are beginning to bear fruit. Again, as Turner (2000:1) succinctly puts it, in a continent short of success stories, Tanzania is beginning to emerge as a potential role model for Sub-Saharan Africa. Perhaps other African countries can learn from Tanzania with respect to effective and appropriate HRM practices in a globalized era. This chapter attempts to trace and analyze the factors responsible for the transformation of personnel management (PM) into HRM in organizations in Tanzania. In so doing, it will discuss the emerging trends in HRM and situate the changes in the context of the changing socio-economic and political environments.

Until the mid-1990s, there was hardly any private sector to speak of in the country as wholesale and retail trade dominated this sector. However, the reform of public services, public enterprises, and privatization is bringing a radically different management pattern to the country. In recent years, a significant number of small and medium-sized enterprises have been set up. Equally, multinational corporations are moving into the economy and, as Mapolu (2000) asserts, are making an impact on the style and pattern of management. However, it is too early to speak of a particular or distinctive HRM practice or style in the private sector. Accordingly, this chapter will focus mainly on the public sector but will make references to the private sector where relevant.

Socio-economic background

Tanzania, a former British colony, is one of the least developed countries in the world. It attained its independence in 1961 as Tanganyika. In 1964, the United Republic of Tanzania was formed following the union of Tanganyika and Zanzibar. Tanzania lies on the east coast of Africa and it covers a total area of 945,087 km^2 (including Zanzibar) (*Financial Times*, 2000; Hill, 1994). It is by far the largest country in East Africa. Tanzania shares borders with Kenya, Uganda, Rwanda, Burundi, the Democratic Republic of the Congo (formerly Zaire), Zambia, Malawi, and Mozambique. It has a population of 32 million (1999 estimate; *Financial Times*, 2000), which is made up of indigenous Africans, Arabs, and Indians. Africans form about 98 percent of the population. The total GDP in 2000 was US$8192 million and the GDP per head was US$240 (*Financial Times*, 2000).

Nearly 85 percent of the people live in rural areas, mostly as smallholder peasants. Accordingly, agriculture is the dominant sector of the economy, accounting for 50 percent of GDP and contributing about 75 percent of foreign exchange earnings. Agriculture is also the main source of wage employment for 80 percent of the population (African Development Bank (ADB), 2000: 8). The sector comprises both smallholders and commercial farmers. Since 1986, the sector has seen some essential policy reforms pertaining to the relaxation of controls on prices, marketing, processing, and input supply. The objective, here, is to provide an enabling environment for private sector led agricultural growth (ADB, 2000). In 1996, the government introduced a Sustainable Industrial Development Strategy (SIDS). This strategy aims to promote high and sustainable growth as a means of improving export earnings. In line with SIDS, manufacturing policy has changed from import-substitution to export-oriented industries (East African Development Bank (EADB), 1999). Other sectors of the economy that have come into prominence in recent years are mining and tourism (Turner and Holman, 2000).

The "African socialism" (Ujamaa) era

In the immediate post-independence period, apart from attempts by the government to Africanize the Civil Service, there was no major change in economic policy. In other words, apart from the Africanization program, economic management was a continuity of colonial policies. However, by the mid-1960s, the government was dissatisfied with the country's economic performance. It was argued that economic activities under a laissez-faire system were creating, perpetuating, and increasing inequality in incomes, wealth and opportunities for most Tanzanians (Kahama et al., 1986).

Hence, in an attempt to rectify the economic problems, the country was declared a one-party state and its socialist government launched the "Arusha Declaration" in 1967. In the words of Bigsten and Danielson (2001), this was a watershed in Tanzania's social and economic development as it moved the economy from laissez-faire to socialism. With the Declaration, the government, through a nationalization policy, assumed control of almost all economic activity in the country. In addition, in 1971, the ruling party guidelines were implemented, asserting the supremacy of the party, and calling for new attitudes and practices in decision making for both management and workers (de Valk, 1996).

The socialist government led by Julius Nyerere created numerous state-owned enterprises (SOEs) to manage the various sectors of the economy. These included banking, manufacturing, insurance, agriculture, and import and export trade (Mapolu, 2000). This essentially killed off the private sector and enabled public enterprises to dominate the modern sector of the economy. In the wake of the nationalization of economic activity, the management style of public enterprises became the dominant influence on Tanzania's management system as a whole (Bol et al., 1997). In other words, public sector management was synonymous with "Tanzanian management."

Other policy directives of the Arusha Declaration were "Education for Self-reliance" and "Socialism and Rural Development." The latter resulted in the "villagization" of rural communities. This took the form of "Ujamaa villages," i.e. cooperative production units. Soon after the Arusha Declaration, the country started to experience economic difficulties. Specifically, the country faced severe balance of payments problems in the 1970s. Furthermore, the East African Community collapsed in 1977 and this had adverse effects on Tanzania's rail, air transport, and communication systems. Also, the second OPEC oil crisis, the Tanzania–Uganda War in 1978 which overthrew Idi Amin, and unfavorable terms of trade, all had severe negative impacts on the Tanzanian economy. In particular, these together limited the expansion prospects of the informal sector and parallel market activities. They also propelled the growth of an underground economy in the state sector, eroding its administrative and productive mechanisms and resulting in high inefficiency and corruption (de Valk, 1996).

The economic crisis intensified in the 1980s as the weak performance of the economy manifested itself in poor and declining productivity. With the economy grinding to a halt, productivity in manufacturing began to decline and, in agriculture, stagnated at best. With declining employment in the informal and public sectors, the government had to pick up the slack in the labor market to avoid civil strife. Hence, employment in the Civil Service expanded considerably during the late 1970s and the early 1980s. However, growth in employment and wages travelled in opposite directions. While employment increased, the average wage for civil servants declined considerably in the 1980s and early 1990s. During this period, government salaries lagged behind those of public enterprises and private sector pay. Consequently, civil servants resorted to other means to increase their incomes. These included rent seeking and corrupt activities, which had adverse impacts on people management. In particular, absenteeism and lateness increased but, unfortunately, were tolerated. The consequence was a decline in productivity and an increase in inefficiency (de Valk, 1996). It is against this background that the economic restructuring programme was initiated. With the economy on its knees, radical and immediate treatment was needed.

Economic restructuring programs

In response to the economic crisis, the Tanzanian government made several attempts to restore economic stability. But with the government still tooting socialist slogans and hence at loggerheads with the IMF over a proposed 15 per cent devaluation in 1978–1979, the Nyerere government had no choice but to implement its own "National Economic Survival Program" (NESP) in the 1981/82 financial year. This reform program, however, achieved limited success. Consequently, the government implemented another "home made/ indigenous" reform program, namely the "Structural Adjustment Program" (SAP) from 1982 to 1985. Sadly, this also achieved limited success. The failure of these reform programs was attributed to the failure or unwillingness of the government to tackle the problems relating to the economic policies associated with the Arusha Declaration.

There was no economic respite until the resignation and subsequent retirement of President Nyerere, the architect of the Arusha Declaration. This smoothed relations with many Western governments and paved the way for Tanzania to seek external assistance from the IMF and World Bank for economic reforms (Bigsten and Danielson, 2001). Thus, during the mid-1980s, the Tanzanian government, with the help and support of the IMF and World Bank, initiated and implemented two Economic Recovery Programs (ERPs) from 1986 to 1992. The aims of the ERPs were to halt the economic deterioration and improve productivity and general economic performance. They initially involved trade and exchange rate liberalization and macro-economic stabilization policies, but the reforms were later broadened to include the banking sector, agricultural marketing, government administration, the Civil Service, and public enterprises (Bigsten and Danielson, 2001).

The ERPs helped to transform the economy and create new jobs in some situations, but unfortunately also paved the way for massive retrenchment of employees in the public sector. Consequently, HR managers had to develop innovative means to deal with new and emergent HR issues. Before discussing the new HRM practices it is necessary to provide a brief overview of PM practices during the socialist period.

Personnel management during the socialist era

The government's strategy to promote economic growth in Tanzania has profoundly reformed the PM system in Tanzania. Current people management initiatives are in sharp contrast to those under the Declaration. In particular, the ideals of the Arusha Declaration required the pursuit of policies aimed at creating equality in all spheres of the socio-economic life (including employment) of all Tanzanians (Kahama *et al.*, 1986). Every effort, then, was made to treat people equally and this was reflected in almost all PM policies and practices.

The socialist government promoted the development of a common language, Swahili, which has helped to achieve a sense of national identity and cohesion unmatched in any other African country with such diverse ethnicity. In Mapolu's (2000) view, it has also fostered national consciousness. This has created a sense of "Tanzanianness" which transcends ethnic identity. Although ethnic tensions and cleavages occasionally erupt, the spirit of nationhood, which is at a high level, prevents violent ethnic clashes. Thus, unlike in many other Sub-Saharan African countries, recruitment, selection, training, and promotion in Tanzania are less influenced by ethnic origin.

Hence, in organizations, the commitment to equality and participation led to pluralistic and inclusive policies without consideration given to the concept of fit. This was because the driving force of PM policies and practices was the trade union movement, which was expected to cooperate with the government's efforts to promote economic development. In the circumstances, joint consultation between employers and employees formed the core of personnel management in Tanzania. Although joint consultation had its origins in the colonial period, the post-independence government reinforced it. The colonial government passed legislation paving the way for the formation of Workers' Committees as part of the trade union movement in organizations. But the friction between the trade unions and the colonial government during the independence struggles weakened the committees and they had become moribund by 1963.

The post-independence government revived the Workers' Committees to supplement the new national trade union movement in order to work towards the achievement of national economic development goals. The Workers' Committees' main objectives were to facilitate better understanding between employers and employees, and to enable employees to discuss and understand employers' problems (Mihyo, 1979). In addition, these committees were intended to facilitate industrial stability and increasing productivity. They were expected to achieve their objectives through active participation in decision making and management of enterprises (Mapolu, 1979). The legislation which gave birth to the Workers' Committees institutionalized the policies and procedures for recruitment, wages, and discipline, the offences which constituted breach of rules in organizations and which required the invocation of various disciplinary actions and their appropriate penalties (Mihyo, 1979).

In 1975, all Workers' Committees were made field branches of the national trades union movement. And, as if this was not sufficient to constrain managerial prerogatives, the government introduced compulsory Workers' Councils in all public enterprises as a form of worker participation. This severely curtailed the power of management in organizations as the directive which set up the Workers' Councils also ordered the reorganization of executive boards and boards of directors to facilitate workers' representation and participation in planning, productivity, quality, and marketing matters. The Workers' Councils were placed under Executive Committees and the latter were given the legal backing to scrutinize the recommendations of the Workers' Councils and to make recommendations on financial, production, quality, and labor matters to the general manager and the board of directors of enterprises.

In effect, then, personnel managers during the socialist era had very little managerial prerogative in the management of people in the enterprise. It is no wonder, therefore, that no serious PM practices existed prior to the 1990s. In many respects, PM in Tanzania suffered from lack of strategy and focus in almost all the PM functional areas discussed in the literature on PM in Africa (see Kamoche, 1993; 2001; Debrah, 2000; Fashoyin, 2000; Kiggundu, 1988). This, however, changed with the liberalization of the economy and the implementation of the ERPs.

Human Resource Management under the liberalized economy

The ERPs ushered in a wide range of changes in the Civil Service and SOEs. This involved the restructuring and privatization of organizations. In response to the employee overstaffing in the public sector, personnel managers were busy retrenching employees. Operating in changed external and internal environments, personnel managers had to find new ways of accomplishing their objectives. Hence, ERPs have contributed to what Mpuya and Mghanga (2001) refer to as a new form of people management in Tanzania. In their view, the main feature of this new management is derived from the Public Service Management and Employment Policy (PSMEP), the implementation of which has resulted in a fundamental shift in the management of people in Tanzania. Organizations now make the best use of resources to recruit, organize, motivate, and develop their staff to obtain optimum effectiveness. Thus, both the public and private sectors are witnessing the demise of the colonial inherited PM practices and the consequent emergence of HRM.

Recruitment, selection and HR planning

Under the PSMEP policy, there is open competition for positions in the public sector. The hiring of new staff is conducted on the basis of an open recruitment approach, without any gender bias and with competition from both inside and outside the public service. This is done through wide sources and methods of recruitment. In particular, there is wide advertisement of vacant positions both within and outside the public service. The recruitment process aims to bring the vacancy to the widest possible field of qualified applicants. Following job posting within the public service, qualified applicants are encouraged to apply for the vacant positions. Selection is based primarily on competency criteria and takes into consideration the job specification and job description. Thus, the job analysis forms an essential part of the rigorous interview for selection.

Job analysis also forms an essential part of the human resource planning (HRP) process. Currently, HRP is used as a basis for assessing future HR requirements. There is more focus on the assessment of future tasks that the organization expects to perform, the skills and competencies required to perform them, and the resources available to pay employees. HRP is now given serious consideration and applied to recruitment, promotion, training and development, retirement, and resignation. In view of its importance to the efficient management of people in the public service, HRP is now integrated into the Public Service Medium Term Expenditure Framework (Mpuya and Mghanga, 2001).

Performance management

There is now emphasis on performance improvement in the public service as HRP is linked to performance and career management. The government is placing emphasis on employees providing the best possible value for money services. In order to ensure that public service organizations provide the highest quality services, performance management systems have been installed throughout the public service, and results-oriented management practices are applied. Effective and efficient functioning of this system requires: (a) the development of programs that support the recruitment and retention of a core of professional, technical, and managerial staff; and (b) installing open performance appraisals to enable the public service to identify and reward good performers while at the same time eliminate, take sanctions or remedial measures against, those that do not perform well (Public Service Reform Program (PSRP), 2001).

Performance-based management requires the support of fair and equitable pay. In this respect, the government is making efforts to streamline the pay structure and rationalize it through applying results of job evaluation and job grading exercise. The public service is also attempting to restore meritocracy. It has been pointed out that over the years of African socialism the ideals of equality in opportunities in employment eroded the meritocratic ethos in the public service, hence, recruitment in the public service was not perceived to be meritocratic. The deterioration in the meritocratic principle also resulted in the prevalence of unethical conduct and a decline in employee morale.

Hence, in its aspiration to promote a quality public service, the government has realized that it is necessary to have a pool of well-equipped, qualified, and motivated staff with unquestionable integrity and professionalism. It has also been realized that such employees should be recruited and/or promoted through meritocratic principles.

It is believed that restoration of meritocracy will ensure the recruitment and retention of dynamic and innovative personnel who will help in the development of a proactive-oriented culture. Restoration of meritocratic principles in the recruitment and appointment procedures entails: (a) open competition for vacancies; (b) selection criteria that maintain an appropriate balance between academic and professional qualifications and other aspects, such as experience, track record, and learning potential; (c) selection criteria which are non-discriminatory; and (d) award of marks to applicants against a predetermined criteria (PSRP, 2001).

Promotion, demotion, and termination are all also now based on merit. Just as in the case of recruitment, vacancies for promotion are filled through open competition, with advertisements aimed at attracting both internal and external candidates. Criteria for selection include suitability for the post as evident from qualifications, skills, experience, and personal qualities. For internal candidates, reference is made to management inventories data obtained from performance appraisals. Although the new performance appraisal system varies from organization to organization and by grades and levels, it generally has the following common elements: (a) job description with specific measurable objectives; (b) interview and feedback mechanism; (c) a copy of the appraisal method given to the employee; and (d) the report reviewed by a senior manager.

Reward management

Arguably, the most appreciated reforms have been in the area of rewards. Tanzanian workers generally suffer from low pay. Trade union leaders point to ILO data to argue that Tanzanian workers are not only among the most poorly paid employees in the world, but also the most heavily taxed. With average monthly wages of US$50 for lower level public servants and US$60 for those in the private sector (Gumbo, 1999), Tanzanian workers are by any measure miserably paid.

Public sector pay in Tanzania dropped drastically in real terms (to one-fifth the level in the 1970s) in the 1980s and 1990s. This was a significant decline in real wages. In fact, in terms of constant prices, it was estimated that, on average, direct pay for civil servants in 1990 was only about 25 percent of the level in 1972 (Mtafifikolo, 1993). In many instances, the remuneration of public sector employees in the 1990s was insufficient to properly feed and clothe the average size household. Consequently, public servants resorted to extensive moonlighting and other unofficial (often illegal) activities to supplement their incomes (Mtafifikolo, 1993).

In addition, there were pay compression problems in the public sector. In an attempt to achieve the socialist ideals under the Arusha Declaration, the government not only controlled wage levels but also adjusted relative levels in favor of junior civil servants. This was sometimes done through "under-the-table" payments and uneven provision of fringe benefits. These features resulted in pay inequity problems and consequent decompression of the pay structure. The problems were particularly severe for senior civil servants and called for a complete overhaul of the pay structure in the Civil Service (Mtafifikolo, 1993). The need for realistic public sector pay was quite urgent in the 1990s in view of its concomitant demotivating factors.

Recently, with some persuasion from the World Bank, the government has been making efforts to enhance public sector pay. The short-term measure for rationalization of the pay structure is the consolidation of direct monetary allowances with basic pay. The government is also making selective adjustment of compression factors in the consolidated salary structure. The government's long-term goals will be: (a) to raise minimum basic salary (MBS) of its employees to the minimum living wage (MLW); and (b) to raise the salaries and other compensation benefits of its top public servants to levels consistent with the feasibility to recruit and retain the best qualified and skilled Tanzanians in its service. It is envisaged that in future the public sector will: (a) be the market leader in the remuneration of unskilled and semi-skilled labor; (b) benchmark public sector pay to that offered by progressive private sector employers for technical, professional, and managerial staff; and (c) implement performance-related award systems throughout the public service (PSRP, 2001).

In relation to compensation/reward management, the government is also making attempts to improve HR practices. These include rationalization of working hours to make it possible for staff to be compensated for extra work involving extra working hours and overtime in general. Leave terms and entitlement have been reviewed in line with the review of retirement and retirement benefits.

Human resource development

Development of adequate and appropriate human resources is necessary for Tanzania to achieve its economic development objectives. Unfortunately, Tanzania witnessed a decline in HRD during the economic crisis period in the 1980s and early 1990s. As Mbowe (1998) rightly points out, in comparison with efforts on the substance of economic policy, institutional and political aspects of development were considered more important than economic and fiscal aspects. Hence, training and development of human resources did not receive adequate consideration. However, in reminding the government that HRD is the linchpin of socio-economic development, Mbowe (1998) comments that HRD is in crisis in Tanzania and the failure of the Tanzanian government to invest in human capital partly explains the backwardness of their economy.

In both the private and public sectors there are critical shortages of skills at almost all levels. In the public sector, this fact has been recognized by the government and it is making attempts to tackle them. In the interest of developing, maintaining, and enhancing the skills and competencies of employees, all public service departments are required to develop and implement training and development programs. These programs are based mainly on the skill requirements identified in their HR plan and on the performance appraisals of employees. Funding for training and development activities are mainly from budget allocations and are geared to meet both the service's human resource capacity and requirements and individual employee's personal and career development goals.

The government has also made capacity building the central focus of the public service reform program. In this regard, programs in leadership and change management have been instituted and staff are undergoing skills development courses. There are attempts to implement systematic training programs in the public sector. Here, demand-oriented training is carried out based on training needs assessment, and on the basis of annual performance appraisals for all public servants. HR development programs are conducted by locally-based institutions such as: the Eastern and Southern Africa Management Institute; the Institute of Development Management; the Institute of Finance Management and the University of Dar es Salaam. In addition, the government has launched the Public Service College (PSC) as an executive agency to provide training in core programs for raising the performance and capacity of public officers.

The PSC is responsible for curriculum development, staff development, and acquisition of up-to-date training materials and resources. It is expected to be the main conduit for the transfer of knowledge, skills, and experiences and for the enhancement of performance and productivity of public officers. The college is charged with instilling professionalism, quality consciousness, innovative thinking, and awareness of technological issues in the delivery of services. It is expected that in the long run the PSC will be able to build adequate capacity to deliver a modern, effective, efficient, and consumer-oriented public service. The PSC will also be involved in providing comprehensive training, consultancy, and applied research interventions (PSRP, 2001).

In this age of globalization and technological advancements it is crucial for employees to be exposed to global issues and developments. In this context, the Tanzanian government, with the assistance of the World Bank, has set up a Global Distance Learning Network (GDLN) facility at the Institute of Finance Management (IFM). The facility connects Tanzanians to the rest of the world. It offers courses developed by the World Bank Institute. The facility is a breakthrough in distance learning and is one of nine such facilities in the world (see also LePine et al., 2002).

Elsewhere in the economy, the privatization program has brought to light lack of some basic skills (Ofori and Debrah, 2002). There are shortages of human resources in areas such as production managers, scientists, technologists, engineers, supervisors, technicians, artisans and skilled workers. There is also a shortage of personnel with skills in fields such as: engineering design, production engineering, testing and quality control, material management and value engineering, research and development, feasibility studies, and consultancy. Equally, there are shortages of personnel trained in survey, exploration, extraction, development and processing of natural raw materials, economics, accountancy, information technology, marketing, finance, and general business administration/management (Mbowe, 1998).

In the private sector, companies are attempting to solve this problem by a variety of means. Some are providing both on-the-job and off-the-job training conducted by external consultants; others are sponsoring their employees for short courses abroad or those conducted locally by the respective professional associations (Ofori and Debrah, 2002). The universities in Tanzania also play leading roles in HRD. Other institutions that provide HR training and development include: technical colleges, training institutions of ministries, ministry of works, communication and transport and national vocational training colleges (NVTCs).

Technical training institutions, which provide trained personnel for the labor market include: those under the Ministry of Science, Technology and Higher Education (MSTHE). Here, the colleges are Dar-es-Salaam Technical College (DTC); Technical College, Arusha; and Mbeya Technical College. These colleges offer engineering technician courses. Institutions operating independently under other ministries include the Rwegarulila Water Resources Institute (RWRI), which trains supervisory personnel in water engineering and laboratory technicians for water analysis; and the Morogoro Works Training Institute (MWTI), which was set up to meet the special need for Ministry of Works' artisans and technicians. The Institute runs technician and artisan courses in the areas of roads, mechanical and electrical maintenance, and building works. Institutions under parastatal organizations include the Saruji Training Institute (STI), which provides trained personnel in skills required by cement, ceramics, and glass factories; it provides preservice and in-service training in more than 20 trades. The Tanzania Electrical Supply Company (TANESCO) Technical Training Institute (TTTI) supplies the industry's need for technicians. Crafts personnel are mainly trained in vocational training centers (VTCs) and trade schools. VTCs operate under the directorate of the National Vocational Training of the Ministry of Labor and Development of Youth, while training schools are run by voluntary agencies, companies, and parastatal organizations. These trade schools are officially registered by the ministry, which also regulates and enforces standards (Regumyamheto and Batalia, 1994).

While all the training institutes, centres and trade schools provide vital HR functions they all share common problems of inadequate staff – both in quantity and quality, lack of modern training equipment, facilities, and lack of teaching material. In this regard, Mwandosya (1998) views HR development as one of the greatest challenges facing organizations in Tanzania. Accordingly, there are calls for the government to allocate more resources to HRD. In particular, Mwandosya (1998) calls for the mobilisation and sensitization of the society (communities, institutions, individuals, endowments) in order to develop awareness of the importance of contributing resources to HRD.

Gender issues

As in most other African countries, there is a predominance of men in management in Tanzania. Women have fewer opportunities than men to move into management and to advance up the managerial ladder. However, as in Ghana, women are not discriminated against in terms of wages and salaries (Debrah, 2000). Nevertheless, women do not have the same opportunities as men, either at the entry level or in terms of the pace of advancement. Mapolu (2000) maintains that even during the socialist period, women were grossly underrepresented in the managerial ranks even in state enterprises. The situation was no better in the private sector and remains the same today.

In the public sector the government is making efforts to address the gender imbalance in managerial staff in organizations. In 1990, a Gender Section was established within the Policy Development Division of the Civil Service Department. The aim of the Gender Section is to ensure that principles and practices of equality of opportunity as regards recruitment, promotion, training, career development, and other conditions of service are enhanced and maintained. This requires the public service to ensure that there is gender sensitivity in its planning, implementation, monitoring, and evaluation of all public service policies, programs, and activities (PSRP, 2001). The long-term objective here is to develop HR systems and practices that are gender sensitive and committed to addressing gender issues.

The Gender Section is in the process of implementing a program of gender mainstreaming and equal employment, aimed at building the capacity of women in the public service to take up the challenge to compete for upward career mobility. It is believed that by such proactive strategies the Public Service will be able to recruit, retain, and develop the required staff to provide an effective and efficient service (PSRP, 2001).

Labor relations

Tanzania has had trade unions since the colonial period when some pioneering labor laws were enacted. The increase in wage employment in the 1950s led the colonial government to create machinery to regulate labor relations. In 1951, the colonial administration set up a Manpower Commission to investigate labor conditions and to propose systems for payment and other means to create a conducive atmosphere to enhance efficiency and productivity (Mihyo, 1979). This commission's report gave birth to two main labor laws: the Minimum Wage, Terms and Conditions of Employment Act of 1953, and the Employment Ordinance of 1955.

The first legislation, in addition to the institution of a minimum wage, established a collective bargaining framework, Workers' Committees, and Joint Consultation Councils of employers and employees. The second legislation introduced minimum standards of employment. These included: restrictions on juvenile employment, the conditions for deductions from employees' pay, leave, transfer and sickness allowances, and the establishment of a provident fund. At about the same time, the colonial government passed legislation on trade union recognition: the Trade Union Ordinance in 1953. This legislation provided the framework for the forming and registration of unions and for setting up the minimum standards in their functioning. Subsequently, the government established trade disputes settlement machinery for dealing with the handling of disputes between employers and employees at both industrial and plant levels.

Like the nationalist political parties, the trade union movement in Tanzania was actively involved in the anti-colonial struggles. However, after independence, relations between the trade union leaders and the government were strained over the future role of the labor movement. Following a military mutiny in 1964 and the alleged involvement of some prominent trade union leaders, the government dissolved and banned the Tanganyika Federation of Labor (TFL). In its place, the government created an "economic development oriented/state institution" union called the National Union of Tanganyika Employees (NUTA).

In 1977, the merger of the political parties on the Tanzanian mainland (formerly Tanganyika) and Zanzibar was accompanied by the merger of the trade unions in both places. The new labor movement was subsequently integrated into the new political party and became one of its mass organizations (Mihyo, 1979). The objective here was to use the union as a vehicle for national economic development.

Upon the advent of multi-party politics, the Tanzanian labor movement freed itself from the state apparatus and become autonomous. It evolved into a number of trade unions under one umbrella organization in April 2001, and in 1998 gained legal status with the enactment of the Trade Union Act (Uiso, 2001), which allowed freedom to form trade unions. As of April 2002, 17 trade unions on the mainland had registered with the Registrar of Trade Unions.

Although trade unions are recognized, the complex dispute settlement procedures make it extremely difficult for unions to call strikes in the public sector and many work stoppages are considered illegal by the public authorities and tribunals. There are procedures for compulsory arbitration or adjudication when bipartite negotiations between employer and employees fail.

In recent years, the trade unions have focused their attention on addressing the problems arising from the ERPs and privatization, child labor, and the impact of HIV/AIDS on employment. As in Kenya, HIV/AIDS are on the increase and affecting workers (International Labor Organization (ILO), 2002). The trade unions are working in conjunction with the government and NGOs to educate workers on prevention measures. Trade union leaders have mounted vociferous attacks on the negative impacts of the ongoing privatization program. They point to the privatization program as the cause of workers' economic hardships. In the views of the leaders, it has brought nothing but woes to ordinary Tanzanian workers. Since the initiation of the privatization program in the 1990s, there has been massive retrenchment of workers in the public sector in Tanzania. The privatization program has resulted in changes in conditions of service resulting in long hours, compulsory night shifts, job insecurity, poor remuneration, forced overtime, and denial of access to trade unions (Panafrican, 2001). In particular, the trade union leaders contend that there is no job security anymore as employers can hire and fire indiscriminately (Panafrican, 2001)

At another level, the union leaders complain that privatization and liberalization of the economy have led to the relaxation of the enforcement of the country's labor laws so as to create a favorable environment for FDI. It is argued that the relaxation of the labor regulations has given employers a loophole to undermine the rights of workers. Moreover, it is asserted that some companies are ignoring laws regarding wages, working hours, and health and safety at places of work (Panafrican, 2001).

The general view of people in the labor movement is that the adoption of market-oriented reforms has resulted in retrenchment and decline in union membership, which have in turn weakened the ability of the trade union movement to fight against practices which are detrimental to the interests of workers. Others, however, argue that the lack of enforcement of labor laws and standards in recent times is a reflection of capacity and budgetary constraints in the Ministry of Labor and Youth Development rather than a deliberate strategy to attract foreign investors.

Child labor issues

In spite of their internal problems, the trade unions are vigorously fighting against child labor in Tanzania. In response to the union's campaign, the government is working with the trade unions, ILO, non-governmental organizations, NGOs, and employers' associations to tackle the problem. Child labor is an extensive problem as 3.4 out of 12.1 million children under the age of 18 are involved (International Labor Organization (ILO), 2002). Children work in almost all sectors of the economy, but the problem is particularly widespread in agricultural work, domestic work, mining, prostitution, and the informal sector. Such children are exposed to risks, dangers, and exploitation, such as physical and sexual abuse by their employers or their family members, and exposure to hazardous chemicals, snakebites, silicosis, etc. (ILO, 2002). The government is working in collaboration with the ILO to eliminate child labor. Programs implemented under the ILO-initiated programs include: education and training programs; capacity building of the Child Labor Unit of the Ministry of Labor and Youth Development; and campaigns to educate and prevent the use of child labor in all sectors of the economy (ADB, 2000).

The increase in child labor is attributed to a number of factors including large family size and the inability of parents to care for all their children; societal norms that discourage the education of girls, hence they acquire limited employable skills and are consequently restricted to domestic work in urban areas; an increase in rural poverty in recent years and hence the push of children to urban centers in search of jobs; the decline in primary school enrolment and high drop-out rate due to the inability of parents to afford school fees; and the worsening HIV/AIDS crisis, which has created a considerable number of orphans who need to work to fend for themselves (Gumbo, 1999: 10; ADB, 1999).

Other traditional customs have contributed to an increase in child labor. In Tanzania, as in other Sub-Saharan African countries, a child from a poor family can be sent to live with relatives who are financially well-off and living in urban areas. In many situations, the child can be treated fairly well, like any other member of the family, and will have the opportunity to go to school. However, with the implementation of SAPs and other socio-economic changes, unemployment, and reduction in incomes, it is argued that societal values and customs are changing. For instance, with parents having to bear the cost of education and health care it is no longer possible for well-off extended family members to assist in the education of children of relatives. Hence, children are increasingly placed in homes as domestic helpers or servants with no opportunity for education (Gumbo, 1999; ADB, 2000: 16).

Another reason for the increase in child labor in the country is the lack of enforcement of legislation. Trade union officials are pessimistic about the possibility of eradicating child labor in Tanzania in the near future. They complain that while there have been significant achievements and successes in trade unions' and the government's attempts to eradicate child labor, it will take many years to fully eradicate the problem as even government ministers, permanent secretaries of ministries, and government supervisors of the ILO programs in Tanzania all use child laborers as domestic helpers in their homes (Gumbo, 1999). What the trade unions need to do is develop appropriate structures and strategies to tackle the challenges arising from the changing political and economic environments.

Conclusion

This chapter has provided a broad analysis of recent developments in the HRM arena in Tanzania. As part of the discussion, the chapter traced the evolution of economic policies and their impact on people management. It has been shown that, while there are still relics of the colonial style people management system in the private sector in Tanzania, the public sector is leading the way in modernizing HRM. Although in its embryonic state, we are witnessing the demise of personnel management and the emergence of HRM. The restructuring of employment in the public sector is expected to be completed in 2011 and, hopefully, Tanzania will have a world-class HRM system which will enable it to recruit, retain, and develop competent employees and to reward them accordingly.

Unlike in the UK, where the new form of public management had its origins in the private sector, in Tanzania the reverse is the case. In other words, it is the changes in the civil service (public sector) management and employment practices which are motivating private sector employers in Tanzania to implement changes in their people management practices. The public sector has taken the lead in innovating HR practices. With pay and conditions of service improving in the public sector, the private sector has to compete vigorously to recruit the best employees. In initiating the transformation in the people management system in Tanzania, the government is, among other things, preparing organizations to respond positively to the challenges of economic liberalization, political and social pluralism, globalization, and the rapidly changing technological environment. It is expected that the private sector will take a cue from the public sector and invigorate its HRM to equally meet the challenges in both the internal and external environments of firms in Tanzania.

To achieve any meaningful and enduring HRM system in Tanzania, there is the need for both public and private sector employers to go beyond the initial changes and develop strategic HRM techniques and practices which will emphasize what Guest (1987; 1990) sees as integration, commitment, flexibility, and quality. More importantly, employers need to regard their employees as a source of competitive advantage (Kamoche, 1996; Barney, 1991; 1995; Hamel and Prahalad, 1989). With increasing competition in the Eastern and Southern African regions, because of the revival of the East African Community and Tanzanian membership of other regional trading organizations, employers will need more than luck to compete effectively.

References

African Development Bank (ADB) (2000) *United Republic of Tanzania: Country Strategy Paper 1991–2001*, Abidjan: ADB.

Barney, J. (1991) "Firm resources and sustained competitive advantage," *Journal of Management* 17: 99–120.

Barney, J. (1995) "Looking inside for competitive advantage," *Academy of Management Executive*, 9 (4): 49–61.

Bigsten, A. and Danielson, A. (2001) Tanzania: Is the ugly duckling finally growing up? Nordiska Afrikainstituted: Research Report no. 120.

Bol, D., Luvanga, N., and Shitundu, J. (eds.) (1997) *Economic management in Tanzania*, Dar-es-Salaam: Tema Publishers.

Debrah, Y.A. (2000) "Human resource management in Ghana," in P. Budhwar and Y. Debrah (eds.) *Human resource management in developing countries*, London: Routledge, pp. 190–208.

de Valk, P. (1996) *African industry in decline: The case of textiles in Tanzania in the 1980s*, London: Macmillan.

East African Development Bank (EADB) (1999) *Annual report and accounts*, Kampala: Uganda.

Fashoyin, T. (2000) "Management in Africa," in M. Warner (ed.) *Management in the emerging countries: Regional encyclopaedia of business and management*, London: Thomson Business Press, pp. 169–175.

Financial Times (2000) "*Financial Times* Survey: Tanzania," 24 July.

Guest, D. (1987) "Human resource management and industrial relations," *Journal of Management Studies*, 24 (5): 503–521.

Guest, D. (1990) "Human resource management and the American dream," *Journal of Management Studies*, 27 (4): 378–397

Gumbo, P. (1999) "Tanzanian unions fight child labour," *Daily Mail & Guardian*, 20 August, Johannesburg: South Africa.

Gurt (2000) *Public Service Reform Program 2000–2001*, Dar-es-Salaam: Mkuki na Nyota Publishers.

Hamel, G. and Prahalad, C.K. (1989) "Strategic intent," *Harvard Business Review*, May–June: 63–76.

Hill, H. (1994) "Tanzania," in *Africa Review, 1993/94*, London: The Economic and Business Report.

International Herald Tribune (1997) "Tanzania," 8 December: 12–13.

International Labour Organization (2002) *IPEC country profile: United Republic of Tanzania*, ILO's International Program on the Elimination of Child Labor (IPEC), Geneva: ILO.

Kahama, G.C., Maliyamkono, T.L., and Wells, S. (1986) *The challenge for Tanzania's economy*, London: James Currey.

Kamoche, K. (1993) "Towards a model of HRM in Africa," in J.B. Shaw, P.S. Kirkbride, K.M. Rowland, and G.R. Ferris (eds.) *Research in personnel and human resource management*, Suppl. 3, Greenwich, CT: JAI Press.

Kamoche, K. (1996) "Strategic HRM within a resource capability view of the firm," *Journal of Management Studies*, 33 (2): 213–233.

Kamoche, K. (2001) "HRM in Kenya," in P. Budhwar and Y.A. Debrah (eds.) *Human resource management in developing countries*, London: Routledge, pp. 209–221.

Kiggundu, M.N. (1988) "Africa," in R. Nath (ed.) *Comparative management: A regional view*, Cambridge, MA: Ballinger, pp. 169–243.

LePine, M., Milkovich, G. Tang, N. Godfrey, L., and Gearhart, R. (2002) "Globalization, global human resource management, and distance learning: a study of the effectiveness of a global learning partnership," in Y.A. Debrah and I.G. Smith (eds.) *Globalization, workplace and employment*, London: Routledge pp. 239–58.

Mapolu, H. (1979) "The organization and participation of workers in Tanzania," in K.S. Kim, R.B. Mabele, and M.J. Schultheis (eds.) *Papers on the political economy of Tanzania*, London: Heinemann, pp. 272–277.

Mapolu, H. (2000) "Management in Tanzania," in M. Warner (ed), *Management in emerging countries*, London: Thomson Learning.

Mbowe, G.F. (1998) "Capacity building and the role of the private sector," in M.J. Mwandosya, J.V. Mwapachu, and S.M. Wangwe (eds.) *Towards a new millennium: perspectives on Tanzania's vision 2025*, Dar-es-Salaam: Centre for Energy, Environment, Science and Technology (CEEST), pp. 125–132.

Mihyo, P.B. (1979) "Industrial relations in Tanzania," in U.G. Damachi, H.D. Seibel, and L. Tachtman (eds.) *Industrial relations in Africa*, London: Macmillan, pp. 240–272.

Mpuya, M.L. and Mghanga, J.D. (2001) *Public sector capacity building through human resource development of personnel for human settlements development: Challenges and experiences of the Ministry of Lands and Human Settlements Development, in Construction Industry Forum Report*.

Mtatififikolo, F.P. (1993) "Reforms in Systems of Governance:The Case of Civil Service Reforms in Tanzania," paper presented at the International Conference on Development Challenges and Strategies for Tanzania: An Agenda for the 21st Century, October, Economic Research Bureau, University of Dar-es Salaam.

Mwandosya, M.J. (1998) "Human resource development in Tanzania: An Overview," in M.J. Mwandosya, J.V. Mwapachu, and S.M. Wangwe (eds.) *Towards a new millennium: Perspectives on Tanzania's vision 2025*, Dar-es-Salaam: Centre for Energy, Environment, Science and Technology (CEEST), pp. 133–138.

Ofori, G. and Debrah, Y.A. (2002) "Establishing a sustainable funding mechanism for training professionals in the construction industry in Tanzania," report submitted to the Commonwealth Secretariat, London.

Panafrican (2001) "Tanzania. Privatization: Trade union leader deplores conditions of workers." Online: http://allafrica.com/storeis/200105010095.html

Public Service Reform Program (PSRP) (2001) *Public Service Reform Program: 2000–2001*, Dar-es-Salaam: Mkuki na Nyota, 2001.

Regumyamheto, J.A. and Batalia, C. (1994) *Consultancy report: A study of human resources in the construction sector*, submitted to the National Construction Council, Dar-es-Salaam.

Turner, M. (2000) "Tanzania: A Sub-Saharan success story," *Financial Times*, World Economy (Africa), 23 September: XIII.

Turner, M. and Holman, M. (2000) "Coming out of the shadows," *Financial Times Survey*: Tanzania, 24 July: 1.

Uiso, D. (2001) "The Trade Union Act 1998." Online: http://Tanzania.fes-international.de/activities/tradeunion.html

6 HRM in Kenya

KEN N. KAMOCHE, STEPHEN M. NYAMBEGERA, AND MUNYAE M. MULINGE

Introduction

Kenya has sometimes been considered a potential engine of growth for East Africa; but this has not been achieved. Kenya thus provides an interesting study of unrealized expectations and poor utilization of human resources. After achieving independence from Britain in 1963, rapid industrial development, tourism, and good prices for agricultural products helped maintain a steady economic growth rate; but throughout the 1980s and 1990s, these gains have largely been reversed and many Kenyans are economically worse off than they were 20 years ago. With a population of 31 million, occupying 582, 650 km², Kenya has very few viable natural resources, except soda ash, limestone, and minor quantities of gold. It relies heavily on crops like tea, coffee, and horticultural products, whose prices are subject to the vagaries of international trade. Tourism has been dented by worries about security following some terrorist attacks and a high level of crime. English and Kiswahili are the official languages, with over 40 other languages and dialects.

The country has gone through substantial changes—in particular, economic and socio-political—particularly since the early 1990s, which have had a dramatic effect on the industrial and managerial scene, with far-reaching effects on the workforce. These changes began with a move toward political pluralism when the government was pressurized into permitting the registration of multiple political parties. This ushered in, in 1991, an era of multi-partyism which was accompanied by wide-ranging economic reforms and liberalization. While, on the one hand, this created a new sense of confidence and hope for a better future, free of the oppressive antics of the erstwhile one-party state, in reality, the country remained under the control of an administration that was still steeped in the old ways characterized by lack of accountability, endemic corruption, and a token acknowledgment of democracy.

Economic liberalization was introduced in 1993 and consisted of the elimination of price controls, import licensing, and foreign exchange controls. The concomitant reforms produced a brief period of economic growth, which in 1995 reached 5 percent. This growth proved to be unsustainable, and in the ensuing years it has fallen to 4.6 percent in 1996, halved to 2.4 percent in 1997, fallen to 1.8 percent in 1998, and 1.4 percent in 1999. In 2000, the economy contracted to –0.3 percent, before registering a precarious recover at an estimated 1.1 percent in 2001, and then falling back to an estimated –0.3 percent in 2002 (Economic Survey, 2002; International Monetary Fund (IMF), 2002). The IMF suspended aid following the government's failure to institute much needed economic reforms in 1997, and again in 2001, when the government failed to institute measures to curb rampant corruption. This has had a devastating effect on the economy and the people's livelihood. The promise of economic rejuvenation following liberalization has not been realized, and much work needs to be done before there can be a sustainable recovery. Some factors that have hampered growth include poor governance and endemic corruption, high corporate taxation and banking interest rates, poor infrastructure (badly maintained roads, an unreliable telecommunications system, expensive and unreliable supply of electricity), and insecurity in the form of a high crime rate occasioned by an unemployment rate estimated at 40 percent (see also IMF, 2002).

These problems result in high operational costs where organizations have to invest in additional infrastructure, providing their own power generation and additional security. The outcome is that the cost of doing business becomes unmanageable, as a result of which Kenya has consistently lost out in terms of competitiveness. It is estimated that in the period 1997–2001 alone, about 120 firms folded and about 100 came under receivership, while the country loses up to 20,000 jobs annually as large multinationals as well as smaller firms relocate to neighboring countries (*The East African*, 2001). Many multinationals are relocating to countries like Zimbabwe, Egypt, and Morocco to take advantage of a new protocol set up within Comesa (Common Market for Eastern and Southern Africa) that allows for zero-tariff exports within member states. Economic liberalization eliminated wide-ranging import duties which led local manufacturers to complain about the dumping of foreign goods at prices that they could not compete effectively with. Business failures resulted in unprecedented levels of unemployment to the extent that about 1,600 people were being laid off every month throughout the 1990s. Kenya finds itself in a vicious cycle because the high production costs drive manufacturers away, denying the State much-needed tax revenues with which to develop the infrastructure, thus leading to even higher costs of production, deteriorating terms of trade, and a drain on foreign exchange reserves following imports.

Corruption has had an extremely dire effect on the economy. In recent independent opinion polls by the Washington-based International Republican Institute, corruption has been mentioned as often as or more often than poverty and unemployment as the single most important issue facing the economy. Research has found that corruption is associated with poorly enforced property rights, weak rule of law, low investment incentives, tax evasion, income inequality, and a lowering of real capita GDP growth (Gupta *et al.*, 1998; IMF, 2002; Mauro, 1996). Efforts to introduce anti-corruption legislation and an independent anti-corruption authority have been derailed by constant political bickering amongst political camps with vested interests in maintaining the status quo, and a lack of political will.

The HR challenge in Kenya today

One of the outcomes of these business woes for HRM is that managers have been forced to shift their attention away from investing in people to cost management. The pressure to remain competitive, and indeed just to ensure business survival, has forced the HR function to undertake drastic cost-reduction measures which inevitably result in pay freezes, pay cuts, reduction in headcounts, and the rationalization of training budgets. The consequences of the economic downturn have been felt right across the public and private sectors. Reforms across the public sector are part of the conditions for resumption of foreign aid. They largely include cutbacks in the Civil Service and government departments, with thousands being retrenched and many more experiencing various forms of restructuring. As a result of economic mismanagement, decline in competitiveness and structural reforms, poverty has worsened, with an estimated 50 percent of the population living below the poverty line (i.e. living on less than US$1 a day). Real GDP per capita stood at US$350 in 1991. Ten years later, it had fallen to US$320 (IMF, 2002).

From the point of view of the working population, these realities have meant a sharpened urge to secure and retain employment, and, in the process, a strengthening of the employers' hands (Kamoche, 2001). Widespread labor cuts, business closures, and concomitant high unemployment have inevitably resulted in a decline in morale and a heightened sense of job insecurity. The challenge for managers is to maintain morale and secure, train, and develop people while working under intense budgetary constraints. Against this backdrop, the country as a whole, and organizations in particular, are under pressure to maintain a competent and motivated workforce to respond to these economic and business challenges. The importance of human capital in the form of knowledge, skills, and competence for economic development and progress is well known (Kamoche, 1997a; Noorbakhsh et al., 2002). The success of institution building and management programs (Horwitz, 1994), as well as the economic transformation process and the realization of strategic development objectives, depend on the effective mobilization, development, and utilization of human resource capacity. According to Noorbakhsh et al. (2002: 110), "human capital allows countries to augment their productive capacities, sustain their growth prospects and attract additional skills from neighbouring regions." The centrality of human capital becomes even more significant "as nations move into knowledge based economies" (Organization for Economic Cooperation and Development (OECD), 1998: 8). Africa faces a difficult challenge of developing and effectively utilizing its human resources (Kamoche, 1997b) if it is to reap the benefits from this stock of knowledge.

The human resources are an extremely vital development input and the one core development resource that most countries have an abundance of. However, the deteriorating human resource situation in Africa as a whole has been noted by the Economic Commission for Africa (ECA), the International Labor Organization (ILO), the United Nations Conference on Trade and Development (UNCTAD), and other international organizations. These bodies have drawn the attention of policy makers not only to the problem itself but also to the dangers it poses to the continent's development (Balogun and Mutahaba, 1990). Within the context of development, the gradual and systematic depletion of the stock of human resources as a result of out-migration of skilled people is a costly form of brain drain, which has been a serious problem in Kenya. We discuss this further below.

Like the rest of Sub-Saharan Africa, Kenya has been seriously hit by the HIV/AIDS pandemic. The most affected are those in the most economically productive age group: 20–50 years. The number of HIV/AIDS cases has shot up drastically since the first was identified in the early 1980s. Over 2.6 million people are infected, while 700 die daily. The life expectancy of Kenyans has fallen from 63 years to 48 years, with a tremendous drain on the economy (Ndichu, 2001). The HIV/AIDS pandemic presents an unprecedented challenge that calls for the development and implementation of appropriate strategies to reduce its rapid spread. It is said that the disease has claimed more lives in Africa than all the wars waged in the continent and is the leading cause of death (Global Issues, 2000). However, there has been very little research into how organizations are coping with the challenge of the depletion of human resource stocks and how this is affecting the labor market and employment relationship. Furthermore, organizations need to devise mechanisms for sensitizing their staff on the effects of the scourge (Baruch and Clancy, 2000).

Current trends in Human Resource Management

Recruitment and selection

In most organizations in Kenya, the management of people has continued to be characterized by an approach that focuses largely on the adoption and use of formal administrative practices as opposed to the strategic development of human resource skills and competencies. Although there is a general awareness of the significance of strategic HRM, the overarching practice resembles personnel administration and recordkeeping and is increasingly characterized by cost-cutting and retrenchment. This view found expression in the 5th National Human Resource Conference hosted by the Institute of Personnel Management in Nairobi in 2001.

A typical recruitment procedure followed by most organizations in Kenya follows the traditional approach of issuing a requisition to the HR department, which consults with top management about whether there is need to hire and whether a budget exists. Officially, recruitment is mainly through advertisements in local newspapers. In practice, common methods include colleges and training institutions, private agencies, headhunting, "poaching" and at-the-gate recruitment, particularly for lower-level and casual workers. While jobs may be advertised in the papers, particularistic approaches are fairly common, and involve nepotism and various other forms of favoritism. This is even more marked in the public sector, which is characterized by unfair recruitment and promotion practices. These practices are brought about by the politicization of the public sector labor market and the lack of respect for professionalism. The former is manifested through the ethnicization of recruitment and promotions. The genesis for this practice is the colonial administrative technique of divide and rule, which served as a tool for subduing and controlling indigenous populations. However, the practice outlasted active colonial rule to permeate the neo-colonial state in the form of ethnicity (so-called tribalism) and/or nepotism (Mulinge and Munyae, 2000; Nyambegera, 2002).

Headhunting and poaching are basically used for high-ranking positions in the organization, especially managerial cadres and professionals with rare skills. Hiring at the gate and by word of mouth are common practices facilitated by a surplus of cheap unskilled and semi-skilled labor. The use of contacts and favoritism is culturally acceptable in a society in which those in paid employment are expected to help family, friends, and tribespeople secure jobs. The use of recruitment agencies and poaching has become common given the high number of entry-level employees, high unemployment levels, and the AIDS scourge which has had a devastating effect on the country's stock of human resources. The scarcity of high-flying managers and highly skilled senior-level professionals has resulted in the increased reliance on headhunting firms like Manpower Services, PriceWaterhouseCoopers, and Deloitte and Touche.

Many private firms and multinational corporations seek to compete for the best workers in the labor market by providing attractive remuneration packages. By using skills and competencies as the basis of recruitment, they eschew the nationwide practice of political patronage, though they are not always immune from favoritism. State-owned organizations, on the other hand, have always been bureaucratic and autocratic and are used to seeking partisan objectives leading to inefficiency and ineffectiveness (Cohen, 1993). Although some of these organizations are now being privatized, they tend to find it difficult to abandon the deeply entrenched practices of employment through systematic corruption and ethnic chauvinism. Like in the public sector, positions are filled by politically connected individuals, and politicians treat these jobs as rewards for relatives and political supporters.

Ferris *et al.* (1999) contend that a focus on fit as a staffing criterion for selection is quite challenging because fit tends not to be well defined and it can be manipulated, managed, and shaped by the conscious efforts of applicants and employees. Managers in Kenya seek to define this fit mainly through selection interviews. This method is known to be of limited value (e.g. Guion and Gibson, 1988), but is convenient to use and it can give managers a supposedly objective defense against charges of favoritism. Other methods like psychological testing have been found wanting, especially when imported from other nations to the African context due to cultural specificity (Bulhan, 1980).

Performance management

In the mainstream literature, performance management has been identified as one of the more problematic activities in HRM. For example, Rice (1990) argues that its unpopularity can be attributed to employees feeling threatened and the possibility that even managers (i.e. the appraisers) themselves are often unsure of what to do. The evaluation of performance in Kenyan organizations is not a uniform process as appraisals differ in aims and procedures. Kamoche (2000) reported that, among the organizations that participated in his study, differences existed both within and across organizations. Practices included: self-appraisal, ranking of performance on an unsatisfactory–outstanding continuum, and making comments on personal achievements and disappointments during the year and suggestions for general improvement. Scholars who have studied performance appraisals in developing countries have found the exercise to be complicated by cultural and social issues (e.g. Mendonca and Kanungo, 1996). Particularism is a major concern, especially in public organizations. This has become more prevalent given the concerns about job security.

Those who know people who can protect them in organizations tend to be spared when performance is used, for example, to select workers for redundancy, which places politics and good interpersonal relationships above organizational goal-oriented performance. Ethnicity and kinship affiliation also play a role here (Nyambegera, 2002). Those who have good interpersonal relationships with the appraiser or come from the "right" tribe can expect to receive favorable assessment. Nyambegera (2002) contends that for organizational effectiveness to be realized in Sub-Saharan Africa issues of exclusion on grounds of ethnicity should be eliminated. At times, appraisals are manipulated by bosses with a grudge against an employee or to pursue a personal vendetta against appraisees. This is by no means unique to Kenya, as authors elsewhere have shown that executives are prone to engage in distorting and manipulating appraisals for self-serving and political reasons, thus losing the expected objectivity (e.g. Cleveland and Murphy, 1992). The high level of job insecurity and unemployment in Kenya has further politicized performance appraisal, and while some multinational firms are bringing in "best practices" from their overseas headquarters, the socio-cultural and economic contexts in Kenya today are such that managers in many organizational forms are under pressure to give favors while at the same time projecting an image of objectivity. These contradictions are increasingly difficult to reconcile.

Compensation

Current thinking on compensation holds that people should be valued for the knowledge they possess and rewarded according to how they apply this knowledge and competencies to productive activities that are consistent with the organization's strategic objectives. Legislation also plays a role through an annually-adjusted minimum monthly wage, which in 2002 was set at the equivalent of US$46 for the two main urban centers, Nairobi and Mombasa, and US$27 elsewhere. However, in some sectors like the agricultural sector and some Asian-owned firms, labor laws including minimum wage legislation are often flouted due to the abundance of cheap labor. In addition to direct financial rewards, firms typically offer a house allowance or a house and transport.

The pressure to cut costs has resulted in many organizations eliminating perks that were previously seen as an entitlement, such as chauffeurs that come with company cars for executives. Pensions are administered through the National Social Security Fund (NSSF) and, increasingly, many firms maintain a provident fund to which the employer and the employee contribute and such benefits are paid on resignation or retirement. Gratuity is also paid by some firms to contract employees. The law requires that all employers contribute to the National Insurance Hospital Fund (NIHF) to cover medical expenses. Private firms normally have separate medical and life insurance cover. Considering the cost of living in Kenya, especially in urban areas, some organizations (especially in banking) provide a number of discretionary benefits such as loans to build or buy a house and education allowances. These "paternalistic services" (Lincoln and Kalleberg, 1990) are an important part of the remuneration package, especially in view of the high cost of living and reduced incomes as retrenchment eats into family incomes. As the society shifts from a collectivist to individualistic ethos, especially for urban dwellers (Nyambegera et al., 2000), many employees are now expecting rewards based on individual performance. Although merit pay is not immune to managerial capriciousness, young professionals believe it offers them some sort of safeguard against the more subjective approaches that are prone to ethnic and political manipulation. Kamoche (2000) also notes that merit is a preferred basis for rewarding employees, especially by the young, well-educated, and skilled personnel; whereas the old, less educated, semi- or non-skilled, and unionized workers prefer seniority and are suspicious of claims to measure performance objectively.

The erosion of absolute values of salaries, particularly in the public relative to the private sector, has negatively affected employee motivation and the possibilities of recruiting and retaining professionals and technical public servants. As such, highly-qualified personnel now prefer to join the private sector when they are suitably qualified. Others have been pursuing opportunities abroad, as we discuss below. The problem of low wages and fringe benefits is compounded by unfair practices in the remuneration of workers. This is manifest in a lack of clear and consistent wage policies, especially in the public sector where arbitrary pay differences for different cadres of workers are very common.

Training and development

Most African countries attained independence with a huge deficit in skilled human resources. However, by the 1980s most countries, save Botswana, Namibia, and South Africa, had managed to meet their manpower requirement in most areas, with deficits existing only in a few professional and technical areas. The void in skilled human resources experienced at independence could be understood within the context of the mainly missionary-sponsored formal education under colonialism, which aimed to equip local people with rudimentary skills that enabled them to serve as clerks and teachers. There was little emphasis on higher education. Post-independence policies in Kenya sought to rectify these imbalances by training Africans to fill public service positions in the quest for the Kenyanization or indigenization of the Civil Service and other private sector positions. The development of human resources became a central objective in the fight against poverty, disease, and ignorance (Bagha, 1990). In the 8th National Development Plan (1997–2001), and Sessional Paper No. 2 of 1997 on "Industrial Transformation to the Year 2020" great emphasis was placed on the central role of human resource planning, development, and utilization on the success of Kenya's industrialization process. In terms of education, between the years 1963 and 2000, primary and secondary school enrolment rose from 891,553 to 5.9 million and from 30,121 to 652,283, respectively. In 2000, a total of 480,996 and 182,863 candidates registered for the Kenya Certificate of Primary Education (KCPE) and the Kenya Certificate of Secondary Education (KCSE), respectively (Kyungu, 2001).

For the last 20 years, Kenya's universities have increased from one to five public and eight privately-chartered universities, with several others being considered for registration. Public and private university level enrolment stood at over 50,000 during the academic year 2001/02. Although information on employment figures of university graduates is scanty, there are indications that those in arts and general sciences take longer to secure employment than their counterparts in other professions. There are over 800 vocational training and technical training institutions at various levels in the country. There is, nevertheless, a major challenge still to be met as only 10 percent of primary and 13 percent of secondary school leavers are absorbed in the post-primary and post-secondary institutions every year. This leaves behind an extremely large number of young people aspiring to enter the labor market without appropriate skills. The labor force is currently estimated at 14.5 million, with about 750,000 new entrants into the labor market annually. Nyambegera *et al.* (2001) point out that many of these people have to endure a poor quality of work life due to the scarcity of alternative job opportunities.

Training and development are considered central to organizational functioning and in particular for helping organizations respond to technological advances. Kamoche (2000: 107) points out that, "the extent to which an organization is prepared to invest in training its employees by way of developing them, is indicative of whether employees are seen as a cost to be rationalized, or a resource that has the potential to contribute meaningfully to the organization." The evidence in Kenya suggests that training is largely treated as a cost, and the economic situation has made it even more difficult for managers to view training as an investment. Kenya's industrial base remains relatively underdeveloped, and is not helped much by a surplus of cheap unskilled labor and relatively low level of technological advancement. The failure to invest systematically in training and development is therefore hurting industrial development and impeding improvements in labor productivity. In fact, the low level of labor productivity is recognized as a major problem in Kenyan industry. It is hardly surprising that the poor state of the economy and constant business failures have forced organizations to slash training budgets. Current efforts at training are limited to equipping employees with narrowly-defined firm-specific skills that facilitate the attainment of short-term objectives. We argue that to develop people and raise labor productivity, organizations will need to transform the way they develop people by nurturing cultures that value the contribution from their employees, undertake cost-efficient training activities that are geared to enhancing labor productivity and product quality, and are consistent with well defined long-term business strategies.

Industrial relations

Siddique (1989: 385) points out that most developing countries exhibit a dualistic economic structure, where a pre-capitalist economic system mainly dominates the scene, with a small industrial sector and a related small numerical size of the working class. Other features include a segmented labor market, with a sharp dualism both between modern and traditional manufacturing sectors and between large and small firms; the dominance of the state in the industrial sector; weak trade unions and weak collective bargaining. Further, Siddique argues that industrial relations in developing country settings can be explained in two ways: the popular cultural based explanation and the role of the state in the industrial relations (IR) systems. For example, in India traditional customs seem to have engendered a paternalistic industrial relations system (Kennedy, 1982) and in Africa reference is made to the traditional African tribal and social systems (Gonsalves, 1974; Diejomaoh, 1979). The State's influence is manifest through the dominant role in industrialization and the labor market, as in Kenya.

The origins of IR in Kenya are traceable to the colonial times when unions emerged as key players in confronting oppressive colonial policies (Singh, 1969). After independence in 1963, the government found it necessary to choreograph the union movement by arguing that the nascent industrialization needed to be protected from activism and disruptive activity. Employer organizations like the Kenyan Federation of Employers were drawn into this effort in order to ensure industrial stability. Kamoche (2000) argues that the government's policy towards IR was that of exercising restraint in order to ensure the industrial stability that was deemed necessary for economic growth.

However, given the deteriorating trust between the government and employees, militancy came to characterize IR. In recent years, this has covered a wide range of industries, for example air controllers and the Kenyan Union of Teachers (KNUT). Factors that have kept the militancy in check include the fear of being sacked in the era of high unemployment and widespread poverty, the prevailing culture of retrenchment, widespread business failures, and the heavy-handed approach by past governments which did not hesitate to interfere in labor disputes "to rescue the economy." Organizations that have recently retrenched staff include Unilever Ltd., Nestlé Foods Ltd., Nairobi Bottlers Ltd., Kenya Breweries Ltd., Unga Group, Standard Chartered Bank, Kenya Commercial Bank, Barclays Bank, and Kenya Power and Lighting Co. The public sector, which previously guaranteed jobs to many graduates and school leavers, has also had to reduce its wage costs and headcounts. In the 2001/02 financial year it retrenched 22,190 employees. About 20,239 are projected to be retrenched in 2003/04. This scenario has strengthened the employers at the expense of trade unions, and this has left the latter at a crossroads with no particular strategy in sight for traversing this unfamiliar territory.

The problem of brain drain and erosion of human resource stocks

In spite of the advances in human resource development, Kenya has fared badly in the area of effective utilization and retention of these resources, especially since the mid-1980s. During this period the country experienced a wave of out-migration of its skilled human resources, especially professionals and other technical personnel, to Europe and America. Most recently, the Southern Africa region and in particular the countries of Botswana and South Africa have become major destinations for Kenyan professionals. Indeed, it is estimated that well over 500 Kenyan doctors now work and live in Southern Africa. These doctors have been educated at huge public expense in medical schools in Kenya. South Africa and Botswana have also become popular destinations for Kenyan academics from the major state universities; other departing professionals include paramedical staff, teachers, engineers, and scientists.

Brain drain is one of the major problems in human resource utilization in Africa (Balogun and Mutahaba, 1990). Indeed, in Kenya, it is now emerging as one of the biggest threats to sustainable economic growth. The problem in Kenya mirrors what is happening across Africa and, therefore, it has to be understood within the broader context of the continent. Noting the huge losses that Africa has incurred as a result of brain drain, bodies such as the ECA, the ILO, and UNCTAD have urged African governments to initiate steps for the return of skills to the continent. What is worrying for Africa is not cross-border migration per se; rather, it is the selective nature of that migration. The new pattern of migration involves the relocation of Africa's highly trained and hard-to-replace professionals to Europe, North America, Asia, and the Gulf region. Many African countries are now losing their professionals to the Southern Africa region (especially Botswana, Namibia, and South Africa). These are the individuals "whose skills seem to be highly appreciated in countries other than their own" (Balogun and Mutahaba, 1990: 66).

Kamoche (2000) found that managers in Kenya, like their counterparts elsewhere, claimed that employees were their most important asset. However, a closer look at what has befallen particularly public sector organizations since the early 1990s renders this position rather ironic. While doing well in training and human resource development, recruitment, remuneration, and promotional practices have tended to undermine the capacity of organizations to attract and, more importantly, retain skilled and specialized workers. This is evident from the exodus of professionals to popular destinations like Europe, North America, and Southern Africa. The unprecedented economic malaise that blanketed the country since the late 1980s coupled with the institutionalization of corruption, political ineptitude, and the gradual erosion of living standards (Kamoche, 2001), has pushed the bulk of Kenyan professionals and skilled workers to seek better opportunities abroad. Most affected by this exodus has been the public sector, which is the dominant employer in the Kenyan economy, as indeed in most African countries (Collins, 1989).

To understand the origins of the problem of brain drain in Kenya, we need to recognize the effect of employment practices and mismanagement. In fact, according to Balogun and Mutahaba (1990), defective employment policies have a lot to answer for in this regard. The continuous skill flight affecting the country is a reflection of the existence of a flawed approach to human resources utilization. More specifically, it demonstrates the absence of a clear and forward-looking employment policy and managerial practices that are conducive to the attraction and retention of skilled and specialized human resources. There are other problems that have been responsible for the brain drain in Kenya. These problems have bred a sense of frustration and resentment, especially amongst efficiency-conscious professionals and skilled technicians. These problems include a general lack of sufficient resources with which to execute tasks effectively (see also La-Anyane, 1985) and inadequate benefits and supportive facilities such as transportation, housing, and funding (Mulinge and Mueller, 1998). The medical profession is a case in point: medical personnel having to work in hospitals that lack essential medical supplies and other essential equipment infrastructure.

What professionals find particularly frustrating is that resources are misappropriated and siphoned away; this may apply to medical supplies, equipment for schools, money set aside for the provision of public amenities, and so forth. Resource inadequacy is known to impact negatively on employee motivation, to lower job satisfaction, and to reduce commitment to the employer. This has been demonstrated in studies by Mulinge and Mueller (1998) and Mulinge (2001), focusing on skilled agricultural workers in the public, parastatal, and private sectors in Kenya. Frustration also comes from lack of autonomy and participation in decision making (Mulinge, 2001). Employees, particularly in the public sector, often endure interference and political meddling, and may be required to implement unpopular and inappropriate externally engineered decisions that may even undermine the organization. Professionals who find themselves treated with disrespect and constantly threatened with dire consequences ultimately vote with their feet. These are some of the factors contributing to the high levels of attrition of professionals in search of better opportunities outside the country.

Conclusions

Kenya is in dire need of human resource reform measures, especially in the public sector, to counter the out-migration trends in skilled human resources and reverse the brain drain affecting the country. This calls for the formulation of a strategic human resource (utilization) policy and the adoption of supervisory and managerial practices which allow staff to realize their maximum potential and contribute to the development of their organizations (Balogun and Mutahaba, 1990). Such a policy is necessary to not only guarantee the country a competitive edge both in the African continent and globally, but also to ensure that Kenya continues to reap returns from the massive investments the country has made in human resource development and training since independence. It is imperative that such a policy be formulated and implemented soon to avert the current brain drain, particularly in those areas that involve high educational and training expenditure and are also the nerve for socio-economic development such as education, medicine, engineering, IT, and business.

To develop such a framework for Kenya requires a proper understanding of rival labor market environments, both within and outside of the African continent. For the framework to qualify to be strategic, it must create a niche for the country that will facilitate the cultivation, nurturing, and sustenance of a competitive advantage. This will be possible if such a policy would have as its purpose the development of an optimal fit between the needs of the employee, the job, the organization, and the environment. By so doing it would guarantee that employees reach their desired level of satisfaction and performance, and organizations, both in the public and private sectors, meet their goals. It would also ensure better and more effective utilization of existing human resource stocks, thus contributing to economic development. A strategic human resources (utilization) policy should ensure that the nation's most important and abundant resource, the people, is utilized effectively to ensure that the country "gains and maintains a competitive advantage" (Blunt and Jones, 1992: 56). As such, the strategic management of people in organizations must entail efforts to make the best use of human resources in the attainment of organizational objectives; i.e. for the public sector, the effective delivery of services. For this to occur, public sector organizations must attract, retain, keep motivated, and effectively utilize various cadres of skilled and professional/specialized workers. An effective human resources utilization framework for Kenya should have the following characteristics to be successful:

- It should be human-oriented. That is, it should take cognizance of the fact that human resources are not limitless (Balogun and Mutahaba, 1990).
- It must pay special attention to HR areas like recruitment and selection, performance management, rewarding, and training. Practices should be systematic, fair, motivational, and merit-based (see also, Kiggundu, 1989).
- Remove organizational constraints on the effective deployment and development of human resources. Balogun and Mutahaba (1990) describe these as arbitrary political interference in professional matters, an overbearing hierarchical order, defective grading and position classification systems, and managerial and supervisory styles which tend to stifle initiative, breed interpersonal conflict, and block creativity.
- Address concerns related to promotional opportunities or career ladders. The proposed framework should transcend staff training to include other elements such as the development of effective and lifelong career development paths for all categories of workers.

- Enhance task performance by employees. The new framework must nurture a work environment that facilitates professionals and other skilled workers to perform their tasks effectively by availing to them the necessary task resources and, generally speaking, creating an enabling work environment.

This is a skeletal view of what the country needs to do to improve the development and utilization of its human resources. In the increasingly competitive and globalized labor market, Kenya needs to take a considered look at the problems and weaknesses in the current efforts to manage people, and recognize that as long as these problems remain it will become increasingly difficult to retain the professional and technical workers that have cost so much to educate and train. Many of these problems are attributable to economic mismanagement, nepotism, and corruption, and have largely been perpetuated by or with the help and blessing of the political establishment. It goes without saying, therefore, that if there is no meaningful change in the political arena, if corruption, nepotism, and related social ills are not eradicated, Kenyans will continue to be exposed to arbitrary and capricious administrative and management practices which ultimately hurt the country's human resources and intensify the current economic malaise.

This discussion ends on the encouraging note that following presidential and parliamentary elections at the end of 2002, and the installation of a new government in January 2003, Kenya stands at the dawn of a new era. Led by noted economist Mwai Kibaki, the new government has promised to fight corruption at all costs and bring the economy back to its feet. After more than two decades of economic degradation, creating a new economic order will take time, commitment, and resources. With a democratic regime at the helm, at least there is now a real chance for Kenya to begin the task of reconstruction. This will also, hopefully, encourage the use of positive practices for managing institutions which will improve the livelihoods of the people. If the foreign investors who have previously abandoned the country can be persuaded to come back, Kenya is likely to experience both capital inflows and an infusion of new management ideas. Hopefully, the issues discussed here will help foreign managers to align their practices to the needs of the local workforce.

References

Bagha, H. (1990) "Human resources development in Kenya," in C. Grey-Johnson (ed.) *The employment crisis in Africa: Issues in human resource development policy*, Mount Pleasant, Harare: African Association for Public Administration and Management.

Balogun, M.J. and Mutahaba, G. (1990) "The dilemma of the brain drain," in C. Grey-Johnson (ed.) *The employment crisis in Africa: Issues in human resource development policy*, Mount Pleasant, Harare: African Association for Public Administration and Management.

Baruch, Y. and Clancy, P. (2000) "Managing Aids in Africa: HRM challenges in Tanzania," *International Journal of Human Resource Management* 11 (4): 789–809

Blunt, P. and Jones, M.L. (1992) *Managing organizations in Africa*, New York: Walter de Gruyter.

Bulhan, H.A. (1980) "Psychological research in Africa: Genesis and function," *Presence Africaine* 116: 20–42.

Cleveland, J.N. and Murphy, K.R. (1992) "Analyzing employee appraisal as goal-directed behavior," in G.R. Ferris (ed.) *Research in personnel and human resource management*, Greenwich, CT: JAI Press.

Cohen, J.M. (1993) "Importance of public service reform: The case of Kenya," *Journal of Modern African Studies* 31 (3): 449–476.

Collins, P.D. (1989) "Strategic planning for state enterprise performance in Africa: Public versus private," *Public Administration and Development* 9: 65–82.

Diejomaoh, V.P. (1979) "Industrial relations in a development context: The case of Nigeria," in U. G. Damachi *et al.* (eds.) *Industrial relations in Africa*, London: Macmillan.

The East African (2001) "Industries quit Kenya as recession bites," 30 July.

Economic Survey (2002), Nairobi: Government Printer.

Ferris, G.R., Hochwarter, W.A., Buckley, R.M., Harrell-Cook, G., and Frink, D.D. (1999) "Human resource management: Some new directions," *Journal of Management* 25 (3): 385–415.

Global Issues (2000) "AIDS: the threat to world security," *Electronic Journal of the U.S. Department of State*, July, 5: 2.

Gonsalves, R.E. (1974) "The politics of trade unions and industrial relations in Uganda," unpublished Ph.D. thesis, Victoria University of Manchester.

Guion, R.M. and Gibson, W.M. (1988) "Personnel selection and placement," *Annual Review of Psychology* 39: 349–374.

Gupta, S., Davoodi, H., and Alonso-Terme, R. (1998) "Does corruption affect income inequality and poverty?" *IMF Working Paper 98/76* Washington: International Monetary Fund.

Horwitz, F. (1994) "Institution-building issues in South Africa," *Public Administration and Development* 14: 187–199.

International Monetary Fund (2002) "Kenya: selected issues and statistical appendix," *IMF Country Report no. 02/84*, Washington: IMF.

Kamoche, K. (1997a) "Competence-creation in the African public sector," *International Journal of Public Sector Management* 10 (4): 268–278.

Kamoche, K. (1997b) "Managing human resources in Africa: Strategic, organizational and epistemological issues," *International Business Review* 6: 537–558.

Kamoche, K. (2000) *Sociological paradigms and human resources: An African context*, Aldershot: Ashgate.

Kamoche, K. (2001) "Human resource management in Kenya," in P.S. Budhwar and Y.A. Debrah, (eds.) *Human resource management in developing countries*, London: Routledge.

Kennedy, V.D. (1982) "Labour policies and Indian Culture," in N.R. Sheth (ed.) *Industrial sociology of India*, New Delhi: Allied Publishers.

Kiggundu, M.N. (1989) *Managing organizations in developing countries*, West Hartford, CN: Kumarian Press.

Kyungu, S.P.M. (2001) Closing speech, 5th National Human Resource Management Conference, Nairobi, Kenya, October.

La-Anyane, S. (1985) *Economics of agricultural development in tropical Africa*, Chichester: John Wiley.

Lincoln, J.R. and Kalleberg, A.L. (1990) *Culture, Control and Commitment: A study of Work Organizations and Attitudes in the United States and Japan*, New York: Cambridge University Press.

Mauro, P. (1996) "The effects of corruption on growth, investment, and government," *IMF Working Paper 96/98*, Washington: International Monetary Fund.

Mendonca, M. and Kanungo, R. (1996) "Impact of culture on performance management in developing countries," *International Journal of Manpower* 17 (4/5): 66–75.

Mulinge, M.M. (2001) "Employer control of employees: Extending the Lincoln-Kalleberg corporatist model of satisfaction and commitment," *Human Relations* 54 (3): 285–318.

Mulinge, M.M. and Mueller, C.W. (1998) "Employee job satisfaction in developing countries: The case of Kenya," *World Development* 26 (12): 2181–2199.

Mulinge, M.M. and Munyae, M.M. (2000) "The ethnicization of the State and the crisis of African development: The Kenyan experience," *Journal of Cultural Studies* 2 (1): 141–159.

Ndichu L. (2001) "Aids pandemic kills 700 Kenyans daily," *Sunday Standard*, 9 December.

Noorbakhsh, F. Paloni, A., and Youssef, A. (2002) "Looking for human capital: Investment in developing countries," in F. Analoui (ed.) *The changing patterns of human resource management*, Aldershot: Ashgate.

Nyambegera, S.M. (2002) "Ethnicity and human resource management practice in Sub-Saharan Africa: The relevance of the discourse of managing diversity," *International Journal of Human Resource Management* 13 (7): 1077–1090.

Nyambegera, S.M., Daniels, K., and Sparrow, P. (2001) "Why fit doesn't always matter: The impact of HRM and cultural fit on job involvement of Kenyan employees," *Applied Psychology: An International Review* 51 (1): 109–140.

Nyambegera, S.M., Sparrow, P., and Daniels, K. (2000) "The impact of cultural value orientations on individual HRM preferences in developing countries: Lessons from Kenyan organizations," *International Journal of Human Resource Management* 11 (4): 639–663.

Organization for Economic Cooperation and Development (OECD) (1998) *Human capital investment: An international comparison*, Paris: Centre for Educational Research and Innovation, OECD.

Rice, B. (1990) "Performance review: The job nobody likes," in G.R. Ferris, K.M. Rowland, and M.R. Buckley (eds.) *Human resource management: Perspectives and issues*, Massachusetts: Needham Heights.

Siddique, S.A. (1989) "Industrial relations in a Third World setting: A possible model," *Journal of Industrial Relations* 31: 385–401.

Singh, M. (1969) *History of Kenya's trade union movement to 1952*, Nairobi: East African Publishing House.

7 HRM in Ethiopia

SEMAW MEKONNEN AND AMINU MAMMAN

Introduction

Over the years attempts have been made by Ethiopia to import public policies and some elements of modern management practices and philosophy such as human resource management. For example, under the concept of New Public Management and Good Governance, the public sector is engulfed by modern management practices and philosophy which usually form the foundation for introducing "hard" Human Resource Management (HRM) philosophy. Armstrong (1992: 202) argued that, "HRM cannot be presented in the form of a universal process for improving the way in which people are managed in organizations." Similarly, Brewster (1993) argued that, "Without some adaptation to take account of the European (and perhaps other?) non-American situations, the HRM concept will continue to attract fundamental critiques. . . ."

Therefore, the main objective of this paper is to review the nature and scope of HRM in Ethiopia and the factors that affect it. The experience of the Ethiopian Evangelical Church Mekane Yesus (EECMY) will be used sparingly to give specific examples to elaborate on the Ethiopian context of management.

The EECMY is an indigenous Ethiopian Church organization that was instituted as a national church on 21 January, 1959 (Andersen, 1980). The EECMY developed its mission statement in line with "wholistic approach." Based on this approach, the Church has developed a theme, "Serving the whole person," which is often referred to as "wholistic ministry." With wholistic ministry, EECMY's objective is to address both the spiritual and physical needs of people. In addressing physical needs, EECMY actively partakes in the development and social work activities of the country.

Currently, the EECMY has over 3,000 employees. As regard to HRM, it has long-standing human resource practices, which include recruitment and selection, training and development, reward management, and performance appraisal.

The chapter begins with the discussion of the significance of human resources (HR) to the development of Africa in general and Ethiopia in particular. We then focus on the context of HRM in Ethiopia. Special sections are dedicated to cultural and political contexts. Finally, given that the adoption of HRM will almost certainly result in some modification of the HRM practices, we recommend how organizations can use some aspects of HRM practices to benefit organizations within the context of the Ethiopian environment.

The strategic imperative and context of Human Resource Management

Strategic imperative

It is now widely agreed that human resources are the most important asset an organization or a nation can have. This is particularly the case for poorer African countries like Ethiopia. However, strictly speaking, the human resource is not just the number of people in an organization or in a country. It is the quality of the people that counts (Kamoche, 1996). Given that almost all human beings have some potential to become resourceful to benefit themselves, the organization they work for, and the country they belong to, the role of government, organizations, and managers in Ethiopia is to turn the population into resourceful beings. To appreciate the significance of human resources at national level, it is necessary to appreciate the significance of HR in the implementation of Ethiopian national development plans. Without a committed and competent workforce, successful implementation of the nation's plans for economic and social development cannot take place. Arguably, the brain drain experienced by Ethiopia in the last two decades does not make this task any easier.

Background

Ethiopia was an ancient African monarchical nation, with significant history dating back to the biblical era. Following the military coup in 1974, a socialist state and later a democratic government was formed. The country has a total area of 1,127,127 km². With a population of 67,673,031, it is one of the most populous countries in Africa. By recent United Nations' estimates, 47.2 percent are between 0 and 14 years old, 50 percent are between 15 and 64 years old, and the rest are over 65 years old. This offers a huge human resource potential.

Ethiopia like many African countries is ethnically diverse. The main ethnic groups are Oromo (40 percent), Amhara and Tigre (32 percent), Sidamo (9 percent). Similarly, the country has two main religions; Muslim (45–50 percent) and Ethiopian Orthodox (35–40 percent). There are also animist (12 percent) and others (3–8 percent). The majority of the people speak Amharic. Other languages spoken by Ethiopians include: Tigrinya, Oromigna, Guaragigna, Somali, Arabic, and other local languages. According to a 1995 United Nations' estimate only 35 percent of the population over 15 years old are literate. The diversity of the population described above is the basis of nepotism affecting many Ethiopian organizations. We will come back to this later in our discussion of the socio-cultural implications of transferring HRM.

The economy, privatization, and HRM

Like many African countries, Ethiopia is a poor country (65 percent live below the poverty line). The economy is largely based on agriculture (52.3 percent). The sector accounts for half of the country's GDP (US$46 billion; 2001 estimate). Agriculture is the main stay of the economy, accounting for 85 percent of exports and 80 percent of total employment. The other significant sector is industry (11.1 percent) and services (36.6 percent). In November 2001, Ethiopia qualified for debt relief from the Heavily Indebted Poor Countries (HIPC) initiative run by the group of industrialized wealthy nations (commonly known as G8). But to appreciate the current economic condition of Ethiopia, it is important to take a historical as well as political perspective. For example, the limited economic growth between 1974 and 1978 was caused by the internal political crisis, armed conflict, and radical institutional reform. This is because the government's nationalization measures and the highly unstable political climate caused economic dislocation in sectors such as agriculture and manufacturing (Ofcansky and Berry, 1991).

The economy began to recover during 1978–1980, as the government consolidated its power and implemented institutional reforms grounded in socialists principles. The improvement of security provided more opportunity for economic growth. However, it was at this time that the country was losing many of its skilled professional labor force, the impact of which took time to manifest. The earlier economic recovery of 1978–1980 was rather short-lived. This is because between 1980 and 1985 the economy experienced a massive set back. Following the persistent down turn, the socialist government publicly declared the failure of the Marxist economic system in a speech to the ruling council on 5 May 1990. The government announced the adoption of a new strategy for the country's future economic development. The strategy included decentralization in planning and a free market, mixed economy in which the private and public sectors would play complementary roles. The new strategy would permit Ethiopian and foreign private individuals to invest in foreign and domestic trade, industry, construction, mining, and agriculture, and in the country's development in general. Although the strategy attracted significant attention, many observers were saceptical about Ethiopia's ability to bring about a quick radical transformation of its economic policies. The plan proved irrelevant given the deteriorating political situation that led to the fall of the military regime in 1991 (Ofcansky and Berry, 1991).

Since the market-oriented economic policy was launched in 1992, privatization of state-owned enterprises was considered an integral part of the broader macro-economic reform. It was aimed at changing the centralized socialist economic system into a market economy by providing the private sector with the major role generating economic growth. Both domestic and foreign investors were encouraged to participate in the privatization process. The Ethiopian Privatization Agency (EPA) was established in 1994 to take charge of the process. So far, 195 units and whole enterprises have been privatized and transferred to domestic and foreign investors. The agency plans to privatize 117 public enterprises in the next three years. The agency also reported that preparations are underway for the privatization of 81 state-owned enterprises.

Another important feature of Ethiopia's social and economic development is the recurring drought. Famine has been a longstanding phenomenon in Ethiopia. Currently, drought has put 14.3 million of the population at risk (Government of Ethiopia, 2002). This, coupled with over 3 million HIV/AIDS-infected people, significantly retards the development of the country. The government has revealed the situation to the international community and launched an appeal. However, if aid does not reach the needy in time, the crisis could be as bad as the famine of 1984, which consumed thousands of lives (South African Broadcasting Corporation, 2002).

Privatization and HRM

The relevance of privatization to HRM cannot be overemphasized. From employees and trade union perspectives, economic restructuring, and privatization in particular, have always been a prelude to the introduction of modern rational management practices. In most cases, privatization leads to loss of jobs in the pursuit of efficiency. To investors/owners, rationalization of employment is necessary to the firm's survival and growth which, they argue, will lead to better pay. The agency (EPA) is aware of this concern. As a result, it has encouraged trade unions to be involved in the process, albeit at a consultative level. Workshops have been organized by the Agency regarding the workers' role in the privatization process. For example, in one particular workshop, more than 100 representatives of trade unions and federations under the Confederation of Ethiopian Trade Unions participated. They were briefed about the Agency's operations, privatization planning and preparation, implementation, post-privatization monitoring, as well as the workers' role in the privatization preparation process by EPA officials. The participants held discussions with the staff of the Agency on the guarantee and security of employees of privatized enterprises, as well as on employees' participation in the process of the privatisation. It is too early to judge the overall consequences of privatization. However, evidence from other countries indicates the following: rationalization of employment; introduction of modern working practices; limited role for trade unions; more redundancies and dismissal; and lack of guarantee for immediate improvement in organizational work performance. For Ethiopia, this is not a recipe for retaining a highly qualified workforce.

Education and training

The quality of the human resources of any country is determined by its formal and informal education system. To appreciate the current level of skills and educational attainment of the Ethiopian labor force, it is essential to understand the historical background of the educational system. Historically, education in Ethiopia was biased toward religious learning. At the beginning of the twentieth century, the education system failed to meet the needs of the nation, especially in the area of statecraft, diplomacy, commerce, and industry. This led to the introduction of a secular educational system. Despite the effort to change the system, by 1974 less than 10 percent of the total population was literate (Ofcansky and Berry, 1991).

In line with socialist principles, in 1977 the government issued a document outlining the main objectives of higher education institutions. The objectives were:

1   the training of individuals in accordance with the national development plan;
2   the provision of qualified medium-level personnel to meet the immediate needs of the economy;
3   the improvement of the quality of education, and the strengthening and expansion of tertiary-level institutions;
4   the establishment of new research and training centers; and
5   the contribution to a better standard of living for people by developing science, technology, the arts, and literature.

In the early 1990s, the problems faced by Ethiopia to make its educational system respond to the nation's needs remained formidable. Social and political change, to say nothing about famine and falling commodity prices, had affected many traditional elements of national life, which ultimately had and continue to have profound effects on the progress of education (Ofcansky and Berry, 1991). In the twenty-first century, the problems still persist. Ironically, some the positive outcomes generated by the previous educational policies are actually benefiting foreign countries instead of Ethiopia. This is because, as we will discuss later, a lot of trained professionals produced by the educational system have migrated to other countries in search of better conditions.

Currently the profile of human resource development (HRD) in Ethiopia is very low. The educational system does not foster the development of adequate and appropriate human resources. The literacy rate is very low. The overall literacy rate in 1996 was 23 percent (Degefe and Nega, 2000). Although it appears that skilled labor is in short supply, paradoxically the unemployment rate for the skilled workforce in Ethiopia is very high too. However, this does not mean that there is no demand for skilled labor, but rather that the skilled unemployed possess the wrong type of skills. In other words, they are trained in the wrong way. The long-standing educational system of the country has being focusing more on theory than practice, which has relevance to the economic development of the country (Denu, 1993).

At present, with the intent of addressing the above-mentioned problems, the government is restructuring the educational system again. One of the objectives is, "To satisfy the country's need for skilled manpower by providing training in various skills and at different levels" (Transitional Government of Ethiopia, 1994: 9). However, unless this effort is fully integrated into the overall national strategy, the same mistake of training people with inappropriate skills which do not meet the needs of the labor market will be made. Again, the concept of HRM can be useful here. The application of the concept can help in the integration of training with labor market needs.

To conclude this section, it is important to highlight the overall limitations of the series of educational reforms in Ethiopia. In our view, the main limitation is the lack of relevance to the socio-economic environment. This is a problem common to most African countries. The second limitation is the lack of stability of reform. This is brought about by the instability of the political economy. The former can be addressed by basic training needs analysis at national level. A educational system developed based on an abstract development plan might not develop the human resource needed. The latter can only be addressed at macro level. Therefore, political and economic stability is essential to developing an effective educational system.

Labour market, brain drain, and HRM

Although there is a surplus of skilled and unskilled workers in the Ethiopian labor market, many of them do not fit the current needs of the economy. Many of those who have the "right" skills have migrated in search of "greener pastures." In a way, this is the failure of both the educational and economic systems. In a lecture delivered to the Annual Conference of the Ethiopian North American Health Professionals Association, David H. Shinn (2002) provided a detailed account of brain drain and its impact on Ethiopian economic and social development. It is an account of how Ethiopian educational policies have become victims of their own success, if it can be called success at all.

Shinn (2002) echoed the views of many experts that, prior to the 1974 revolution almost all Ethiopians who attended university in the country remained on completion of their studies and most of those who studied overseas returned to Ethiopia. He argued that the anecdotal information since 1974 is consistently depressing, especially in the areas of science, engineering, and medicine. He also cited a study by Ethiopian institutions which indicated that of every 100 professionals sent overseas for training between 1982 and 1997, only 65 percent returned. The consequences of brain drain to the Ethiopian economy and organizations is very clear. However, as indicated by

Degefe and Nega (2001: 118), "In addition to the economic, social, political, physiological and administrative impediments that tend to push out the highly skilled manpower, globalisation poses a challenge by providing the ways for the furtherance of brain drain." According to Shinn (2002), the causes are remarkably similar across Africa and developing countries. They can be summarized in terms of push and pull factors. The former relates to the economic and political conditions in the country that force professionals to venture out for better security of employment and working conditions. The latter relates largely to the enticement of better standards of living and working conditions offered by other countries, especially in developed countries.

Undoubtedly the Ethiopian labor market is seriously affected by brain drain, and this has continued into the twenty-first century. This has provided a serious challenge for organisations and HRM professionals. The model of HRM which emphasizes commitment and loyalty is very relevant here. The extent to which the model can be applied would largely depend on the economic condition of the nation in general and organizations in particular. In other words, the national government, human resource professionals, and theorists have a major role to play addressing the problem of brain drain in Ethiopia by applying HRM principles. Shinn (2002) provided some suggestions on how governments can address the problem of brain drain. He argues that, at the most general level, countries that are serious about reducing the outflow of professionals need to strengthen their economy across the board, improve governance, and increase political freedom. As far as Ethiopia is concerned all three are essential for stemming the tide of brain drain. A conference sponsored by the Economic Commission for Africa (2000) offered suggestions on how developing countries can address the issue of brain drain. Some of the recommendations of the conference which are relevant to Ethiopia include:

- provision of funding to investigate the extent and impact of brain drain;
- cooperating with African countries to address the problem of human capital development and utilization at sub-regional level;
- addressing the non-recognition and utilization of the expertise of women;
- more involvement of the private sector to serve as the engine of economic development;
- increasing focus and use of non-conventional resource mobilization approaches by tertiary institutions;
- increased budgetary allocation to higher education and research.

From the HRM perspective, the issue will be addressed in the following sections.

HRM and brain drain in Ethiopia

Undoubtedly, Ethiopian organizations can play a significant role in addressing the problem of brain drain. This can be achieved by adopting the model of HRM which focuses on commitment and loyalty. However, this calls for organizational changes that value, reward, develop, and challenge skilled Ethiopians (Shinn, 2002). From the Ethiopian perspective, the Japanese model of HRM is also relevant to ensure commitment and loyalty. In other words, a good dose of paternalism as applied in Japanese firms would seem appropriate in the Ethiopian context. For example, providing interest-free loans or decent housing and transportation will ensure that the commitment and loyalty of employees are gained. In fact, evidence indicates that wages and salaries are not the main determinants of employee retention. The main factors that retain employees in their jobs are extra benefits. For Ethiopian professionals who aspire for a better and higher standard of living, provision of fringe benefits such as housing, car loans, and decent working conditions will be major factors in retaining them.

It is important to note, however, that the ability of Ethiopian organizations to apply the model of HRM and its subsequent impact would largely depend on wider national factors. In other words, the political, economic, and social condition of Ethiopia at any point in time will influence not only the willingness and ability of organizations to apply best practice in retaining its employees, but also influence professionals' willingness to stay. Although it is true to say that most professionals who migrate would rather stay in Ethiopia, bringing them back and retaining those who are still in Ethiopia will require a joint effort from organizations and government at all levels.

On the whole, there is a lot government could do to enable organizations to address the problem of brain drain by applying good HRM practices. For example, tax incentives can reduce financial burden and enable organizations to provide benefits to their employees. The ability of government to support organizational efforts to address brain drain will depend on the economic condition of Ethiopia. This is because the provision of a good and relevant educational system would depend on sound economic conditions.

Trade unions

Although some argue that HRM does not see trade unions as partners to managing employees, the role of trade union role in Ethiopia cannot be underestimated. This is partly because unions have legitimate status in Ethiopia. The right of workers' association in Ethiopia has been guaranteed since 1955. It was not until 1962, however, that the government issued the Labour Relations Decree, which allowed the establishment of trade unions. The first trade union, the Confederation of Ethiopian Labor Unions (CELU), was recognized by the imperial authorities in 1963. CELU was made up of 22 industrial labor groups. The lack of national structure and constituency has affected its effectiveness. In fact, like many trade unions in Africa, CELU was bedevilled by the problems of corruption, embezzlement, election fraud, ethnic, and regional discrimination.

CELU tried to be independent, both under the imperial regime as well as under the military regime. For example, some of its members supported the overthrow of the imperial government, but it was the first trade union to reject the military junta and to demand the creation of a democratic government. As a result of this opposition, the incoming military government temporarily closed CELU headquarters in May 1995, on the grounds that the union needed to be reorganized. Also, the government authorities insisted that workers should elect their future leaders according to the aims and objectives of Ethiopian socialism. This is an indirect way of using trade unions as another arm or mouthpiece of the socialist government. Although the rights to organize freely, to strike, and to bargain collectively over wages and working conditions still remained, CELU rejected these actions and continued to demand democratic changes and civilian rights. It has been argued that the failure to follow the government's demands lead to the abolishment of CELU (Ofcansky and Berry, 1991). It was replaced with the Ethiopia Trade Union (AETU) in 1977. The intention of the government was made clearer when it declared that the main purpose of AETU was to educate workers about the need to contribute their share to national development by increasing productivity and building socialism.

Further restructuring of AETU took place in l982, with the Trade Unions' Organization Proclamation. By the late 1980s, the AETU had failed to regain the activist reputation its predecessors had won in the 1970s (Ofcansky and Berry, 1991). This is perhaps the indication of the intervention and interference by the socialist government. Following the overthrow of the socialist government in 1991, trade unions in Ethiopia have become relatively more independent. However, they still remain polarized and ineffective, largely due to internal strife, national economic problems, and the increasing marketization of the economy. These conditions make it difficult for unions to organize effectively in the interest of their members. In fact the high unemployment and the growing privatization of state-owned enterprises has resulted in lower trade union membership. Despite all these problems, trade unions still play and will continue to play a vital role in the labor market. This is necessary in order to check the excesses of privatization and the market economy. It should be pointed out, however, that the weakness of trade unions in Ethiopia, coupled with the growing influence of the market economy, guarantees that the HRM model will find its home in Ethiopian economic environment. This is because the model is more unitary than pluralist in perspective. In other words, the industrial relations (IR) context would seem to suggest that unitarist elements of the current mainstream HRM approaches can be adopted within Ethiopian organizations. The success of the model (HRM) would depend on the socio-cultural context of Ethiopia. This is the subject of our discussion in the next section.

National culture and Human Resource Management

Of all the factors affecting HRM in Ethiopia perhaps none is more potent than the national culture (i.e. collectivism, power distance, uncertainty avoidance). This is because the values underlining HRM are not based on Ethiopian values. As Kanungo (1995: 11) pointed out:

> . . . because many of our human resource management tools have been developed primarily within a context of economically developed nations, most have never been appropriate for use in developing countries. Traditional U.S.-based HRM theories, with their lack of contextual embeddedness, their strong individualistic orientation, and their emphasis on freewill . . . , mismatch what is most salient about the nature of work and human systems in developing countries.

Collectivism

Collectivist cultures view people largely in the terms of the groups to which they belong. Ethiopia is a collectivist society. Social groups such as family, social class, organizations, and teams all take precedence over the individual. In Ethiopia, one's identity is based on group membership and collective views are considered better than individual opinion. Similarly, in Ethiopia membership of a group protects individuals in exchange for their loyalty to the group.

Undoubtedly, these collectivist values have major implications for the HRM practices of Ethiopian organizations. For instance, in recruitment and selection, family relations and ethnic and tribal interests play a major part in the process. This is because assisting relatives and tribe members is expected and highly valued. Although the organizational policy might not encourage such practices, managers are not penalized if they recruit people on the basis of nepotism.

It can be argued that hiring persons from a specific group familiar to the members of the organization can reduce risk and help to maintain loyalty (Hofstede, 1991). Nevertheless, such practice can be counter productive if unqualified persons are employed to do the jobs. Within the context of Ethiopian collectivist culture, managers will find it difficult to take disciplinary action against employees they are intimately related to. For example, firing relatives or persons with whom managers have special relationships can be intimidating in Ethiopian society. Moreover, hiring relatives can lead to conflict and low trust among other members of the organization. This is particularly the case because as we have demonstrated, Ethiopia has high ethnic diversity.

Along with this cultural context, organizations have other in-group selection criteria apart from academic qualifications and skills. For example, EECMY membership and faithfulness to the doctrine of the Church, good testimony of character and contribution of the candidate are examples of selection criteria. This in fact promotes commitment of members to the organization and it helps to recruit members who share similar values. However, this criteria is not confined to EECMY alone. Many Ethiopian organizations intuitively, because of collectivism use criteria such as character and other non-job-related factors to choose candidates for employment, for example family history is one of them. However, this runs counter to rational individualistic model of HRM, where the objectives of the organization and the job should be the deciding factor in recruitment and selection. In other words, the rationalist model under HRM can sometimes conflict with collectivist values, where caring for each other and the common good take precedence over organizational economic interest.

Another area of HRM practice affected by collectivism is performance appraisal. The main aim of the activity is to provide information to determine promotion, transfers, salary increases, and to supply data to the management on performance of the employees to determine training needs (Harrison, 1993). In principle, performance evaluation of employees is supposed to be undertaken regularly. However, in practice, organizations such as EECMY do not undertake performance evaluation regularly. There is potential and covert resistance to evaluating and discussing individual performance in Ethiopian organizations. Evaluating the work of groups, sections, or departments is more acceptable than evaluating the performance of an individual worker. The tendency for collective as opposed to individual evaluation is not entirely contrary to the HRM model. The idea for self-managing teams and participation advocated by some proponents of HRM assumes collective evaluation of performance. However, individual evaluation is sometimes necessary in order to determine training and development needs of employees. Collectivist values, however, sometimes militate against this.

Training and development is also another area of HRM practice affected by Ethiopian values of collectivism. For example, EECMY has a human resource development program (HRDP). This program includes in-country and international scholarship schemes. If the organization utilizes the program properly, it can benefit a lot from it. However, the program has not been fully aligned to the needs of the organization. Scholarships have been granted to employees as per their request, not based on organizational need. This practice can be considered a form of reward to employees who have served the Church for a long time. The tendency of maintaining relationships by granting scholarships regardless of organizational needs is considered important. Again, this is not confined to EECMY alone. Many organizations across Ethiopia offer training opportunities as a means of reward and maintaining social relationships. This practice is in conflict with the concept of "hard" HRM. Hard HRM models require HRM decisions such as training and development to be aligned to organizational strategy.

For the most part, there are certain aspects of collectivism which do not sit well with the model of HRM. Most of the key levers of HRM as identified by Storey (1992) assume individualism. Employees are viewed as individuals and treated accordingly.

This pertains to all the functional areas of HRM such as recruitment, selection, and training. As we have just seen, nepotism in Ethiopian organizations would make the application of this approach to managing people very difficult indeed.

Power distance

This pertains to how cultures deal with inequality. Ethiopia is a high power distance country. It has norms, values, and beliefs which assume that people have their station in life and inequality is fundamentally acceptable. It is also acceptable that Ethiopians should be dependant on the privileged and powerful. The powerful are entitled to privileges as well.

In line with high power distance, most organizations are characterized by hierarchical decision-making systems. Inequality pervades not only across roles but also within roles. This is true in the public as well as in the private sector. For example, EECMY believes that its members are part of the body of Christ, equally important, but with different functions geared towards the same goals (EECMY, 1999). EECMY has a formal structure which is relatively decentralized. The Church units are autonomous. Nevertheless, contradiction exists between being and what is claimed to be. For instance, decisions made by executives or top management lack consultation with other staff. Privileges for members of top management, such as vehicle usage and housing allowance (EECMY, 1995), are provided based on power distance not based on needs of the job. Similarly, office sizes and furnishings are also based on power distance. This attitude and behavior pervades many Ethiopian organizations. HRM, as an approach to managing people, considers employee participation as central to gaining employees' commitment and productivity. As demonstrated above, the large power distance in Ethiopian society sometimes militates against the application of employee participation.

One of the key levers of the HRM model is few job categories. This is supposed to ensure flexibility and a flatter structure. This is why de-layering has found favor within organizations operating the HRM model. However, this idea runs counter to a culture characterized by large power distance. This is because the need for status and image which characterizes a large power distance culture like Ethiopia demands vertical differentiation to justify or maintain status and image.

Uncertainty avoidance

This relates to norms, values, and beliefs regarding tolerance for ambiguity. A strong uncertainty avoidance culture seeks to structure social systems (politics, education, and business) where order and predictability are paramount, and rules and regulations dominate. In such a culture, risky situations create stress and upset people. Consequently, people avoid behaviors such as changing jobs.

Strong uncertainty avoidance societies like Ethiopia have norms, values, and beliefs that view conflict as unnecessary and needing to be avoided. Because of strong uncertainty avoidance Ethiopians sometimes prefer people who are cautious, not risk-takers. Similarly, rules and regulations are considered very important and should be followed. The role of experts and people with authority is considered very important, and their views are considered correct. Consensus making is considered vital for the health of society. The respect for experts would sit well with the idea of learning and the learning organization; however, whether this is applied for the benefit of organization is a matter of debate. This dimension of Ethiopian culture is reflected in organizations as well. According to an analysis of a survey of members of public sector organizations in Ethiopia, 56 percent of them indicated that the degree to which the climate of their organizations encourages risk-taking is low (Dadi, 1997).

One of the differences between the HRM model and the traditional personal management and IR model pertains to the value attached to rules. While the latter views rules as important in managing employment relationships, the former is "impatient" with rules (Storey, 1992). Strong uncertainty avoidance typified by the Ethiopian culture would not fit the idea of impatience with rules. This is because, as we have stated earlier, societies with strong uncertainty avoidance are uncomfortable with ambiguity and therefore insist on rules to ensure certainty in behaviors. Thus, managers and employees in Ethiopia are more comfortable with operating under rules. Arguably, mainstream HRM with its impatience with rules would not sit well with Ethiopian organizations. However, it should be pointed out that the rules followed in Ethiopia are both formal and informal.

Government polices and HRM

In Ethiopia the majority of modern organizations are in the public sector. This guarantees high political interference in the management of organizations. As Kanungo (1995: 250) pointed out: "A major actor in developing country environments is the government, to the point where many organizations are dependent on it for survival." The private sector has less political interference from the government. Nevertheless, it has been noted that the government restricts the capacity of private sectors by rejecting permits for importing items (Kanungo, 1995).

In Ethiopia, politicians frequently interfere in the operation of public organizations. Sometimes even private-sector organizations do not escape interference; for instance, managers do not have the autonomy to recruit and select employees. Dadi (1997: 29) pointed out: ". . . the management autonomy managers have is not adequate. To assure that order is maintained and social interests are protected the interference of government is appropriate. But interference in placement and other similar operations is a hindrance."

Non-governmental organizations have also been facing direct and indirect interference from the government. During the previous military regime (1974–1991), many indigenous and international NGOs operated under the restricted control of the government. The government was openly against international NGOs from the West (Campbell, 1996) and indigenous NGOs who had an affiliation with Western ideology.

The EECMY has experienced the same problems faced by other NGOs; for example, its headquarters was confiscated by the government in 1979. The labor law restricted its ability to carry out its HRM functions effectively' for example, the labor law states that "Every undertaking shall employ workers only through the employment office. . . . Every undertaking shall report all job vacancies to an employment office as soon as they occur" (Negarit Gazeta of the Socialist Ethiopian Provisional Military Government, 1975).

The current government of Ethiopia has also introduced restrictions which limit the capacity of organizations, even though it seems that there is improvement. For instance, many NGO representatives have felt that the current government attempts to impose greater control on their operations (Campbell, 1996). It is quite difficult to get permission from the government to invite expatriate personnel. The Church was also asked to be registered as a new organization after over four decades of operation in the country.

On the issue of recruitment and selection, the government has allowed organizations to hire their own personnel, although it has set policies, rules, and procedures to be followed (Negarit Gazeta of the Tranitional Government of Ethiopia, 1993). The privatization policy in the country has created competition among organizations in the labor market, whilst on the other hand the structural adjustment policy has resulted in unemployment. Above all, lack of political stability in the country coupled with frequent changes of policies, rules, and procedures has been creating uncertainty and problems in the operation of organizations.

The above discussion highlighted the significant impact of the government in organizational life in Ethiopia. The key question is "how conducive is this environment for the implementation of HRM?" The best way to answer the question is to look at some of the assumptions of HRM. The most popular assumption is that organizational strategy should determine HRM strategy. Clearly, this assumption is not easily achievable when the government continuously intervenes in organizational affairs. In fact, developing consistent and effective organizational strategy would be difficult under persistent government intervention. The insistence by the government of the establishment of a trade union in EECMY is an example of how the government's role in the economy can make it difficult, if not impossible, to implement one of the cornerstones of HRM.

Closely related to the issue of "fit" between organizational strategy and HRM strategy is the idea of along-term proactive approach to managing people. Again, Ethiopian organizations will find it very difficult to use a long-term and proactive approach to managing their HR when the government regularly intervenes. In fact, short-term and reactive orientation is what characterizes the management of people in most Ethiopian organizations.

Another strategic aspect affected by government influence is decision-making. According to Storey (1992), decision-making under HRM model is supposed to be very fast. This assumes that organizations operating with an HRM model have the freedom and independence to make fast decisions on issues relating to HRM. As we have seen, the Ethiopian government's frequent intervention does not make it easy for organizations to make quick and independent decisions. This is particularly the case in the public service. On the whole, it can be concluded that government policy is one of the most important factors influencing HRM in Ethiopian organizations. Unfortunately, this influence can conflict with the implementation of HRM principles.

Conclusion

The main aim of this chapter is to review the nature and scope of HRM in Ethiopia and factors that affect it. From the beginning, we have seen that human resources have strategic importance to the social and economic development of Ethiopia. More specifically, the success of the current structural adjustment and privatization effort embarked upon by the government depends on the effective management of human resources. The key contextual factors highlighted in this chapter are economic, labor market, education and training, labor unions, national culture, and political environment. It is not our intention to review these factors again, suffice it to say that the extent to which a modern system of management (e.g. an HRM model) succeeds would depend on these contextual factors. We have seen, for example, that the problem of brain drain can be addressed by applying the concepts of loyalty and commitment as the centerpiece of HRM. However, the depressing economic environment affecting organizations make it rather difficult to provide the rewards and working conditions that will ensure commitment and loyalty.

It is not all bad news as far as the contextual factors are concerned. The government and organizations can turn the unique socio-cultural and economic environment to their advantage. We do not believe that it is possible to change the environment overnight in order to accommodate HRM. However, it is possible to make a gradual shift in that direction. But in the short term, at least, we advocate the modification of an HRM model to fit the environment. For example, it is impossible to eradicate nepotism overnight in Ethiopia, therefore managers should ensure that if they have to hire their relatives, only the qualified and those that can be controlled are hired. Also, the extended family should not have undue influence on how the hired family member is treated.

Different environments can provide different opportunities. These may differ from country to country, from organization to organization. Therefore, Ethiopian organizations may have opportunities and prospects which are favorable for adapting

HRM. For example, the collectivist culture can be utilized to maximize teamwork and participatory management. A high level of collectivism fits with participative management. Participative management emphasizes teamwork, group harmony, and task interdependence rather than individual work (Kanungo, 1995: 189). Performance can be geared towards a team rather than to an individual. The low masculine cultural dimension of Ethiopia also can foster team motivation rather than individual motivation. To conclude, we advocate that theorists and practitioners should try to develop creative ways of using the contextual factors to implement good HRM practices.

References

Andersen, K. (1980) *Brief history of the Mekane Yesus Church*, Modersmalets Trykkeri Als: Haderslev.

Armstrong, M. (1992) *Human resource management: Strategy and action*, London: Kogan Page.

Brewster, C. (1993) "Developing a European model of human resource management," *International Journal of Human Resource Management* 4 (4): 765–84.

Campbell, W. (1996) *The potential for donor mediation in NGO-state relations: An Ethiopian case study*, Sussex: Institute of Development.

Dadi, B. (1997) "Enabling Environment for Managerial Capacity Building in Ethiopia," Paper presented at the 3rd annual conference on management in Ethiopia, 21–23 November, Nazreth.

Degefe, B. and Nega, B. (eds.) (1999/2000) "Ethiopian Economy Association Annual Report on the Ethiopian Economy," Volume I.

Degefe, B. and Nega, B. (eds.) (2000/2001) "Ethiopian Economy Association Annual Report on the Ethiopian Economy," Volume II.

Denu, B. (1993) "The acquisition and utilization of tertiary level trained manpower in Ethiopia With Particular Reference to Addis Ababa Commercial College." Addis Ababa Commercial College, Proceedings of the 1st Symposium of Human Resource Development in Business and Commerce, pp. 148–191.

Economic Commission for Africa (2000) *Conference report on brain drain and capacity building in Africa*, Addis-Ababa, 22–24 February.

Ethiopian Central Statistical Authority (2001) "Report on the Year 2000 Welfare Monitoring Survey Statistical Bulletin (259)," Volume 1.

Ethiopian Evangelical Church Mekane Yesus Central Office (EECMY) (1995) *Personnel Manual*, Addis Ababa.

Ethiopian Evangelical Church Mekane Yesus (1999) *Constitution*, Addis Ababa.

Government of Ethiopia (2002) "Ethiopia: Emergency assistance requirements and implementation options for 2003—A joint government/UN appeal." Online: http://www.reliefweb.int/w/Rwb.nsf/6D79DE95095655F249256C8A002D3274s

Harrison, R. (1993) *Human resource management: Issues and strategies*, Harlow: Addison-Wesley.

Hofstede G. (1991) *Cultures and organizations. Software of the mind: Intercultural cooperation and its importance for survival*, London: McGraw-Hill.

Kamoche, K (1996) "Strategic HRM with resource-capability view of the firm," *Journal of Management Studies* 33 (2): 213–33.

Kanungo, R. (ed.) (1995) *New approaches to employee management: Employee management in developing countries*, Greenwich, CT: JAI Press.

Negarit Gazeta of the Socialist Ethiopia Provisional Military Government (1975) "Labor Proclamation," No. 64, Articles 3.4 and 4.1, Addis Ababa.

Negarit Gazeta of the Transitional Government of Ethiopia (1993) "Labor Proclamation," No. 42, Addis Ababa.

Ofcansky, T.P. and Berry, L. (1991) *Ethiopia: A Country Study*, Washington, DC: Federal Research Division.

Shinn, D. (2002) Lecture delivered to Annual Conference of the Ethiopian North American Health Professionals Association on 23 November, *Addis Tribune,* 6 December.

South African Broadcasting Corporation (2002) "The year in review: Drought in Ethiopia could lead to disaster." Online: http://www.sabcnews.com/africa/west_africa/0,1009,47449,00.html

Storey, J. (1992) *Developments in the management of human resources*, Oxford: Blackwell.

Transitional Government of Ethiopia (1994) "Education and Training Policy," Addis Ababa.

8 HRM in Ghana

SAMUEL ARYEE

Introduction

Ghana attained political independence from British colonial rule in 1957 and became a republic in 1960. Until its independence, Ghana was known as the Gold Coast. It is located on the west coast of Africa, bordered on the west by Ivory Coast, on the east by Togo, and the north and north-west by Burkina Faso. Administratively, Ghana is divided into ten regions, with Accra as the seat of government and the commercial heart of the country. According to 2002 estimates, Ghana's population stands at 20.2 million, with over half (56.1 percent) in the 15–64 years age bracket, 3.5 percent in the 65 years and over age bracket, and the rest (40.4 percent) in the below 15 years age bracket (CIA: *World Factbook*, 2002). Although the population is multi-ethnic, each with its own language, English is the official language.

Ghana's economy is based primarily on the production of agricultural products and minerals. Cocoa, a primary foreign exchange earner, is produced by small-scale farmers. Other notable agricultural products are coffee, kola nuts, shea nuts, pineapples, oil palm, cotton, and rubber. Minerals like gold, diamond, bauxite, and manganese have traditionally being mined, while oil and natural gas have only recently been discovered. The country's tropical forests yield timber, which is a major foreign exchange earner. The domestic economy is based on subsistence agriculture, employing about 60 percent of the workforce, and accounts for 36 percent of GDP. Of the rest of the estimated 9 million workforce, 15 percent are employed in industry and 25 percent in services. The estimated unemployment rate was 20.3 percent in 2001 (CIA: *World Factbook*, 2000; GhanaHomePage, 2002).

At independence and the early years that followed, Ghana was widely considered the world's largest producer of cocoa, had the highest per capita income of all countries in Sub-Saharan Africa, and external reserves the equivalent of three years of imports (Nowak *et al.* 1996: 22). However, by 1982, years of inappropriate economic policies (e.g. government intervention in the economy through price and import controls, deficit financing leading to high rates of inflation, and an overvalued cedi, the national currency), coupled with political crises that precipitated frequent changes in government, led to a steady decline in the economy.

To revive its economy, Ghana, in collaboration with the World Bank and the International Monetary Fund (IMF), implemented an economic recovery or restructuring program (ERP) in 1983. In tandem with the ERP is a government blueprint, Vision 2020, which aims to transform Ghana into a middle-income country by 2020. The attainment of this objective is, however, dependent on the success of the ERP. Most economic indicators suggest impressive improvements in the country's economic performance following the launching of the ERP. For example, it has resulted in a consistent 4–6 percent growth in GDP, major improvements in infrastructure, annual inflation has dropped from 123 percent per annum in 1984 to 32 percent in 1991, growth in foreign investment (particularly in banking, mining, construction and telecommunications), and increased industrial capacity (Konadu-Agyemang, 2001: 25). However, failure to attract foreign investment on the scale expected and the deteriorating terms of trade for Ghana's primary products constitute threats to the continued success of the program and, with that, the translation of Vision 2020 into reality.

The formidable task of transforming Ghana into a middle-income country is aggravated by its high external debt (estimated at US$5.96 billion in 2001), which now absorbs a huge percentage of its export revenues. Consequently, Ghana opted for debt relief under the Heavily Indebted Poor Country (HIPC) program in 2002. It is against the backdrop of a difficult economic environment characterized by high unemployment, heavy external debt, and deteriorating standards of living for a large segment of the population that we discuss HRM in Ghana and its potential role in enhancing organizational effectiveness.

The political-economic environment

Ghana started life as an independent country under the leadership of Kwame Nkrumah, whose government adopted a socialist model of economic development. Under this model, the government invested heavily in the development of social infrastructure and sought to diversify the economy through an import substitution industrialization program. The initial post-independence period witnessed an unprecedented growth in wage employment in both the private and public sectors, with the government as a major employer. The growth in wage employment gave a fillip to the personnel management function, which was among the earliest management functions to be indigenized. During this period, the personnel management function was primarily concerned with administrative and welfare activities, as well as ensuring industrial peace. By the mid-1960s, most economic indicators pointed to a declining economy. Inflationary pressures, coupled with massive layoffs following the failure of many of the state-sponsored industrialization projects, created considerable economic hardship. Dissatisfaction with the government's economic performance, among other factors, triggered the overthrow of Nkrumah's government in 1966, and the formation of the National Liberation Council (NLC).

The NLC government marked the beginning of the alternations between the three military and four civilian governments that have punctuated the post-independence political history of Ghana. With the exception of the Provisional National Defence Council (PNDC), the military regimes saw themselves as caretaker governments and did not therefore pursue long-term economic development as a primary objective. Further, successive governments (with the exception of the Busia government) pursued a policy of direct intervention in the economy through the establishment of state enterprises and tended to rely on administrative rather than the market as a resource-allocation mechanism (Huq, 1989).

The PNDC, formed after a military coup in 1981, appears to have had the most far-reaching effect on the political-economic environment of HRM in Ghana. With the economy teetering on the brink of collapse, the PNDC government, in collaboration with the World Bank and IMF, launched an economic recovery program (ERP) in 1983. The underlying objective of the program was to move away from controls and centralized regulation in favor of a more liberal, market-oriented approach (Abbey, 1990). The key elements of the program were:

1 realignment of relative prices to encourage more productive activity, promote exports, and strengthen economic incentives;
2 a progressive shift away from direct controls and intervention toward greater reliance on market mechanisms;
3 early restoration of fiscal discipline, an increase in public saving and reduced recourse to bank financing of the government;
4 rehabilitation of economic and social infrastructure;
5 implementation of structural and institutional reforms to enhance efficiency in the economy (Nowak *et al.*, 1996: 23).

The initial phases of the adjustment program were concerned with: (a) economic stabilization, which entailed the dismantling of exchange and price controls, a discrete devaluation of the cedi, and restoration of fiscal discipline; and (b) addressing the underlying causes of imbalances in the economy and rebuilding the productive base. Specific policies included privatizing state-owned enterprises (SOEs) and workforce restructuring and retrenchment as elements of a comprehensive reform of SOEs

Of particular relevance to our purposes are the privatization, and workforce restructuring and retrenchment programs. By 1998, a total of 212 SOEs in such sectors as banking and finance, hotels and tourism, transport, telecommunications, and mining had been privatized (Haruna, 2001). Most if not all the privatized SOEs are now foreign owned. The restructuring of the workforce was precipitated by inappropriate skill mixes and staffing ratios, as well as to expose SOEs to competitive market forces in order to stimulate cost-effective and financially responsible management (Davis, 1991). Although the ERP envisaged that retrenched workers would be absorbed into the private sector, that has not been the case because of its small size and under-capitalization. Paradoxically, the high rate of unemployment and the general sense of job insecurity have curtailed absenteeism but have, instead, increased presenteeism—a phenomenon which describes a situation whereby employees may be at work but are unmotivated to perform their prescribed roles.

An integral feature of the adjustment program which has implications for the quality of the country's human resources is the restructuring and financing of education. In order to make education more relevant to the country's human resource requirements, the British-style secondary school system has been replaced with a junior and secondary school system. Additionally, undergraduate education has been extended from three to four years. The emphasis in pre-university education is now on technical or vocational skills. In terms of financing of education, government expenditure has been substantially reduced and user fees introduced. For the working poor, the introduction of user fees has increased the financial burden of educating their children, leading to high dropout rates in pre-university education. These dropouts, many of whom are unemployable, participate in the informal sector of the economy hawking myriad consumer goods. Additionally, cuts in government expenditure have meant deteriorating conditions of employment for teachers at all levels of the educational system. Like professionals in other fields, many teachers have joined the brain drain, thus depriving the country of the human resources required for socio-economic development.

The political and economic context of HRM in Ghana—characterized by economic stagnation, limited growth in the formal sector of the economy, and high unemployment—strengthens an employer's hand when dealing with employees. This is because such a dismal economic context reduces the bargaining power of employees, as well as the appeal of industrial action as a means of protecting their interests. However, motivating employees whose real incomes and, therefore, standard of living is steadily declining constitutes a major HRM challenge. This challenge stems from the difficulty faced by organizations with declining profits in using monetary incentives to enhance employee motivation and, ultimately, productivity. Given that indigenous employers are unlikely to acquire the technology to compete with their foreign competitors, effective management of the workforce constitutes a realistic source of competitive advantage. Consequently, the creative management of the motivation, development, and utilization of the workforce should go a long way in determining the status of the HRM function as a strategic partner in achieving organizational effectiveness in an increasingly competitive global marketplace.

The socio-cultural environment

In view of the recognition that management practices do not exist in a vacuum, the socio-cultural context and how it impinges on the management of people has become a recurrent theme in the cross-cultural management literature (Kanungo and Jaeger, 1990; Kuada, 1994; Munene et al., 2000). Cultural values, defined as the mental programming of the mind, are structurally expressed in the ways that institutions function and in the justifications that the leaders and members of organizations provide for their behavior (Assimeng, 1981; Schwartz, 1999).

The cultural values that provide the organizing framework for a discussion of the socio-cultural context of HRM in Ghana are collectivism and power distance (Hofstede, 1980). As a collectivist society, Ghanaians seek meaning in life largely through social relationships, through identifying with the group in which they are embedded, and participating in its shared way of life. This group is defined in terms of the extended family into which all Ghanaians are born and whose interest they are socialized to promote. The extended family is characterized by a high degree of reciprocity in the exchange of both moral and material support. For example, it is the moral obligation of employed members of the family to financially support the aged and less fortunate members. When exported into an organizational context, the distinctions between in-group and out-group, and the associated obligation to help one's in-group members, have been noted to undermine the goal-oriented meritocratic purposes of a bureaucratic organization. This is because it encourages particularistic rather than universalistic organizational practices. For example, the decision to hire, reward, and promote should be based on the universal principle of an employee's contributions to organizational goal attainment. However, in a particularistic context, such personnel decisions are based on non-merit considerations such as kinship ties.

The emphasis on the family leads to the perception of the organization as an extension of the extended family or organizational familism. Organizational familism has implications for the nature of exchange that Ghanaians expect to characterize the employment relationship. Much like the extended family, there is the expectation that the organization will take care of the material and socio-emotional needs of employees, in addition to considering their family circumstances when making personnel decisions. Further, as a member of the organization's extended family, employees expect help in times of bereavement. A major feature of Ghanaian culture is the emphasis on funerals and elaborate rituals of mourning. In addition to expecting a period of absence from work, employees expect financial assistance to help them meet the cost of funerals. Gardner (1996) noted that organizations have a legal obligation under the terms of the collective bargaining agreements to buy a coffin for a deceased employee or members of his/ her immediate family, make a cash donation, and to provide transport for colleagues who wish to attend the funeral. The obligation to attend funerals of deceased colleagues, members of the extended family, and close friends constitutes a cultural constraint on the productivity of the Ghanaian employee.

Ghana is a high power distance country (Hofstede, 1980), a value orientation that finds structural expression in authoritarian leadership and an emphasis on status differences. Kuada (1994) described the dominant leadership style as authoritarian-benevolence, which is characterized by close supervision of subordinates, elaborate instructions on all matters, and disapproval of deviations from such instructions. Although decision-making is by consensus in traditional Ghanaian society, this cultural practice has not found expression in organizational life. Instead, there is a preference for centralized decision-making, with subordinates reduced to implementing decisions and a "check with the boss" mindset.

Organizations in Ghana have adopted the bureaucratic means of formalism and hierarchy. However, the cultural emphasis on interpersonal relationships has meant that these bureaucratic means have been harnessed to particularistic ends. Organizational life in Ghana is therefore, characterized by dependence, deference, and particularism. The centralization of decision-making authority has made employees aware of the need to have a good relationship with their supervisor if they are to have a successful career. Consequently, deference and ingratiation constitute influence strategies that employees use to manage the subordinate–superior relationship. The benevolence component of the dominant authoritarian-benevolence leadership style (Kuada, 1994) is manifested in the supervisor's development of a patron–client relationship with his or her subordinates. In this patron–client relationship, superiors provide extra opportunities, privileges, and protection to a select group of subordinates who reciprocate the superior's patronage with loyalty, compliance, and subservience to the superior's interests. The subordinate–superior relationship in Ghanaian organizational life is, therefore, more personalized than contractual.

The cultural emphases on hierarchy and social relationships through group identification, as detailed in the preceding discussion, have implications for how employees expect to be treated and, therefore, strategies for the effective management of people. Leonard (1987: 901) noted that, ". . . the differences in organizational behavior between Africans on one hand, and the United States and Europe, on the other . . . are not due to managerial failures but to fundamental dissimilarities in the value priorities of the societies that encapsule them." In the succeeding section we examine how these value priorities have shaped HRM practices in Ghana.

HRM practices

As previously noted, the HRM/personnel function received a major boost during the post-independence expansion in the public sector and government enactments (e.g. Industrial Relations Acts) to regulate the employment relationship. The description of HRM practices here applies to medium and large organizations, both locally and foreign-owned, where the HRM function is more formalized.

Pertaining to recruitment and selection, most organizations tend to place advertisements in local newspapers and professional magazines for managerial and/or professional positions. In a recent study that examined HRM practices in Nigerian and Ghanaian organizations, Arthur et al. (1995) reported that newspaper advertisement was the most frequently used form of recruitment, followed by written notices in and around the organizations, and visits to university and college campuses, in that order. In the context of high unemployment, HR managers increasingly receive unsolicited applications but visits to university campuses for recruitment purposes are now a rarity. In Arthur et al.'s (1995) study, they reported that selection interviews constitute the most frequently cited selection method, followed by academic qualifications and letters of recommendation. They also reported that psychological tests, work samples, and work simulations were less frequently used. The decision to hire operatives is usually made by the HR manager, while the decision to hire professional and/or managerial level employees is made by top management in consultation with the HR manager (Debrah, 2001). Arthur *et al.* (1995) noted that even among organizations with a formal selection process, the vast majority did not collect information to ascertain the predictive validity or effectiveness of the selection system. In spite of the formal trappings of the selection system, HRM practices/decisions in Ghana are underpinned by particularistic rather than universalistic norms (Kuada, 1994). Particularism in selection decisions does not suggest a de-emphasis on merit, but rather highlights the importance of personal influence in such decisions. Blunt and Popoola (1985: 51) noted that: "In settings where paid work is scarce, and where there are strong pressures to allocate jobs in a particularistic fashion, the selection process constitutes a prime means for fulfilling one's obligations to kin and other personal contacts."

Performance appraisal is also widely practiced in medium to large organizations. Usually, performance appraisal is conducted on an annual basis. Arthur *et al.* (1995) reported that a majority of the organizations that participated in their study used a formal system for evaluating employee performance. They further reported that appraisals are based on supervisor ratings and used primarily for such personnel decisions as promotions and transfers. In view of the general absence of systematic planning, performance goals are not set and, therefore, performance criteria are vaguely defined. Vagueness in terms of performance criteria, encourages subjectivity in the performance appraisal process. Cultural norms not only impact on the process but also the form of performance appraisal. For example, the tendency to avoid confrontation makes critical or negative face-to-face feedback an unpleasant task for managers. Additionally, the hierarchical structuring of interpersonal relations suggests that newer forms of performance appraisal, such as 360-degree feedback, are unlikely to be adopted in the Ghanaian context.

As an HR activity, training and development has traditionally been accorded considerable importance in the public sector and in large locally and foreign-owned organizations (Debrah, 2001). Government-sponsored training institutes such as the Ghana Institute of the Management and Public Administration (GIMPA), Management and Productivity Development Institute (MDPI), and the Civil Service Training Center provide courses for middle-level managerial employees in the public sector. In addition to these organizations, training may be funded or sponsored by overseas development agencies or technical aid programs like the United Nations Development Program (UNDP), the International Labor Organization (ILO), and the World Bank. Large private sector organizations like Ghana Airways, Barclays Bank, Ghana Commercial Bank, and Standard Bank have training schools where low to middle-ranking employees are periodically sent for refresher courses. Senior employees in these organizations are routinely sent overseas, especially where the organization is a subsidiary of a multinational. Arthur *et al.* (1995) reported that the majority of participants in their study had some form of employee training. These organizations reported having a formal policy on training, a separate training budget, and utilized external training specialists and consultants. Until the recent spate of redundancies, public sector employees generally enjoyed lifetime employment. For this reason, they tended to depend on their organizations for career development rather than adopt a proactive orientation to the management of their careers. For the vast majority of small to medium-sized organizations, the tendency is to buy rather than to invest in training and development of employees. Whatever training occurs in such organizations, it is usually through some form of unstructured on-the-job training.

Wage and salary determination in Ghana comprises basic wages and benefits/allowances. The basic wage for unskilled and semi-skilled employees is based on the national minimum wage. This is determined by the Tripartite Committee on Salary and Wages, and takes into account the state of the economy and the ability of employers (including the government as the largest employer) to pay (Obeng-Fosu, 1991). The national minimum wage forms the basis for wage negotiations by both trade unions and staff associations and their employers. Generally, most medium to large organizations have a salary structure, so what is negotiated is annual increments to keep pace with inflation. Starting salaries are determined largely on the basis of educational qualification and initial point of entry. Given the absence of performance-related pay, annual increments are seniority rather than merit based. In spite of the male-dominated nature of Ghanaian society, there are no gender-based differences in earnings. Although women tend to drift into feminized occupations (such as primary school teaching and nursing), they earn the same salary as their male colleagues when they perform similar or the same jobs. In the face of declining real wages, benefits and allowances have become primary means of extrinsically motivating employees. Benefits offered by many medium to large organizations include housing allowance in lieu of accommodation, loans for the purchase of cars or company cars (for senior employees), and medical/ health benefits. Other benefits which are legally mandated include paid annual leave and maternity leave.

The preceding discussion suggests that the HR function in Ghana constitutes a series of discrete operational and administrative/maintenance activities, not driven by the strategic goals of the organization.

Industrial relations

Ghana's industrial relations system is based on the tripartite cooperation of the labor market partners—government, trade unions, and employers. The Industrial Relations Act of 1965 defines the dynamics of industrial relations and, by implication, the nature of the relationship between the labor market partners. This Act consolidated the law (Industrial Relations Act of 1958) relating to trade unions, collective bargaining, settlement of disputes involving certified trade unions, strikes and lockouts, and unfair labor practices (Kusi and Gyimah-Boakye, 1994; Obeng-Fosu, 1991).

Trade unionism in both the private and public sectors has existed in Ghana since the introduction of wage employment by the colonial government and a labor federation, the Trades Union Congress (TUC), was established in 1945. The early unions operated autonomously and were concerned primarily with issues relating to the employment relationship. However, the cooptation of trade unions into the struggle for independence marked the beginning of an exchange relationship between the government and the labor movement. This exchange relationship entailed the labor movement advancing the interests of their membership through legislation in return for embracing the development objectives of the government. While the 1965 Act sought to conform to International Labor Organization (ILO) regulations, it is fair to suggest that it represents a positive outcome of the political exchange between the labor movement and the Nkrumah government.

The Act provides for the recognition of a central labor movement, Trades Union Congress (TUC), as the sole representative of the labor movement and the structure and functioning of the labor movement. To address the fragmented state of the labor movement, the 1965 Act structured unions along industrial lines and allowed for the affiliation of 17 national industrial unions to the TUC. A noteworthy feature of the Act, which may be indicative of the political exchange between the labor movement and the government, is the legally mandated check-off of union membership dues. This ensures the financial security of the unions. Although the compulsory check-off is a potential solution to the free rider problem, it has been noted to contravene ILO standards (Panford, 1993). The TUC does not, however, participate in the negotiation of collective bargaining agreements on behalf of its affiliates. Instead, it provides advice on issues relating to the employment relationship, coordinates the activities of its affiliates, and represents the interests of workers through its membership of various national bodies.

Collective bargaining, as a cornerstone of the regulation of the employment relationship, was consolidated by the Act. For the purposes of collective bargaining, the 1965 Act provides for the formation of a standing joint negotiation committee comprising representatives of a certified union and of the employer, on the basis of parity of representation. Collective bargaining is at the enterprise level and covers both procedural and substantive issues. Of interest here is the substantive component of the collective bargaining agreement, which defines the conditions or terms of employment such as basic salary, annual increments, allowances, benefits, and subsidies. The core allowances include housing, annual leave, medical care, and transportation. The housing allowance does not exceed 20 percent of an employee's basic salary and it is usually tax exempt (Kusi and Gyimah-Boakye, 1994). In addition, there are "generic allowances" like the supply of a coffin, a shroud, schnapps and beer for the funeral of a deceased employee, education allowance for children of employees, subsidized canteens, and the provision of interest-free loans for employee purchases of cars or motorcycles, appliances, and furniture (Davis, 1991). The 1965 Act provides for procedures governing terminations, and dismissals, issues which are also covered in the collective bargaining agreement under discipline. The Act also provides for mechanisms for dispute resolution. Disputes that are not successfully settled at the level of the enterprise are referred to the Minister of Labor through the Chief Labor Officer. The Minister then appoints a conciliator and, if necessary, an arbitrator. Disputes which are not settled even after arbitration may then lead to strikes or lock-outs.

As an instrument for regulating the employment relationship, collective bargaining is not restricted to trade unions. Although senior staff associations and other identifiable groups such as the Civil Servants' Association, Ghana National Association of Teachers, and Ghana Registered Nurses Association do not have collective bargaining certificates, they negotiate collective bargaining agreements with the government. Parties to a collective bargaining are required by law to submit their collective bargaining agreements to the Prices and Incomes Board (PIB) for vetting and approval.

As a labor market partner, the Ghana Employers Association (GEA) has a major influence on the practice of HRM. Established in 1959, the GEA represents employers' interests to the government, promotes good relations and better understanding between employers and employees, and assists affiliated employers in negotiations with organized labor (Obeng-Fosu, 1991). The GEA also promotes consultation among its members and adopts a coordinated approach to matters of concern to its members. Specifically, the GEA coordinates and represents the views and reactions of its members on industrial relations problems, reactions to proposed legislation, and methods of improving both the climate for and efficiency of business affairs to the government (Kusi and Gyimah-Boakye, 1994). The GEA also provides training, not only in industrial relations but also aspects of personnel management. Through the ILO's "Improve your Business" project, the GEA has helped its members to address the business and management problems of small enterprises. The GEA represents 330 members, drawn from diverse industrial sectors such as banking and finance, manufacturing, transport, forestry, tourism, and mining (Kusi and Gyimah-Boakye, 1994).

Given the close link between socio-economic and political factors and industrial relations, the implementation of the ERP continues to impact the practice of industrial relations. Panford (2001) noted that the downsizing in the public sector, the traditional bastion of unionism, has led to a decline in unions from a membership of 635,000 in 1985 to 520,936 in 1996. The economic crisis requires not only a cooperative labor–management relationship but also new strategies to address the challenges of increased productivity, efficiency, and competitiveness.

Management of human resources and organizational effectiveness

Recognition of employees as a source of competitive advantage (Pfeffer, 1994) suggests a need to move away from the discrete, operational, and administrative focus of HRM activities in many indigenous organizations to more integrated, strategically-oriented activities. Kiggundu (1989: 158) captured the changing focus of the HRM function thus:

> As organizations in developing countries become more complex, and as they begin to operate in a less protected and increasingly uncertain, competitive, and often hostile environment . . . they are going to need more than ever before carefully crafted missions and strategic business plans.

Strategic management enjoins the management of indigenous organizations in Ghana and, indeed, Africa to address two interrelated issues: (1) "what business are we in?" and (2) "how do we compete?" The impetus for strategic human resource management (SHRM) stems from the human resource deployments and activities needed to implement the organization's strategy. This calls for the development of competencies needed to implement an organization's strategy as encapsulated in a resource-based view (RBV) of the firm. Essentially, RBV provides a "framework for viewing human resources as a pool of skills that can provide a resource to serve as a sustained competitive advantage" (Wright and McMahon, 1992). Kamoche (1996) illustrated the application of RBV to an understanding of the role of human resources in strategic management in terms of a resource–capability approach. This approach integrates the knowledge, skills, and abilities (KSAs) of employees and the organizational capability for managing them through its HRM practices. Given the dependence of indigenous organizations on imported Anglo-Saxon HRM practices, HRM practitioners and their organizations are confronted with the choice of appropriate practices to manage the skills or competencies required to execute a given organizational strategy.

Institutional theory provides a framework for the diffusion of HRM practices to indigenous organizations in Ghana. It is concerned with organizational–societal relations in terms of the pressures for acquiring and maintaining legitimacy in relation to the environment (DiMaggio and Powell, 1983; Powell and DiMaggio, 1991; Scott, 2001). Institutional theory focuses on two central issues: (1) how organizational forms in the broader social structure are reproduced within organizations; and (2) the degree of congruence between normative structures in organizations and society, through a variety of mechanisms like coercion, normative regulations, and imitation leading to similarities. The underlying principle of institutional theory that an organization's survival requires it to conform to societal norms of acceptable behavior has precipitated a culture-fit perspective in the diffusion of HRM practices (Beugré and Offodile, 2001; Harvey, 2002). For example, Beugré and Offodile (2001) examined the extent to which modern management practices like employee participation and empowerment, and performance-based compensation fit into the African value or thought system.

The growing conceptualization of the employment relationship as a social exchange is congruent with the collectivist ethos of Ghanaian and, for that matter, African society. Social exchange describes an informal, open-ended relationship between two parties in which the exchange goes beyond monetary inducement to include socio-emotional elements (Blau, 1964). When a party benefits from another's action, it engenders a feeling of obligation to reciprocate the favor. From an organization's perspective, this entails the consideration of employees' well-being and an investment in their long-term employability. These beneficial actions create an obligation on the part of employees to reciprocate with attitudes and behaviors that promote organizational effectiveness. A social exchange relationship has been variously described as mutual investment or a high commitment employment relationship. A configuration of HR practices that define such an employment relationship include performance-related compensation, developmental appraisal, participation and empowerment, and training and development.

There is research evidence linking social exchange-based employment relationship to organizational effectiveness (Huselid, 1995; Tsui *et al.*, 1997). A social exchange-based employment relationship is congruent with the reciprocal obligations that exist between members of an extended family. Accordingly, the effectiveness of indigenous organizations in Ghana may be contingent upon the adoption of a configuration of HR practices suggested by this form of employment relationship.

Conclusion

The adoption of an import substituting industrialization policy at independence and in the early years that followed created a stable and predictable environment for organizations in Ghana. That environment facilitated the adoption of HRM practices concerned with administrative and operational issues with little consideration for how they impact on organizational effectiveness. However, the liberalization of trade following the ERP has created a dynamic and competitive environment, as evident in the flooding of the domestic market with competitively priced, high quality imported products. The inability of indigenous organizations to acquire the technological sophistication of these foreign-based organizations suggests that they will have to depend on the skills, creativity, and motivation of their employees as a source of competitive advantage. As argued in this chapter, this requires a rethink of the employment relationship and the way employees are managed. Underpinned by a strategic orientation, it has been argued that indigenous organizations will need to consider their employees as resources to be developed (RBV) and the resulting skills deployed to implement the organization's strategic objectives. Given that HR practices are usually adopted from Anglo-Saxon countries, institutional theory was proposed as an underlying framework for the adoption of culturally congruent practices. Consistent with the theme of cultural congruence or fit, a social exchange-based employment relationship was argued to provide the configuration of HR practices that will facilitate the development of the competencies and the motivation to apply these competencies to enhance the effectiveness of indigenous organizations. In summary, this chapter has provided a contextual discussion of HRM practices in Ghana, and how human resources could be managed to promote organizational effectiveness in an increasingly competitive and globalized marketplace.

References

Abbey, J.L.S (1990) "Ghana's experience with structural adjustment," in J.Pickett and H. Singer (eds.) *Towards economic recovery in sub-Saharan Africa,* London: Routledge, pp. 32–41.

Arthur, W., Woehr, D.J., Akande, A., and Strong, M.H. (1995) "Human resource management in West Africa: Practices and perceptions," *International Journal of Human Resource Management* 6: 347–367.

Assimeng, M. (1981) *Social structure of Ghana*, Accra: Ghana Publishing Corporation.

Beugré, C.D. and Offodile, O.F. (2001) "Managing for organizational effectiveness in sub-Saharan Africa: A culture-fit model," *International Journal of Human Resource Management* 12: 535–550.

Blau, P.M. (1964). *Exchange and power in social life*, New Brunswick, NJ: Transaction Publishers.

Blunt, P. and Popoola,O.(1985) *Personnel management in Africa*, London: Longman.

CIA (2002) *World Factbook*. Online: www.cia.gov/cia/publications/factbook/geos/gh.html

Davis, J.T. (1991) "Institutional impediments to workforce retrenchment and restructuring in Ghana's state enterprises," *World Development*, 19: 987–1005.

Debrah, Y.A. (2001) "Human resource management in Ghana," in P.S. Budhwar and Y.A. Debrah (eds.) *Human resource management in developing countries*, London: Routledge, pp. 190–208.

DiMaggio, P.J. and Powell, W.W. (1983), "The iron cage revisited: Institutional isomorphism and collective rationality in organizational fields," *American Sociological Review* 48: 147–160.

Gardner, K. (1996) "Managing in different cultures: The case of Ghana," in B. Towers (ed.) *The handbook of human resource management*, Oxford: Blackwell, pp. 488–510.

Ghana Home Page (2002) Online: www.ghanaweb.com/GhanaHomePage/economy/statistics.php

Haruna, P.F. (2001) "From a developmental to a managerial paradigm: Ghana's administrative reform under structural adjustment programs," in K. Konadu-Agyemang (ed.) *IMF and World Bank sponsored structural adjustment programs in Africa: Ghana's experience, 1983–1999*, Aldershot: Ashgate, pp. 111–139.

Harvey, M. (2002) "Human resource management in Africa: Alice's adventures in wonderland," *International Journal of Human Resource Management* 13: 1119–1145.

Hofstede, G. (1980) *Culture's consequences: International differences in work-related values*, Beverly Hills, CA: Sage.

Huq, M.M. (1989) *The economy of Ghana: The first 25 years since independence*, London: Macmillan.

Huselid, M.A. (1995) "The impact of human resource management practices on turnover, productivity, and corporate financial performance," *Academy of Management Journal* 38: 635–672.

Kamoche, K. (1996) "Strategic human resource management within a resource–capability view of the firm," *Journal of Management Studies* 33: 213–233.

Kanungo, R.N. and Jaeger, A.M. (1990) "Introduction: The need for indigenous management in developing countries," in A.M. Jaeger and R.N. Kanungo (eds.) *Management in developing countries*, London: Routledge, pp. 1–19.

Kiggundu, M.N. (1989) *Managing organizations in developing countries*, West Hartford, CT: Kumarian Press.

Konadu-Agyemang, K. (2001) "An overview of structural adjustment programs in Africa," in K. Konadu-Agyemang (ed.) *IMF and World Bank sponsored structural adjustment programs in Africa: Ghana's experience, 1983–1999*, Aldershot: Ashgate, pp. 1–15.

Kuada, J. (1994) *Managerial behavior in Ghana and Kenya: A cultural perspective*, Aalborg, Denmark: Aalborg University Press.

Kusi, T.A. and Gyimah-Boakye, A.K. (1994) "Collective bargaining in Ghana: Problems and prospects," in *Political transformations, structural adjustment and industrial relations in Africa: English-speaking countries*, ILO Labor Management Relations Series, No. 78, Geneva: ILO.

Leonard, D.K. (1987) "The political realities of African management," *World Development* 15: 899–910.

Munene, J.C., Schwartz, S.H., and Smith, P.B. (2000) "Development in sub-Saharan Africa: Cultural influences and managers' decision behavior," *Public Administration and Development* 20: 339–351.

Nowak, M., Basanti, R., Horvath, B., Kochhar, K., and Prem, R. (1996) "Ghana, 1983–1991," in IMF (ed.) *Adjustment for growth: The African experience*, Occasional paper 143, Washington, DC: IMF, pp. 22–47.

Obeng-Fosu, P. (1991) *Industrial relations in Ghana*, Accra: Ghana Universities Press.

Panford, K. (1993) *African labor relations and workers' rights*, Westport, CT: Greenwood Press.

Panford, K. (2001) "Structural adjustment programs, human resources and organizational challenges facing labor and policy makers in Ghana," in K. Konadu-Agyemang (ed.) *IMF and World Bank sponsored structural adjustment programs in Africa: Ghana's experience, 1983–1999*, Aldershot: Ashgate, pp. 219–239.

Pfeffer, J. (1994) *Competitive advantage through people: Unleashing the power of the workforce*, Boston, MA: Harvard Business School Press.

Powell, W.W. and DiMaggio, P.J. (1991) *The new institutionalism in organizational analysis*, Chicago: University of Chicago Press.

Schwartz, S.H. (1999) "Cultural value differences: Some implications for work," *Applied Psychology: An International Review* 48: 23–47.

Scott, W.R. (2001) *Institutions and organizations*, Thousand Oaks, CA: Sage.

Tsui, A.S., Pearce, J.L., Porter, L.W., and Tripoli, A.M. (1997) "Alternative approaches to the employee–organization relationship: Does investment in employees pay off?" *Academy of Management Journal* 40: 1089–1121.

Wright, P.M. and McMahon, G.C. (1992) "Theoretical perspectives for strategic human resource management," *Journal of Management* 18: 295–320.

HRM in Ivory Coast

CONSTANT D. BEUGRÉ

A country of just over 16 million people, Ivory Coast gained its independence from France on 7 August 1960. Although French is the official language, more than 60 ethnic languages are spoken in the country. Ivory Coast has the third largest economy in Sub-Saharan Africa, behind South Africa and Nigeria. The country accounts for 40 percent of the economic output of the West African Monetary Union and is the world's biggest producer and exporter of cocoa beans. It is also the third largest producer and exporter of coffee, and exports palm oil, cotton, and pineapples. The agricultural and related sectors employ about 68 percent of the labor force. There is, however, an attempt to diversify the country's economic structure. The country enjoys effective infrastructures, such as paved roads linking major cities and commercial centers, telephone, and electricity. For instance, by African standards, the telephone system is well developed, although it operates below capacity (CIA, *World Factbook*, 2002).

Ivory Coast has heavily invested in education since independence, although the total literacy rate is relatively modest, 48.5 percent (57 percent for men and 40 percent for women). There are six public institutions of higher education, five universities or university centers and a major polytechnic institute that graduates mostly engineers. Ivory Coast has also several private institutions of higher education offering two-year degrees. Despite this effort in education, more remains to be done. Indeed, unemployment is relatively high, averaging 13 percent in urban areas (CIA, *World Factbook*, 2002). However, by African standards, the modern economic sector is relatively developed and makes the country a regional economic powerhouse, especially in the francophone zone.

A key factor in ensuring the country's economic development is the prosperity of the private sector. However, no economic advantage can be gained from local companies unless they effectively manage their workforce. As Pfeffer and Veiga (1999) contend, human capital is key to building competitive advantage for any organization. Therefore, organizations should consider their human capital as an asset rather than a cost to reduce.

The present chapter is divided into three sections. The first section analyzes key cultural patterns in Ivory Coast. Specifically, the section develops a triadic model of cultural patterns in the country. Understanding the cultural underpinnings of a country is key in managing its workforce. The second section discusses current human resource management practices in business organizations. Finally, the third section suggests several strategies for better Human Resource Management.

Understanding cultural patterns in Ivory Coast: a triadic model

Before discussing human resource practices in Ivory Coast, the chapter analyzes the cultural characteristics of the country. Although several authors have discussed the impact of cultural patterns on management in Sub-Saharan Africa (see Beugré and Offodile, 2001; Blunt and Jones, 1997; Mangaliso, 2001), very few have exclusively focused on Ivory Coast as a country. It is safe to say, however, that the cultural patterns in Ivory Coast are not dramatically different from those of other countries in Sub-Saharan Africa. Like other Sub-Saharan African cultures, the Ivorian culture is characterized by a respect for elders, importance of the extended family, collectivism, and deference to authority (see Beugré, 1998; Beugré and Offodile, 2001; Mangaliso, 2001). According to Hofstede (1993), West Africa (of which Ivory Coast is a part) ranks high on power distance, low on individualism, and long-term orientation, but moderate on both quantity of life and uncertainty avoidance. These cultural values, undoubtedly, influence human resource practices in business organizations in the country. Indeed, Noe *et al.* (2000) note that cultural characteristics influence the way managers behave in relation to subordinates, as well as the perceptions of the appropriateness of various human resource practices.

However, two key cultural and ethnic composition characteristics set Ivory Coast apart from other African countries. First, despite a mosaic of ethnic groups in the country, its culture can be categorized along three dimensions: the Akan culture, the Kru culture, and the Northern/Muslim culture. These three subcultures can have a tremendous impact on human resource management practices in modern organizations. Second, the French cultural influence is nowhere more vivid and felt in Africa than in Ivory Coast. Not only is French the official language for business and government, but also the educational system, the values shared by Ivorians, and the scheme of reference are French-based. Thus, the Ivorian culture is a French-dominated culture. This cultural triad and its potential impact on human resource practices are explained in the following lines.

The Akan culture

The Akans represent the dominant ethnic group in Ivory Coast, accounting for 42.1 percent of the total population. The Akans live mostly in the center, the east, and the southeast of the country. Recently, however, most Akan farmers have moved to the midwest and southwest to exploit agricultural opportunities offered by vast forestlands. Due to professional mobility, no ethnic group is confined to a specific geographic location even though it may be the dominant group in some areas. The traditional societal organization of this ethnic group is based on chiefdoms and/or small kingdoms. In these kingdoms, power is generally vested in a king, usually called "*nanan*." According to traditions, the *nanan* derives his power from God and/or ancestors. The Akan culture is characterized by deference to authority and a relative tolerance for injustices, especially emanating from rulers. Rulers are expected to exercise absolute power and questioning their values and behaviors is considered an offense and is severely punished.

The Akan culture is also characterized by obedience to authority and competition among "subjects" to gain the attention and favor of the ruler. Even in today's "modern life," these traditional beliefs still prevail and the Akans are known for their deference to authority and respect for traditions. Personality cult is a normal practice in the Akan culture. The chief is powerful and considered infallible. Rarely do followers question the chief's behaviors. Doing so is perceived as a transgression of traditions and customs. As an example, the former president, Houphouet Boigny, who single-handedly ruled the country from 1960 until his death in 1993, was venerated and viewed as infallible. He was known to say that Akan rulers (he was Akan himself) do not designate their heirs while they are still in power. However, he changed the constitution to ensure that Henry Konan Bedié succeed him. Mr Bedié was president from 1993 to 1999, when he was ousted by a military coup on 24 December 1999.

The Kru culture

The Kru represents 15–18 percent of the general population of Ivory Coast. They are generally Christians or animists. They are mostly located in the midwest and the southwest. They enjoy the richest lands, allowing for cocoa and coffee production, the main commodities exported by the country. However, as in the case of the other major ethnic groups, the Kru are not confined in these specific geographic areas and can be found in other parts of the country, especially as employees or civil servants.

The Kru culture is *ahierarchical* (no rigid hierarchy exists among its members) and heavily influenced by a traditional democratic system at the village level (Beugré and Offodile, 2001). In this culture, the village chief acts as a spokesperson rather than a ruler whom villagers have to blindly obey. In the Kru culture, the village chief is held accountable for his deeds (rarely do women get selected as village chieftaines). Elders select the village chief for a limited term, generally five years, after which he can be re-appointed or another person can be selected. This selection process is not based on kinship or a family of rulers, but on the person's character and skills. In general, the Kru resent authority. A key belief in the Kru culture is that everyone should gain his or her recognition in society based on his or her skills and deeds. Power is not considered an important indicator of societal differentiation. The power holder is perceived as a spokesperson. Modern Kru tend to resent autocratic leaders and expect treatment with respect and dignity from those in power.

The Northern/Muslim culture

The northern part of the Ivory Coast includes mostly people from the Senoufo ethnic group and Muslims. Although this subculture is characterized as Northern/Muslim, not everyone in the north is Muslim. Indeed, several people in the north are Christians and animists. However, Muslims tend to dominate the region not only in numbers but also in culture. Muslims account for 30 percent of the total population of Ivory Coast. Most Muslims in the north are immigrants or descendents of immigrants from neighboring countries, mostly Burkina Faso, Guinea, and Mali. The dominant cultural pattern is obedience to authority and the belief that the chief derives his power from God. For Muslims, the chief is a prophet and followers should comply with his orders. In the Muslim culture, there is a strong disposition toward the great or prophetic leader, who is perceived as a worker of miracles (Pillai *et al.* 1999), as well as the ordinary or *caliphal* leader who rules by coercion and fear (Dorfman, 1996). Although Muslims in Ivory Coast do not practice Sharia laws, they tend to view themselves more as Muslims than as citizens of Ivory Coast. Such a mindset may be explained by the fact that migrants from neighboring countries are overwhelmingly Muslim (more than 70 percent).

These three cultural patterns characterize what we may call the Ivorian culture. The Akan and Northern/Muslim subcultures may be considered as high on power distance, whereas the Kru subculture may be considered as low on power distance. While in the first two subcultures injustices tend to be tolerated, especially when they originate from leaders, in the Kru culture injustices are not accepted or tolerated.

Do these cultural differences explain the attempted military coup of 19 September 2002 that led to near civil war? The answer is probably yes, since most leaders of the rebellion are from the Muslim north and have the backing of northern Muslim countries such as Burkina Faso and Mali. The main reasons for this crisis, however, are more political than religious; discussion of these political ramifications is, however, beyond the scope of this chapter. The focus here is more on how these cultural differences may shape HRM practices in Ivory Coast. Without negating the economic impact of this crisis, it is fair to point out that more than 90 percent of the Ivory Coast economy is not affected by the current crisis since the vital economic areas are still under government control. Moreover, government controlled areas include more than 82 percent of the total population of Ivory Coast.

Gundykunst and Ting-Toomey (1988) noted that cultures that inculcate an acceptance of power differences lead individuals to expect, take for granted and, therefore, not get angry about injustices. Such a tendency may be applicable to African organizations, where prevailing cultural patterns make powerholders more powerful and often unaccountable to their subordinates and/or constituencies. African leaders bestow favor and expect and receive obedience and deference (Blunt and Jones, 1997). A better understanding of the Ivorian culture requires an understanding of these three cultural patterns.

Table 9.1 Cultural patterns in Ivory Coast: a triadic framework

Akan	Kru	Northern/Muslim
Autocratic	Ahierarchical	Autocratic/submissive
Follow the "*nanan*" mindset	Independant mindset	Follow the chief mindset
Deference to authority	Resent authority	Obedience to authority/chief as prophet
High tolerance to frustrations	Low tolerance to frustrations	High tolerance to frustrations
High power distance	Low power distance	High power distance

A cultural value that Ivorians tend to share together is the tendency to bury their dead in their native villages. Although a person may die far away from his or her native village, the corpse is brought back to the village for burial and funerals. This practice is costly in terms of financial resources, time, and human resources. Relatives and friends of the deceased take part in the ceremonies. This practice leads to what I label "mourning absenteeism." Mourning absenteeism refers to absences due to an employee's attendance of funerals. Indeed, out of moral or family obligation, employees feel compelled to take part in the burial ceremonies. For this purpose, they will miss work to go to the deceased's native village. Although no systematic study has assessed the impact of this practice on organizational productivity, it is obvious that it may undermine employee performance.

Table 9.1 depicts the three subcultures along with their dominant characteristics. As explained previously, the Akan and Northern/Muslim cultures tend to be autocratic, whereas the Kru culture tends to be ahierarchical and therefore more flexible. However, this characteristic does not imply that every Akan or Northern Muslim is autocratic and every Kru is flexible. Respecting hierarchy and formal position is more vivid among the Akans and the Northern Muslims than among the Kru. Similarly, in these high power distance cultures there is a tendency for high tolerance for frustrations, whereas there is a low tolerance for frustrations in the Kru culture.

Human resource practices in Ivory Coast

The human resource function in most organizations in Ivory Coast is traditional in the sense that human resource managers focus exclusively on recruiting and selecting employees, and compensating them.

Recruitment and selection

Employee recruitment and selection in most business organizations in Ivory Coast follow formal procedures. Employees are often hired based on objective criteria such as education, experience, skills, etc. However, job applicants often complain about the lack of fairness in the hiring process. Critics of the hiring process contend that employers prefer to hire people they know or who have political connections. The role of the *invisible power* or connections seems important in the hiring process. Under these conditions, getting hired depends more on who you know rather than what you know. Although no systematic study has been conducted (to the best of my knowledge) on the influence of nepotism and corruption on the hiring process in Ivory Coast, anecdotal evidence suggests that most of the time employees tend to be of the same ethnic group as those who hold powerful positions within organizations. As Takyi-Asiedu (1993: 95) put it, "there is a conviction that to give a job to a fellow tribesman is not nepotism, it is an obligation." It is even a moral obligation to help those tribesmen who are less fortunate to find a job.

Two reasons may help explain such a practice. First, managers may consider having a moral obligation to help their less fortunate relatives or tribesmen. Providing them with a job is a way of playing their role of social support. Second, by recruiting or helping to recruit relatives and fellow tribesmen, managers may build a power base within their respective organizations. To the extent that these employees owe their jobs to the "benevolence" of their manager, they will tend to remain loyal to him or her. The influence of nepotism on the hiring process, however, may be more salient in state-owned enterprises than in private business organizations. Empirical studies are needed to ascertain the spread of this practice across organizations in Ivory Coast. Relying on such practices may lead to the "management of affection" based on a social network of people related by ethnicity, family, or regional ties.

Nepotism may also affect managers' behavior towards their employees depending on whether those employees are members of the same ethnic group or not. Although no empirical studies have been conducted in Ivory Coast to assess the effect of "ethnic proximity" on managers' behavior toward employees, one may speculate that managers' behavior toward same ethnic group employees and other ethnic group employees may differ. Thus, employees may be divided into two groups, in-group members and out-group members. In-group members are employees who are from the same ethnic group as the manager, whereas out-group members are employees who are not from the same ethnic group as the manager. It is anticipated that the manager's treatment of these employees would depend on their status as in-group or out-group members. In-group employees may develop and maintain closer relations with the manager than out-group employees (see Table 9.2). To the extent that in-group employees enjoy close relations with the manager, they may communicate more frequently with him or her, feel a sense of security and protection, and develop trustful relations with the manager.

Table 9.2 Hypothesized relations between managers and employees based on ethic affiliations

In-group members	Out-group members
Close relations with supervisors	Formal relations with supervisors
Sense of job security and protection	Sense of insecurity/protection
Frequent communications with supervisors	Formal communications with supervisors
Trust	Lack of trust/suspicion
Important extra benefits	Limited extra benefits

Out-group employees, however, would have formal relations with the manager, communicate less frequently with him or her, and express feelings of insecurity. Out-group members may not be trusted and may not benefit from extra tangible and intangible rewards from the manager. Since particularistic personnel practices may derive from such dichotomy, trust and perceptions of fairness may be affected. Particularistic personnel practices refer to human resource practices that focus on the type of relationships with subordinates (friendship, kinship, etc.). In such a situation, human resource practices such as selection, compensation, performance appraisal, and promotion are based on subjective measures. Pearce *et al.* (2000) found that trust and commitment were lower and shirking greater in those organizations with relatively more particularistic personnel practices. Those employees not benefiting from management's favors had a tendency to shirk.

Table 9.2 summarizes the hypothesized relationships between a manager and employees based on their ethnic proximity with the manager. In-group members would entertain close relations with their supervisors, whereas out-group members would have only formal and work-related interactions with their supervisors. Likewise, in-group members would also experience a sense of job security and protection, and frequent communications with their supervisors compared to out-group members. Such frequent interactions with supervisors may instill trust and provide important tangible and intangible benefits to in-group members. Out-group members, however, may tend to suspect their supervisors and may not enjoy extra benefits as opposed to in-group members.

Compensation

The compensation system in most business organizations in Ivory Coast is not different from that of Western companies. It includes two aspects, monetary compensation (salary, bonus) and benefits, such as health insurance and pension contributions. Compensation in the private sector generally tends to be higher than in the public sector, although it may seem low compared to the cost of living, especially in Abidjan, the largest city and the economic capital of Ivory Coast. Employees often request the services of human resource managers to receive loans or advance on pay since they are often cash-strapped before the end of each month. Employers also contribute to pension plans for their employees and provide tuition aids. Factors determining compensation policy include seniority, status, and experience. Compensation practices, such as performance-based pay, stock options, and cost of living adjustments, are virtually unknown in Ivory Coast.

Expatriate managers tend to earn more than local managers. In such a situation, local employees may experience feelings of unfair treatment. Beugré (2002) suggested that this apparent difference in compensation might create feelings of deprivation among local employees. To the extent that local employees experience distributive unfairness compared to expatriates, negative attitudes and reactions in terms of reduced effort, turnover, lack of commitment, and strikes may occur. This is particularly salient in the private sector, which employs more expatriate employees and managers.

Performance appraisal

Performance appraisal in Ivory Coast is often limited to written statements and evaluations from managers as in most West African countries. In a study of HRM practices in West Africa, especially in Ghana and Nigeria, Arthur *et al.* (1995) found supervisory ratings the most frequently cited source of performance information, accounting for 81 percent of the responses. Since Ivory Coast is at the same industrialization level as Ghana and Nigeria, one may expect the same pattern. Performance appraisal tends to be dominated by written statements from managers and rarely integrates employee input. Moreover, performance appraisals are rarely used as a basis for compensation and promotion. Promotion is often seniority based. Here, again, the process may be biased by ethnic considerations and loyalty to the manager.

Managers may tend to positively evaluate the performance of employees who are their *protégés*. Since managers assess employees' performance without their input, the fairness of the evaluation process is problematic. However, this form of evaluating employee performance can best be understood by relying on prevailing cultural values. Indeed, in Ivory Cost, a West African country that ranks high on power distance, there is a status gap between managers and employees. Managers tend to be powerful and rarely seek input from their employees in making job-related decisions. "In an authoritarian setting the appraisal system is unavoidably one-sided. In such a case, the supervisor's view of the subordinates' performance prevails" (Waiguchu, 1999: 198). It is also safe to say that in a culture of nepotism, performance is often largely based on compliance rather than productivity (Thairu, 1999). "Because management in Africa is more attuned to self-management and empowerment, it may require adjustment of some aspects of managerial practices in Africa (Waiguchu 1999: 199). Although Table 9.1 indicated that the Kru culture tends to be lower on power distance, no empirical research to the best of my knowledge, has compared Kru managers and other managers on this cultural dimension. As indicated earlier, empirical research is needed to ascertain the extent to which the Akans, Kru, and Northern/Muslim cultures lead to different behaviors in the workplace.

Labor relationships

The workforce in Ivory Coast is unionized, although no statistics related to the number of unionized workers compared to the total workforce are available. Labor and management have different, if not opposite, views. Like in every country, unions aim to improve working conditions, secure decent pay, and minimize the effects of layoffs on workers. Management, however, seeks to reduce costs by an efficient use of human resources, while trying to minimize the effects of employee dysfunctional reactions, such as work stoppages and strikes.

There are several unions in Ivory Coast. The major unions are UGTCI (General Union of Workers of Ivory Coast), Centrale Dignité (Dignity Central), SYNARES (a union of university professors), and the SYNESCI, to name the most popular (a union of middle school and high school teachers). Although these unions did not play a key role during the independence struggles, they were instrumental in contributing to multi-party elections and democracy in the early 1990s. Specifically, the SYNARES and the SYNESCI were instrumental in allowing the multi-party elections in 1990 and the liberalization of the political discourse.

The labor–management relationship may symbolize a cultural pattern in that it helps understand how those who have power and control resources view employees in the workplace. In countries where labor–management relations are adversarial, one may expect a "them versus us" mentality. Current relations between unions and management in Ivory Coast can be characterized as adversarial. This may be explained by the autocratic management styles local managers use. These autocratic management styles confirm Kiggundu's (1988: 223) contention that, "in Sub-Saharan Africa, there are sharp distinctions and status differences between management and workers. Management has the power, the controls, the authority, and the rewards and punishments. The workers are expected to do their work and obey management's instructions and directives." One of the consequences of this adversarial relationship is the frequency of strikes and work stoppages.

Since this adversarial relationship is detrimental to both parties, management and unions should develop cooperative relations, if not partnerships. There are two objectives for this transformation. First, it is important to increase the involvement of individuals and work groups in overcoming adversarial relations and increasing employee commitment, motivation, and problem solving. Second, it is important to reorganize work so that work rules are minimized and flexibility in managing people is maximized (Noe *et al.*, 2000).

Another concern of unions in Ivory Coast is the perceived gap between local employees' and expatriates' compensations. The private sector is mostly dominated by subsidiaries of European companies, although subsidiaries of American, Canadian, and Japanese companies are also operating in the country. These subsidiaries employ local employees and managers as well as expatriates. Expatriates often earn more than locals. This disparity in compensation raises fairness issues and is a concern for unions.

Training and development

Training in organizations in Ivory Coast includes in-house and off-site training. The former includes on-the-job training, on-site training, and corporate training centers. In on-the job training, more experienced employees help newcomers learn their tasks by observation and on-hands experience. Such training is less costly and easy to implement. On-site training involves outside consultants and/or internal trainers but the training occurs within the company. Some companies operate internal training centers combining the use of internal and outside trainers. Examples of such companies include CIE (Compagnie Ivorienne d'Electricité), a utility company, *SOTRA* (Société des Transports d'Abidjan), a public transportation company, and SIR (Société Ivorienne de Raffinage), an oil refinery. These companies operate their own training centers using internal trainers as well as college professors and outside consultants.

Organizations in Ivory Coast also use off-site training to meet their training needs. Such training occurs in institutions of continuous education. There are currently two highly regarded institutions of continuous education in the country, the CAMPC (Centre Africain et Mauricien de Perfectionnement des Cadres) and the CUFOP (Centre Universitaire de Formation Professionelle) affiliated with the university of Cocody. These institutions focus on the continuous education and development of managers. In some cases, when specific training is not available in Ivory Coast, subsidiaries of multinational corporations often send their employees overseas, usually to France, the UK, or the USA.

Improving human resource practices in Ivory Coast

To better manage their workforce, business organizations in the country should integrate new management practices and information technology. Such new practices include outsourcing human resource activities through the creation of human resource centers, using 360-degree feedback as a performance evaluation technique, and introducing performance-based compensation. These techniques are explained in the section that follows.

Introducing performance-based compensation

Few organizations in Ivory Coast use merit pay as a compensation technique. However, well implemented, merit pay can help motivate employees and induce a sense of distributive fairness. A performance-based compensation system would help employees understand the existence of a direct link between effort and performance. Merit pay may include direct compensation, as well as cash benefits and stock options. Although investing in the stock market is not part of the Ivorian culture, providing such compensation measures may help familiarize employees with the stock market. However, to successfully implement merit pay, organizations would need to establish high and challenging performance standards, develop accurate performance appraisal systems, and train managers in the mechanisms of performance appraisal and in the art of giving feedback to employees (Cascio, 2003).

In addition to monetary compensation, business organizations in the country should also use non-monetary compensation as a way of motivating employees. Recognition for work well done and annual prizes, such as employee of the year, are important incentives. Several organizations already use such non-monetary rewards. They need, however, to completely integrate such practices in their formal compensation packages. Employers should also consider cost of living in determining compensation levels. Most employees are paid monthly, generally at the end of the month. To help employees better manage their pay, which is often insufficient, a bi-monthly payment would be preferable. However, the success of such payment installments will depend on the characteristics of each company and the potential costs involved.

Using 360-degree feedback for better performance evaluation

To reduce potential bias in existing performance evaluation measures, the use of 360-degree feedback would help improve the effectiveness and objectivity of the evaluation process. There are four components of a 360-degree feedback: boss, self, peers, and customers. These programs can involve feedback for a targeted employee or manager from four sources: (1) downward from the target's supervisor, (2) upward from subordinates, (3) laterally from peers and coworkers, and (4) inwardly from the target him or herself (Waldman *et al.*, 1998). This performance measurement technique can foster individual development and improve performance. Three-hundred and sixty-degree feedback should be used for developmental purposes and tied to organizational goals and strategies; it can promote individual development and improve performance if linked to developmental planning, goal setting, and organizational support (Tornow and London, 1998).

However, 360-degree feedback is not a panacea. What gets measured and rewarded drives behavior (Waldman *et al.*, 1998). Even when 360-degree feedback ratings are used for developmental purposes, individuals will tend to modify behaviors in ways to receive more positive ratings (Waldman *et al.*, 1998). In the context of Ivory Coast, the upward rating process (employees rating bosses for example) may well be challenging, since employees rarely rate their managers in African organizations.

Outsourcing the human resource function

Outsourcing refers to the performance by outside parties, on a recurring basis, of human resource tasks that would otherwise be performed in-house (Greer *et al.*, 1999: 85). There are two factors essential to the outsourcing of human resource activities in Ivory Coast. First, most business organizations in Ivory Coast are small or of medium size, employing fewer than 500 employees. Therefore, their HRM departments are generally small. Second, existing human resource departments lack a strategic focus and are more preoccupied with managing internal and routine activities. Third, these human resource departments often employ individuals who lack the appropriate credentials and skills and therefore are less responsive to their internal and external customers. Thus, to realize economies of scale, business organizations may outsource the human resource functions by using collaborative management. Collaborative management implies that organizations can pool their resources to create a human resource center that will manage their respective human resource activities. Collaborative management may help reduce costs and improve efficiency in managing human resources. Using collaborative management to manage human resources would require a high degree of coordination and trust among participating organizations. Such trust can be instilled by fair treatment and training in cooperation. In addition, clearly explaining the advantages of collaborative management may help improve its success.

Creating human resource centers

A human resource center is a center created by two or more companies to perform their human resource activities. In the case of business organizations in Ivory Coast, suppose, for instance, that ten companies employing on average 250 people join forces to create a human resource center. This human resource center will oversee 2,500 employees. Using this human resource center will reduce the costs of operating individual human resource departments within organizations. It may also improve efficiency because fewer staff members will be needed. The center may be physically located in the facilities in one participating company or participating companies may rent or build a common facility. Wherever the physical location of the human resource center, it should be easily accessible to employees and managers of the participating companies.

Information technology would help improve the efficiency of these human resource centers. A human resource information system is a systematic procedure for collecting, storing, maintaining, retrieving, and validating data needed by an organization about its human resources. A human resource information system can be informal as in small companies or sophisticated and complex as in large corporations. Whatever the human resource information system, it helps effectively manage a company's workforce. Human resource information systems involve such activities as long range planning, supply and demand forecasts, recruitment and hiring, compensation, and occupational accidents, to name just a few. The purpose of a human resource information system includes providing information that is required by human resource stakeholders and supporting human resource decisions. A human resource information system has several advantages including reducing costs and time, helping to improve decisions, and producing more accurate and timely information.

There are three key components of a human resource information system: input, data maintenance, and output. Input typically takes the form of data entry activities such as recording and editing. It involves capturing information that can be processed by the system. Data maintenance implies that the data collected should be stored and updated when the need arises. A continuous process of correcting and updating output activities must maintain the quality of any data stored in a human resource management information system. However, the most important element of a human resource information system is information. The goal of a human resource management information system is the production of appropriate information for human resource-related decisions. Outdated and inaccurate information may not be useful. Information is critical because it allows the opportunity to assess the existing workforce, its nature, qualifications, as well as training and promotion needs. Information also helps determine the future workforce. Therefore, it is important to focus on the accuracy, validity, reliability, and utility of the information collected. In a human resource information system, people collect data and transform these data into information. This information is then transformed into knowledge that can be acted upon. Knowledge without action cannot help improve decisions. Despite its advantages, a human resource information system may face some obstacles. Two of the obstacles include lack of money and lack of top management support. As in any change effort, top management support is crucial for the success of the system.

A human resource information system is an investment. As such, we must consider the costs of this investment at four levels: software, costs of hardware, maintenance, and training. The problem then is how to measure the benefits of the system in terms of return on investment (ROI). The benefits of the system would be measured by the quality of decisions, user satisfaction, system usage, and overall efficiency. If most people use the system, they may imply that the system has a wide acceptance and is needed by these people.

Conclusion

Introducing the proposed changes in the management of human resources in Ivory Coast represents a challenge. As in most Sub-Saharan African countries, innovation, entrepreneurship, risk taking, and individualism are not valued or rewarded (Kiggundu, 1988). Thus, introducing changes would be a challenge for both employees and managers. For instance, introducing performance-based pay in a country where there is a centralized allocation of resources may constitute an insurmountable challenge.

Similarly, developing human resource centers requires a change in current practices. Top management should be involved in the introduction of such changes. For instance, CEOs and top executives of local companies may have to make the decision of using human resource centers to effectively and efficiently manage their workforce. The management of such centers would require hiring and training human resource managers, but also developing a strong coordination and instilling trust among participating organizations. The effective management of people requires a more comprehensive and systematic approach (Pfeffer and Veiga, 1999).

Although some of the changes may be difficult to implement, evolving societal trends may facilitate their long-term application. Societal changes, including information technology, the quest for democracy, and the development of a more educated workforce, may contribute to changing the workforce of the twenty-first century in Ivory Coast. For instance, the development of the Internet allows employees to have access to more information and knowledge, leading to more autonomy in regard to management. Such trends may allow employees to request more involvement in decisions concerning their jobs and how their work performance is assessed. Also important are social and political changes leading to more political democracy since the early 1990s. Beugré (1998; 2002) notes that political and social changes on the African continent are likely to spill over into the workplace in the form of a quest for more justice and freedom, translating into demands for fair wages, unbiased performance appraisal, and more involvement in organizational decisions.

Empirical research, however, is needed to help human resource managers in Ivory Coast to understand their own culture and its impact on HRM practices. For instance, this chapter contends that Ivory Coast does not have a single culture but three different subcultures. The extent to which these subcultures affect work behavior warrants empirical investigation. How should a manager who is Akan manage employees who are Kru and vice versa? Undoubtedly, research is needed to provide Ivorian organizations with strategies and insights to better manage their workforce.

References

Arthur, W., Jr., Woehr, D.J., Akande, A., and Strong, M.H. (1995) "Human resource management in West Africa: Practices and perceptions," *International Journal of Human Resource Management* 6 (2): 347–366.

Beugré, C.D. (1998) *La motivation au travail des cadres Africains* [The work motivation of African managers], Paris: Les Editions L'Harmattan.

Beugré, C.D. (2002) "Understanding organizational justice and its impact on managing employees: An African perspective," *International Journal of Human Resource Management* 13 (7): 1–14.

Beugré, C.D. and Offodile, F.O. (2001) "Managing for organizational effectiveness in sub-Saharan Africa: A culture-fit model," *International Journal of Human Resource Management* 12 (4): 535–550.

Blunt, P. and Jones, M.L. (1997) "Exploring the limits of Western leadership theory in East Asia and Africa," *Personnel Review* 26: 6–23.

Cascio, W. (2003) *Managing human resources: Productivity, quality of life, profits*, 6th edition, New York: McGraw-Hill.

CIA (2002) *World Factbook, Cote d'Ivoire*. Online: http://www.cia.gov/cia/publications/factbook/geos/iv.html

DeNisi, A.S. and Kluger, A.N. (2000) "Feedback effectiveness: Can 360-degree appraisals be improved?" *Academy of Management Executive* 14 (1): 129–139.

Dorfman, P. (1996) "International and cross-cultural leadership research," in B.J. Punnet and O. Shenkar (eds.) *Handbook for international management research*, Cambridge, MA: Blackwell Publishers, pp. 267–349.

Greer, C.R., Youngblood, S.A., and Gray, D.A. (1999) "Human resources management outsourcing: The make or buy decision," *Academy of Management Executive* 13 (3): 85–96.

Gundykunst, W.B. and Ting-Toomey, S. (1988) "Culture and affective communication," *American Behavioral Scientist* 31: 348–400.

Hofstede, G. (1993) "Cultural constraints in management theories," *Academy of Management Executive*, February, 81–94.

Kiggundu, M.N. (1988) "Africa," in R. Nath (ed.) *Comparative management: A regional view*, Cambridge, MA: Ballinger, pp. 169–243.

Mangaliso, M.P. (2001) "Building competitive advantage from Ubuntu: Management lessons from South Africa," *Academy of Management Executive* 15 (3): 23–33.

Noe, R.A., Hollenbeck, J.A., Gerhart, B., and Wright, P.M. (2000) *Human resource management: Gaining a competitive advantage*, 3rd edition, New York: Irwin/McGraw-Hill.

Pearce, J.L., Branyiczki, I., and Bigley, G.A. (2000) "Insufficient bureaucracy: Trust and commitment in particularistic organizations," *Organization Science* 11: 148–162.

Pfeffer, J. and Veiga, J.F. (1999) "Putting people first for organizational success," *Academy of Management Executive* 13 (2): 37–48.

Pillai, R., Scandura, T.A., and Williams, E.A. (1999) "Leadership and organizational justice: Similarities and differences across cultures," *Journal of International Business Studies* 30 (4): 763–779.

Takyi-Asiedu, S. (1993) "Some socio-cultural factors retarding entrepreneurial activities in sub-Saharan Africa," *Journal of Business Venturing* 8: 91–98.

Thairu, W. (1999) "Team building and total quality management (TQM) in Africa," in M. J. Waiguchu, E. Thiaga, and M. Mwaura (eds.) *Management of organizations in Africa: A handbook of reference*, Westport, CT: Quorum Books, pp. 267–279.

Tornow, W.W. and London, M. (eds) (1998) *Maximising the value of 360-Degree Feedback*, San Francisco: Jossey-Bass.

Waiguchu, M.J. (1999) "Performance appraisal," in M.J. Waiguchu, E. Thiaga, and M. Mwaura (eds.) *Management of organizations in Africa: A handbook of reference*, Westport, CT: Quorum Books, pp. 197–208.

Waldman, D.A., Atwater, L.E., and Antonioni, D. (1998) "Has 360-degree feedback gone amok?" *Academy of Management Executive* 12 (2): 86–94.

10 HRM in Tunisia

MAHMOUD YAGOUBI

Introduction

A former French colony, Tunisia has been a democratic republic since 1956. Islam is officially the state religion and Arabic is the national language. With an area of 163,610 km² and an estimated population of 9.6 million in 2001, Tunisia is the smallest of the four countries composing the Maghreb in North Africa. Bordered to the west by Algeria and by Libya to the south and the east, Tunisia benefits from a large opening on the Mediterranean Sea and a close proximity to Europe. Lacking natural resources, Tunisia has relied heavily on human resources to develop its economy. Tunisia has now transformed itself from a protected economy into a newly industrialized and opened economy in order to attract more foreign direct investments. As foreign firms increase their involvement in Tunisia, they will need to build capabilities and utilize local skills. Knowledge of HRM and, more importantly perhaps, knowledge of the factors that have an impact on HRM in Tunisia, will become increasingly critical to the way business is done there and ultimately to its success. Thus, since 1995, Tunisian firms have been burdened outwardly by the need to compete simultaneously with firms in advanced countries and internally by the need to change the organizational structure and human resources systems. In addition, the recent economic directions and the increase in income provide a chance for the people to change their mentality and their quantity-oriented way of thinking to a quality-oriented approach. People, and employees in particular, were expected to become more self-reliant rather than looking to the state or their trade union for assistance. So we can see that, as firms and people's way of thinking and behavior go through drastic changes, present day HRM is also going through a significant transformation.

This chapter, therefore, discusses, within a socio-economic context, a number of factors that influence human resource policies and practices and highlights the new trends in HRM in Tunisia. It begins with a discussion of the past and the present Tunisian economy and enterprises. This is followed by a description and discussion of internal and external factors influencing HRM in Tunisia. The next section discusses the development of HRM functions in Tunisian organisations and is followed by the concluding section which provides a brief summary and some recommendations concerning the issues covered.

Economic crisis and liberalization of the Tunisian economy

Until 1986, the regime of a partly controlled, partly free economy realized very satisfactory performances. However the context became less favorable in the 1980s, notably between 1984 and 1986, because of several negative factors (the fall in oil prices, the return of 30,000 workers who had emigrated to Libya, the conflicts between government and trade unions in January 1978, January 1980, and January 1984). These events and the emergence of a strong radical "Islamist group" have constituted an obstacle for economic development. The political instability scared foreign and Tunisian investors and deterred them from creating projects, a fact which has reverberated negatively on growth and job creation. In addition, as the State continued a very important public investment policy despite these handicaps, it was obliged to borrow massively, including from commercial banks, so Tunisia was threatened by a financial crisis. This situation resulted in the eviction of President Bourguiba and his replacement by Prime Minister Ben Ali in November 1987. This political change allowed Tunisian authorities to accept conditions imposed by the World Bank and the IMF in exchange for financial assistance.

By adopting the structural adjustment program (SAP) in 1987, the Tunisian government turned towards liberalization of the economy, redirecting its development strategy in order to give more importance to the private sector. In addition, on 17 July 1995, Tunisia became the first country in the Middle East and North Africa region to sign a free trade agreement with the European Union. The increasing openness of the world economy necessarily implied alignment of the national economy to world performance with regard to prices and quality. Reforms introduced under the Ninetieth Plan (1997–2001) therefore led, according to the National Institute of Statistics (NIS), to impressive macro-economic performances. These performances have also been accompanied by important social achievements; these include the intensification of job creation and particular attention to social welfare expenditures. Income seems to be more evenly distributed than in most comparable countries and the incidence of poverty to be correspondingly low. The rate of literacy decreased from 46.2 percent in 1984 to 24.7 percent in 2001.

At the end of the 1980s, the Tunisian economy was increasingly well diversified. The agricultural sector's share in value-added had fallen from about 17 percent in 1990 to 14 percent in 2001, while the manufacturing sector's share rose from 19 percent to 21 percent over the same period, and non-government services expanded from 37 percent to 45 percent. Industries such as textiles, clothing, leather goods, and electrical and mechanical components are important to the export-oriented manufacturing sector, and tourism is an important component of the service sector.

Tunisian firms

The Tunisian economy is composed, according to the NIS (1998), essentially of small and medium-sized enterprises (SME) that represent approximately 96 percent of the total, with a strong proportion of firms depending on the "micro" or the informal sector. Their structure and their organization indeed present the advantage of flexibility. Nevertheless, a great number of them are handicapped by the weak capacities of their management. The managers of private firms are in general artisans, exporters, those wanting to exit the public sector, and immigrants that have chosen to return to Tunisia to create their own firms (Denieul and B'Chir, 1996). The majority of these entrepreneurs are unqualified; they are not professional managers and they count on their technical knowledge. Meddeb (1999) notes that the majority of Tunisian employers have received on-the-job training. Their success is based on family capital and friendship networks.

By benefiting from a protected market until 1995, most Tunisian firms have neglected quality improvement and technological modernization, since they could sell their products on the local market even if the quality was mediocre and the price was high. Consequently, firms are often not equipped or managed in order to compete on quality, but rely on occupying domestic market niches. Export performance has been fairly consistently strong since the 1970s, and most of it has been due to the private sector; however, all the main traditional exports face constraints. Almost all manufacturing exports, with few exceptions, are technically simple, requiring little skill and yielding a low added value. The main source of growth, "textiles, clothing, and footwear," soon met competition from East European and Asian producers with higher skill levels and/or lower wages once the European Union members' quotas that protected Tunisian exports were removed with the ending of the Multifiber Agreement. Studies conducted in 1991 by the Promotion Industry Agency show that the majority of firms use traditional technology (Hannachi, 1991); for example, in 1990, the mechanical sector counted only 40 digital machines. This technological weakness is closely linked to the utilization of a less skilled workforce. Indeed, a study by Ben Zakour (2000) indicates that the average rate of top management and engineers in Tunisian firms represents only one-sixth of the rate existing in industrial countries.

To meet the competitive challenge of the European Union, the Tunisian government adopted the industrial restructuring program in 1994–1995 ("program de mise à niveau") to help the manufacturing industry to adapt and upgrade its methods and practices of organization and management.[1] The program includes a component for environmental

---

1 The program is managed by the COPIL, which is attached to the Ministry of Industry and is composed of 16 members representing the government, the employers' association, banks, and the labor union. The COPIL approves financing for 70 percent of the cost of an initial diagnostic study to develop the restructuring plan for the enterprise. The enterprise itself, financial institutions and the government finance this plan. The contribution of the government takes the form of a premium; this premium varies between 10 and 20 percent of the total investment envisaged in the restructuring plan.

restructuring, aimed at improving basic and technological infrastructure and at upgrading institutions providing support. The program also includes a component for enterprise restructuring which envisages: immaterial investments (enterprise organization, human resource management, quality plans), material investments (modernization of technological and technical processes), and financial restructuring (reducing the debt load of firms).

In addition to the main "mise a niveau program," other programs are under design or being implemented. The government has recently established a "mise a niveau program for services" tied to industry. These include the key services that are important in improving the productivity and competitiveness of the industrial sector: business services, information technology, training, telecommunication, and transportation. In addition, an appropriate number of professional teams have also appeared and apply their knowledge to a specific subject. As a result, the mobilization of the consulting firms has had to be undertaken. These firms provide professionals with the opportunity to increase their specialization and, likewise, the performance and competitiveness of the firm are increased correspondingly (for example, the use of consulting firms to recruit and select candidates).

Thanks to these programs, Tunisian organizations have rapidly evolved their working methods. They experiment with new microprocessor technologies. In particular, computer-aided design and computer-aided manufacturing systems have been used to provide firms with flexibility and cost-effective shortened production runs. In addition, new organizational methods and management practices that are generally based on Western principles—such as quality control and just-in-time inventory control—have been introduced because they offer a viable and inexpensive path for upgrading Tunisian industry in order to survive in increasingly competitive market conditions (Yagoubi, 2001). Each of these innovations involves changes in traditional techniques, but do they entail modifications in HRM practices?

Factors affecting HRM in Tunisia

This section discusses Tunisia's labor market developments, education and vocational training, industrial relations, socio-cultural factors, and management style and their impact on HRM.

Labor market developments

In July 2001, the Tunisian labor force was estimated at about 3.3 million out of a population of about 10 million. The minimum employment age in Tunisia is 16 years. The size of the economically active population rose from 1.8 million in 1984 to 2.5 million in 1997. Official statistics show that the unemployment rate decreased from 16.4 percent in 1984 to 15.9 percent in 1997.

Data from the 1989 and 1994 censuses and the 1997 employment survey (NIS) show robust growth in employment opportunities in Tunisia, averaging 3 percent a year. This record of employment generation is very encouraging, especially in comparison with the previous year, when employment grew at 2 percent on average. Job creation, however, slowed during the most recent years, averaging 2.6 percent between 1994 and 1997. The implied income elasticity of employment was also significantly lower, at 0.51 for 1994–1997, compared to 0.63 for 1989–1994. Throughout the period, female employment grew more rapidly than male employment, reducing the unemployment rate for female workers from 21.9 percent in 1989 to 17.44 percent in 1997. This development in female participation is due to the increase in the cost of living, the change of values regarding the role of women in society, and the increase in the number of well-educated women.

Recent labor market studies also reveal that the workforce is becoming more educated. In 1994, about 36 percent of the workforce received secondary or higher education, compared to 28 percent in 1989 and 24 percent in 1984. Nonetheless, 24 percent of the workforce is still unable to read or write (mainly concentrated in agricultural and construction activities). Over 1989–1997, the sectors with the largest annual growth rates were also those with above average improvements in the education levels of their workers. As it becomes more educated, the Tunisian workforce is becoming more productive. The added value per worker increased by 17 percent over 1989–1997.

To increase the flexibility of labor regulations, the labor code was revised in 1994 and again in 1996. As a result, in some sectors, fixed-term contracts and sub-contractual arrangements now account for 90 percent of labor contracts.[2] Although increasing each year, the number of workers laid-off due to the privatization and restructuring of public and private enterprises remains small and has had a negligible impact on labor market developments. In 1996, 3,900 workers were laid off; in 1997, 6,000; and in 1998, 5,100 (World Bank, 2000). Public sector retrenchment was responsible for 2,000 layoffs a year during that period. Studies also find an important proportion of "Black-market workers," who are not declared, and a high turnover rate in Tunisian enterprises (Ben Zakour, 2000).

Recognizing that the country's demographics would make youth unemployment a serious social problem, the government established some youth employment programs to provide jobs and training for young people and students. These programs failed to meet their objectives. They have allowed enterprises to profit from qualified and less expensive employees and they have thereby increased flexibility and precariousness. There are other initiatives destined to helping the unemployed to start their own businesses, especially in agriculture, industry, and service sectors. According to Letaief Azaiez (2000), the

2 Indeed, we indicate that Tunisian labor legislation allows firms to recruit by fixed term contracts and seasonal personnel, and to dismiss them without paying any indemnity at the end of their contracts.

bad choice of beneficiaries, the embezzlement of funds, difficulties in identifying new opportunities for investment, the impossibility of repaying loans, and the failure of some projects led to the failure of these programs.

Education and vocational training

Education has been one of the most important areas of progress in Tunisia over the past few decades. Achievements in education have not only helped reduce poverty, but have also created an increasingly educated and productive workforce. Indeed, Tunisia annually devotes almost a third of its budget and 6 per cent of GDP to education. However, the predominantly public education system was slow in responding to the demand for new skills until the end of the 1980s. As a result, the mixed skill of the workforce remains inadequate for firms' needs (World Bank, 2000). In July 1989, the government launched a major reform of the education system that increased the basic education cycle to nine years and introduced free compulsory education until the age of 16.[3] The reform also aimed at reducing the number of school dropouts. The government has embarked on other large-scale activities in this area, such as the computerization of schools and an overall assessment of the basic education system. As a result of these measures, dropout rates have decreased steadily. For example, for grades 1 to 6, about 48,000 pupils dropped out of school in 1996–1997, compared to 97,000 in 1989–1990. In 2001, there were 4,476 public primary schools, 1,065 public high schools and colleges, and 2.4 million pupils—which constitutes up to 25 percent of the total population.

Education is still heavily influenced by the French system. As in France, there is a great emphasis on passing examinations. The baccalaureat is the examination taken at the end of four years in a secondary school, before being admitted to university. University education has grown rapidly since the 1990s, increasing from 85 establishments (university and high school) (or sixth form college for The UK) in 1993 to 121 in 2001. The number of higher education students rose from 96,101 in 1993 to 226,102 in 2001 (Ministry of Higher Education, 2001).

The Tunisian government is also placing increasing emphasis on vocational training, which fulfils the double objective of educating and preparing workers for a modern job market. There are several institutions dedicated to vocational training, ranging from technical centers to newly established professional centers. The government has recently created a program to rehabilitate vocational training and employment, called "Mise à Niveau de la Formation Professionnelle et de l'Emploi" (MANFOPME), which goes hand-in-hand with the enterprise "mise à niveau program." MANFORME

---

3 The reform introduced a nine-year basic education cycle. Pupils enrolled in this new system reached their 9th grade examinations and those who passed entered the first year of the four-year secondary cycle.

covered 1996–2002 and aimed to make vocational training more useful for enterprise and to link it to a nation-wide employment creation strategy. The program is being implemented in collaboration with vocational training institutions (VTI) and the Ministry of Vocational Training and Employment (MVTE). Moreover, the program introduces specific agreements between MVTE and VTI, and it is run by a committee of representatives from both sides. In 1998, the number of vocational training students was 14,126 (MVTE, 1999).

Despite these reforms, the suppression of the six-year technical education cycle in 1990, the main source of technicians training in various areas such as administration, industry and management, constitutes a great error. For example, according to the Gherzi Organization (1999), the Tunisian textile and clothing industry, the main exporting sector, suffers from a deficit of technicians estimated at 497 in 1998.

Industrial relations

Before the installation of the French protectorate, industrial and professional relations were strictly regulated by corporation norms. During the colonial period, economic and social struggle was confused with the national struggle for independence. All social victory strengthened the action of the political group in its struggle for independence, and each political group came to reinforce the workforce in its struggle to put an end to the harshest forms of exploitation. Once independence had been acquired, Tunisian social policy continued to be characterized by the pursuit of great reforms. However, according to Lamouri (2000), Tunisia has long had incomplete labor legislation.

Labor market negotiations are governed by an extensive set of rules contained in the labor code and in various collective agreements which are negotiated by tripartite committees every three years with the aim of avoiding industrial conflicts.[4] Collective agreements determine, among others things, the level of wages and their growth over the next three years. This policy has succeeded in making labor disputes very rare in recent years, and has been an asset in attracting investments. Tunisian unionism has been characterized by the domination of a single national organization (The Tunisian General Employment Union (UGTT)) that was created on 20 January 1946. This organization represents 30 percent of the Tunisian workforce; 60 percent of members belong to the public sector and 40 percent to the private sector. The UGTT is composed of 7,000 unions distributed throughout the country, of which, 23 are regional unions, 20 are professional federations, 30 are national unions, with the rest being local unions.

4 The committees include representatives of the government, the employer's association and the labor organization.

During French colonial rule, the UGTT played an important role in mobilizing workers to fight for independence. After independence, the UGTT became more an administrative institution than an independent organization of workers, and its leaders have belonged to the government structure and occupied some high functions in the national and regional administration. At the end of the 1970s, the development of the industrial sector—incited by the law of 1972 and destined to encourage direct foreign investment and exports—has led to a more interdependent round-up of workers. This labor population increased the degree of unrest (in 1978 and 1984) and forced the UGTT to put an end to its complicity with the government. There were over 240 strikes in 1979, more than in 2002 (124). Today, Tunisian unionism is undergoing a deep transformation; so while strikes used to be the privileged instrument of the union struggle, the union is now found to be involved in a contractual policy, through periodic negotiations with the employers' association under government control. At the enterprise level, despite social and economic changes, the union still occupies a less important place. Indeed, since 1994, the legislator has left the resolution of collective conflict to the Enterprise Consultative Committee and not to the trade union. This revision of the labor code suffers from three limitations. First, we observe that the number of members (40 permanent employees) of this committee is incompatible with the Tunisian economic structure, composed as it is essentially of small enterprises and a great proportion of fixed-term contracts. Furthermore, this committee is "consultative," therefore how can it sign agreements? Finally, the third limitation concerns the role of the union. Indeed, the collective conflict is between the employer and the union as the single legally chosen institution to defend workers' interests, but it is the committee that negotiates with the employer to solve this conflict.

National socio-cultural factors

Using national socio-cultural factors as a way to understand HRM style can be extremely useful, because even if Tunisia evolves rapidly under the effect of economic liberalization, we can imagine that cultural characteristics are anchored in the population, and will take a certain time to evolve. Economic development will thus be more rapid than cultural evolution (D'Iribarne, 1993). Consequently, it is judicious to study the influence of culture on the functioning of enterprises. We will mainly develop: the respect for age, the hierarchical position, and the system of interpersonal relationships.

The respect for age is important for Tunisians and it is inculcated very early in Tunisian children, who must respect their parents and grandparents. The hierarchical position is also taken into account for the appraisal of individuals. For example, the function of senior management represents a criterion of fundamental power and authority because it creates a position of superior decision-making in the mind of Tunisians. One can thus observe a certain condescension from Tunisian managers with regard to their subordinates. This attitude is strengthened if an important difference of age exists. Indeed, the respect of hierarchy maintains power at the center. The best means for a Tunisian worker to indicate that respects their chief is to accept the totality of that chief's decisions. This means that the subordinate becomes a task executor. They avoid being creative and using initiative, fearing to disrupt a system where ideas circulate from top management to simple workers. In addition, according to Letaief Azaiez (2000), this hierarchy is established not according to the importance of assumed responsibilities or official skills, but according to the tightness of the relations woven with the "owner." As a result, the particular secretary or the chauffeur of the employer often has more influence and weight than the general manager of a department. The respect for age and hierarchy also generates communication problems between the different departments in Tunisian firms. The Tunisian employee demonstrates a commitment to their direct boss, with whom they are in permanent interaction. Conversely, they reject other commitments, even within the same firm. If they follow the instructions of the manager of another department, they feel that they are breaking the bond which links them to their direct chief. Consequently, the Tunisian employee has difficulty integrating a quality task force team that is horizontally organized, for example.

In Tunisian organizations, networks of individual relations have great importance. These relationships are especially based on family relations, but other relationships exist, for example the village or the industrial group. Tunisian entrepreneurs resort to the help of friends to repair a machine or to find a replacement piece. The Tunisian family is very extended; relatives can live with their oldest son and married couples can live with their parents. It is also necessary to note that family relations are very solid. This solidarity is tested in different events: family members accept responsibility for a wide range of relatives for financial support, job seeking, and other support. This relation system functions thanks to an obligation of reciprocity. In the professional framework, the person who finds a job for someone expects some reciprocity from the candidate. For example, Tunisian managers may obtain a substantial gift from the person they recruit.

In addition, there is a high sense of collectivism in Tunisia, which views workers largely in terms of the group to which they belong. This supremacy of the group over the individual discourages the establishment of individualized reward systems based on individual performance, and considers creativity and initiative an opposition to the group. These particular socio-culture factors have had disastrous effects on HRM, on employee attitudes at work, and on their productivity, and have introduced serious distortions in the functioning of the labor market. Indeed, job allocation is decided by a complex web of social connections where the employee is not an isolated individual but part of a collective grouping.

Tunisian management style

The Tunisian entrepreneur is essentially enclosed, frequently in a family SME which supposes a direct, personalized, and autocratic management style (Denieuil, 1992). Many founder-owners have handed over the enterprise to the eldest son in the family because of their belief that the enterprise can be managed more effectively with the loyalty of and the hierarchy within the family. In most cases, the employers assume all the functions in the firm alone or with family members (Dhaoui, 1996). Their subordinates do not take any decisions without authorization from the summit of the hierarchical pyramid, even routine and simple decisions. According to Zghal (1987), these problems of power centralization, standardization, and the high degree of specialization reduce the chances of learning by doing and destroy the diffusion of acquired knowledge in Tunisian enterprises. Dhaoui (1996) also finds that Tunisian enterprises do not have flowcharts or procedures manuals defining objectives, tasks, and specifying responsibilities. This absence of formal procedures creates many difficulties for the Tunisian management style. Information is always considered to be confidential, so Tunisian enterprises, notably the small ones, sometimes have no structure which would allow information to circulate. This lack of information creates no incentive for employees to provide their best effort, and consequently it causes a climate of antagonism.

Development of HRM practices

The Western system of HRM in Tunisian organizations has evolved from the systems implemented by the French colonial administration; traditional personnel management, however, existed in some form during both the colonial and post-colonial periods (Zghal, 2000). We have divided the development process of HRM in Tunisia into three stages.

Stage 1: French colonial administration

In this period, the French colonial administration created political and economic conditions that would guarantee an abundant workforce in order to introduce some industries into Tunisia. These conditions aimed at expropriating the farmers, deteriorating artisans' corporations by encouraging the consumption of industrial products and, consequently, impoverishing farmers and the middle class. This policy, associated with the encouragement of the immigration of foreign qualified workers (essentially from Italy), succeeded in satisfying the personnel needs of colonial industry in cities. A fundamental HRM problem, namely "to attract and retain workers," was posed, particularly in mines. Miners considered the work in mines as an extra activity that they neglected easily when the crop was good. So, those in control of the mines developed a management system aiming to ensure the stability of the personnel by combining incentive systems such as worker loans, premiums for assiduity, and the gratuitous distribution of land in exchange for a number of days of work per year. Where there was training, it was mainly informal (on-the-job training), only foreign workers benefiting from off-the-job external training, performance appraisal, and career planning.

Stage 2: 1956–1995

The second stage began after independence and lasted until the mid-1990s. The departure of foreign employees and the processes of "Tunisification" propelled the HR function to the forefront in the early 1950s. The new government's objective was to replace the foreign staff with Tunisians in both the private and public sectors. This policy contributed to the emergence of new senior managers responsible for the correct functioning of numerous organizations created by the State. These managers were appointed according to their allegiance to the political group and not for their managerial skills. Consequently, their major concern was to take advantage of the situation and to offer a "payback" to specific groups and individuals who had previously provided support. This led to significant departures from stated policies regarding recruitment, promotions, and reward allocations. It is for these reasons, according to Letaief Azaiez (2000), that an important public sector exists today. Thus, the image of the personnel function suffered as the managers were incapable of running it competently.

The personnel function gained more importance in organizations in the mid-1960s and 1970s as a result of several events: the enactment of the labor code in 1966, the growth of the number of employees, the increasing importance of the role of the UGTT as a social partner, the recrudescence of work conflicts, and the need to find a workforce adapted to industry (Zghal, 2000). However, during this period, the role of personnel managers was to do some administrative, tasks according to an essentially accounting, administrative and judicial logic. The profile of the person who directed this function corresponded entirely to the marginality of this service. They had no professional training in HRM. Indeed, according to Boukhris-Elmajdi (1998), the personnel function was restricted to a secretary or to the accountant who counted days of presence and absenteeism in order to prepare wages. On the other hand, the hierarchy took the important decisions concerning, for example, recruitment or training. This administrative role or the contract administrators' idea of the personnel managers' role continued to dominate in the majority of public and private Tunisian organizations during the 1980s, especially with the signature, on 7 November 1988, of a national pact between the Ben Ali government and unions, and the installation of a contractual policy (Zghal, 1998). This national pact linked development to the necessity to overcome conflicts and to reconcile the different social partners. It clearly mentions the involvement of employees and employers to work towards free negotiation, with the result that each part "accepts with conviction necessary sacrifices." The evocation of the word "sacrifice" makes reference to the serious social and economic crisis which occurred in the 1980s.

In terms of recruitment, the decision to hire a candidate was usually made by the top management and the selection was based on personal connections and academic background. Although most enterprises used familiar procedures of recruitment and selection such as job advertising, interviews, and testing candidates, many vacancies were reserved for friends, family, and customers. According to Denieuil (1992), an employer said, "When I recruit, I must know the name of the candidate, his father and his mother." Thus, there have been many cases of vacancies being filled before they were advertised, recruitments being realised even if they were in excess, or if the candidate occupied a non-existent job or lacked the skill demanded. Consequently, this lack of objectivity in recruitment and selection affected job analysis and human resource planning. With the exception of a few enterprises in the private sector, job analysis and human resource planning were generally not considered important in organizations. According to Letaief Azaiez (2000), as the top management employees of public enterprises are always changing, we witness the constitution of different clans in the personnel composition of these organizations (i.e. each top manager recruits from among their family or friends).

There were many training programs in Tunisia but most of the training activities actually fell within two major programs. The first encouraged training through a mechanism of tax rebates for eligible firms that had to pay a vocational training tax along with social security. Manufacturing firms were to pay 1 percent of total salaries, and others 2 percent. Any eligible firm obtained a rebate whenever it spent on training its employees, (and proved that it did) up to the limit of its own contribution. Therefore, there were no subsidies; it was meant to be an obligatory mechanism. The Tunisian employer sees training as a cost rather than an investment. Budgets for training are very limited and there is a lack of awareness of the importance of continuous training. Only 1,000 firms used this system, compared to approximately 10,000 eligible firms. Noticing that the smallest firms hardly conducted any training, the Tunisian government introduced the second major program designed exclusively for SMEs. In this case, training activities were strongly subsidized when approved, but the number of participants was still rather small: less than 1,000 compared to tens of thousands of SMEs operating in the country.

According to Ben Zakour (2000) and Boukhris Elmajdi (2000), in most cases training was mainly informal, on-the-job and without well structured internal training programs. It consisted of learning when a new worker observed a more senior machine operator or the line manager. In this case, a new worker benefited from the insight and experience of older workers, but the program resulted in at least two potential problems: this process also transferred personal habits, some of which may be undesirable or inefficient, and merely imitating operations without any theoretical foundation reduced the person's capacity to formulate creative solutions to unexpected situations.

The wage policy applied in Tunisia since 1973 has essentially aimed at increasing the minimum wage and improving the pay of less skilled workers, who constitute the basis of the trade unions. This wage policy, which predominated in Tunisia until the mid-1980s, has allowed the development of premiums, which are generally granted according to no clearly defined rules. The consequence of these developments is that, for political reasons (i.e. complicity between government and trade unions) less skilled workers, a large category of workers, benefit from a wage abnormally superior to the wage rate negotiated in the sector. Conversely, the wages of skilled workers, a small category, are low. As a result, firms are obliged to use illegal processes to recruit skilled workers, such as the attribution of fictitious functional jobs and the multiplication of premiums to preserve them. To counterbalance the excessive wage growth of the first half of the 1980s, the wage policy adopted after the SAP has opted for a slowing of wage increases and for a reconciliation of improvement in purchasing power and national performance. However, the wage structure remains very rigid because it prevents a close link between base wage and bonuses for in-company performance. It discourages workers and prevents them from improving their skills. Indeed, for the same job, we can observe that the wage is not the same for two workers; the longest-serving has a higher wage than the new recruit even if the latter makes more effort than the former. Wages, therefore, do not reward individual performance. Furthermore, it is necessary to note that the applicable wages in Tunisia are those annexed to sectoral collective agreements (Belhareth and Hergli, 2000). These agreements apply wage increases to all firms in the sector without taking their situation into account. To adapt the wage structure to the firm's situation, social partners can establish a collective agreement with the firm. However, this remains influenced by either the absence of trade unions in the majority of Tunisian firms or by their complicity with the employer (Zghal, 1998; Lamouri, 2000).

Boukhris Elmajdi (2000) finds that only a few enterprises can rationally appraise their employees because they use appraisal formalities conceived by collective agreements. These firms can thus determine skills lacking for each employee as compared to their job. They can also determine their training needs according to these insufficiencies. Other enterprises annually make a global evaluation of their personnel according to vague qualitative and quantitative criteria such as absenteeism. Thus, performance appraisal poses a major problem in Tunisian firms because it takes into account the respect of hierarchy and not real performance as evaluation criteria. Indeed, in such a system, the good employee is the one who respects their superior, not the one who executes their tasks correctly. Difficulties of evaluation, therefore, simultaneously imply both reward and sanction problems for employees.

As a result, some forms of recruitment and promotion practiced in Tunisian firms introduce important modifications in the functioning of the labor market, by creating a parallel market where recruitment is realized by co-option from relatives and friends. Similarly, the firms, especially public ones, have become a real social institution: recruitment beyond needs and without planning, remuneration unrelated to output or productivity, and vertical and horizontal promotion related to seniority that often does not take into consideration either competence or skills (Letaief Azaiez, 2000). This particular design of work relationships in the country and the behavior of managers has had disastrous effects on employee attitudes to work and on their productivity, and has introduced serious distortions in the functioning of the labor market. Indeed, disenchantment and frustration have been widespread within enterprises, where there is bitterness and resentment towards owners and much indifference with regard to the future of the organization. Workers prefer to reserve all their energy for other jobs outside working hours, and sometimes even during working hours using the equipment of the firms that employ them. Thus, wages gradually lost their economic character to be conceived as a simple "recognition of presence."

Stage 3: Post-1995

The transition from what may be described as "traditional" personnel management to HRM was the result of particular environmental challenges faced by Tunisian organizations from the mid-1990s (see Table 10.1). It is now commonly accepted in Tunisia that human resources are an important source of competitive advantage, so past human resource practices must change in some way if survival is to be ensured.

Tunisian studies conducted by Belhareth and Hergli (1997) and Yagoubi (2001) show that the human resource function is developing increasingly in Tunisian organizations and some human resource departments are even involved in the formulation of business strategies. In this respect, personnel managers are changing their role from personnel administration to personnel mobilization through development of competence and motivation. More and more Tunisian organizations are creating a separate HRM department. These departments have begun with job analysis and job standardization in order to clearly define the activities performed by a worker, and to eliminate superfluous activities. Consequently, job analysis is misused in the name of downsizing.

Tunisian enterprises currently use a selective staffing practice where "selective" can be thought of as two distinct search processes: extensive search (variety of recruiting sources) and intensive search (via interviews and tests). With the converging forces of more flexible labor legislation and the diffusion of new manufacturing practices, firms are becoming more selective in their hiring criteria. Consequently, the workforce profile has considerably changed. Today, enterprises prefer to recruit young people with the highest skills, without professional experience, but with the capacity to collaborate and to work in teams.

Table 10.1 Environmental challenges faced by Tunisian organizations in the mid-1990s

Economic	*Cultural*	*Labor market*	*Political*
Economic liberalization	Individualism	High unemployment	Market mechanism
Industrial restructuring	Self-help	Flexibility	Privatization
		Dual-labor market	Unions weakened

There has been a significant increase in the level of well-structured training programs in order to improve professional skills. Tunisian firms today invest more in "comprehensive" training efforts, thanks to subsidies offered to enterprises in the framework of the industrial restructuring program and governmental programs designed exclusively for SMEs. In particular, training comprehensiveness seems to take two primary forms: intensity and scope. Training intensity includes such things as the percentage of employees who attend training programs and the amount of money spent on training. Training scope focuses on skill variety in training efforts. There are also indications of a movement towards performance-based wages and promotion, introducing incentive systems such as profit sharing, the diversification of performance appraisal methods, and the introduction of performance-based factors. Tunisian firms have also opted for a flexible work organization, which allows them to rapidly adjust to fluctuations in demand and products. This flexibility has been concretized through the installation of teams, linking workers of different services and hierarchical levels, as well as through the reduction of the number of hierarchical levels and the number of managerial and supervisory staff. Workers in each of the teams are cross-trained to perform a series of different tasks within the team.

Despite these changes, studies show that HR managers do not have very high-level qualifications and the majority of them are not specialists in HRM (Belhareth and Hergli, 1997). In most Tunisian organizations, the final decision concerning HRM practices is still made by top management. In addition, despite the organization of the work into teams, the cycle of tasks remains standardized and repetitive, with little if any opportunity for individual workers to have input into variations on the design of the job task. The hierarchy occupies an essential role concerning distribution of tasks between operators. The new technology enables managers to control their workforce more subtly in ways that mask discipline under the cloak of microelectronic rationality. This raises the question of knowledge diffusion (Nordman, 2001); if workers identify job losses and disadvantages with the restructuring program, then they are likely to resist the program itself. Consequently, the rates of turnover and absenteeism are high in Tunisia. For example, Meddeb (1999) argues that absenteeism is at the rate of approximately 25 percent within Tunisian firms. Boukhris Elmajdi (2000) also estimates a turnover rate of 13 percent. This mobility is essentially spontaneous, especially in small enterprises where 87 percent of departures are voluntary. Ferguene and Hsaini (1998) also show a degradation of work conditions, with excessive dismissals, delay of wages payment, and no respect for legal working hours.

Conclusion

This chapter has argued that economic and socio-cultural factors and industrials relations have had a significant impact on the Tunisian HR function in the past and will continue to do so in the future. The chapter has allowed also to observe the tendency, slow but positive, of organizations towards a better recognition of their HRM. Unfortunately, many organizations are still progressing fairly slowly in this area. Both trade union and labor legislation is the most serious hindrance in this regard. However, if Tunisian organizations want to compete with their foreign counterparts, there is a strong need for HR managers to seriously emphasize a number of issues. For instance, clear and simple employment regulations should be introduced to change the less productive work culture to a more productive one. There is also a need for competent managers who understand, develop, and implement adequate employment policies.

References

Belhareth, M. and Hergli, M. (1997) *The impact of external competition on firms' human resource strategies: The case of Tunisia*, Tunis: ARFORGHE.

Belhareth, M. and Hergli, M. (2000) *The adaptation of the Tunisian labor market to the new economic context*, Tunis: Centre de Publication Universitaire.

Ben Zakour, A. (2000) "Tunisian small and medium size enterprises in the storm of internationalization," paper presented at the conference on Globalisation and Development, 9 June, Paris, IRD.

Boukhris-Elmajdi, A. (1998) "Textile: From national performance toward international competitiveness by the involvement of human capital," *Les Cahiers de l'ISCAE* 1: 22–41.

Boukhris-Elmajdi, A. (2000) "Human resources development: From training to employment in Tunisia," unpublished Ph.D. Thesis, University of Paris 1.

Denieuil, P.N. (1992) *The entrepreneurs of development: Search on the Tunisian ethno-industrialization, the dynamic of Sfax*, Paris: L'Harmattan.

Denieuil, P.N. and B'Chir, A. (1996) "Tunisian SME," *Annuaire de l'Afrique du Nord* 35: 181–193.

Dhaoui, M.L. (1996) *Restructuring program and industrial firms' competitiveness in Tunisia*, Tunisia: Arabesques.

D'Iribarne, I. (1993) *The logic of honor*, Paris: Seuil.

Ferguene, A. and Hsaini, A. (1998) "Flexible productive organization and the dynamic of local industrialization: The supple specialization system of El-Jem (Tunisia)," *Revue de Tiers Monde* 39 (156): 905–921.

Gherzi Organization (1999) "Strategic study of Tunisian textile sector," working paper, Zûrich: Gherzi Organization.

Hannachi, S. (1991) "Portrait and tendency of Tunisian industry," working paper, Tunis: Industry Promotion Agency.

Lamouri, H. (2000) "Tunisian Labour Regulation," working paper, National Institute of Labor and Social Studies.

Letaief Azaiez, T. (2000) *Tunisia: political changes and employment (1956–1996)*, Paris: L'Harmattan.

Meddeb, R. (1999) "Textile and clothing industry in Tunisia: firm owners' needs and women's working conditions in the SME," working paper, 136, Geneva: ILO.

Ministry of Higher Education (2001) Online: www.ins.nat.tn

MVTE (1999) *Employment conjuncture*, no. 12.

NIS (1998) *Enterprises repertory*.

Nordman, C. (2001) "Human capital development and knowledge diffusion within enterprise: Econometrics analysis of Tunisian and Moroccan data," unpublished Ph.D. Thesis, University of Paris1.

World Bank (2000) *Republic of Tunisia: Social and structural review 2000*, Washington, DC: World Bank.

Yagoubi, M. (2001) "The behavior of Tunisian manufacturing firms adhered to the IRP under the New Economic Model," in O. Alphonso (ed.) *Advancing knowledge development in African business*, Proceedings of a conference held on 4–7 April 2001 at Saint Joseph's University and Erivan K. Haub School of Business.

Zghal, R. (1987) "Cultural conditions of technology production," *Travail et Développement* 9.

Zghal, R. (1998) "New Orientations of the Tunisian trade union," in The French Documentation (ed.) *Arabic world Maghreb-Machrek*, 162, Paris.

Zghal, R. (2000) *Human resource management*, Tunis: Centre de Publication Universitaire.

11 HRM in Libya

ABDOULHAKEM ALMHDIE AND
STEPHEN M. NYAMBEGERA

Introduction

Globalization of the world economy and marketplace has necessitated that HRM interventions in other contexts be investigated (see, for example, Roberts and Boyacigiller, 1984; Adler and Boyacigiller, 1995) due to differences in context. Human resource management is now not a new concept, as it has been over 20 years since it first became a major area of interest in the 1980s. The concept attracted extensive discussions by both academia and practitioners (e.g. Legge, 1989; Guest, 1989; Pfeffer, 1994). The discussion indicate that efficient management of human resources enables an organization to have a competitive advantage (Pfeffer, 1994; Poole and Jenkins, 1996). However, researchers have acknowledged that one of the main challenges organizations face is that of managing this resource because of the constraints by national and cultural variations (e.g. Trompenaars, 1993; Adler and Boyacigiller, 1995; Banutu-Gomez, 2002). The importance of HRM was first recognized in the West but is now spreading globally, although the focus of research has been more on developed rather than developing economies. The reason for HRM research being limited to developed economies is well captured by Pieper (1990). He argues that there is not much similarity between developed and developing countries because such economies are more concerned with survival issues than implementing complex human resource practices. This chapter examines the national influence, especially the political, cultural, and religious dimensions, on HRM policy practice in Libya. In order to appreciate the contextual influences of HRM in Libya, a brief historical overview of the country is necessary.

Libya attained independence from Italy on 24 December 1951. Peters (1982) points out that it is during this period that Libya came into existence, when three provinces of Tripolitania, Fezzan, and Cyrenaica were amalgamated to form the state of Libya. Although prominent in the Arab world, Libya is not, in many aspects, an Arab indigenous state because of its history (Birks and Sinclair, 1980). The Arab world is defined as a group of 22 countries sharing a common language and culture, as well as a set of values. These countries include Algeria, Bahrain, Djibouti, Egypt, Iraq, Jordan, Kuwait,

Lebanon, Libya, Morocco, Mauritania, Oman, Palestine, Qatar, Saudi Arabia, Somalia, Sudan, Syria, Tunisia, United Arab Emirates (UAE), Western Sahara, and Yemen (Krieger, 1993). Libya has been occupied by several foreign powers, for example Phoenicians, Greeks, and Arabs, among others (Bruce, 1998). Before the Arab invasion in the seventh century, Berbers mostly inhabited the land we now know as Libya, later renamed the Socialist People's Libyan Arab Jamahiriya. Descendants of the original inhabitants of North Africa, the Berbers, resisted the Arabs at first but eventually converted to Islam and adopted Arabic as their language. Berbers are found throughout North Africa, with the largest concentrations in Morocco and Algeria (Wright, 1982). However, six ethnic categories are still present in Libya, and most of the language distinctions, which characterized them in the past, still persist. Libya occupies a land area of 1,759,540 km^2, bordered by the Mediterranean Sea in the north, Chad and Niger in the south, Egypt and Northern Sudan in the east, and Tunisia and Southern Algeria in the west. The country has a population of 5,368,585 (July 2002 estimates) and its main religion is Islam, which is professed by 99 percent of the people. Arabic is the national and official language, with English used as a second language.

After independence, the country was ruled by a monarchy until 1969. On 1 September, 1969, in a daring coup d'état, a group of about 70 young army officers and enlisted men seized control of the government and, in a stroke, abolished the Libyan monarchy. Colonel Muammar Abu al-Qadhafi took over as leader of the Revolutionary Command Council (RCC) (Blundy and Lycett, 1988). At the onset of RCC rule, Qadhafi and his associates insisted that their government would not depend on individual leadership, but rather on collegial decision making. A broad-based political party, the Arab Socialist Union (ASU), was created in 1971 and was modelled after Egypt's Arab Socialist Union. Its intent was to raise the political consciousness of Libyans and to aid the RCC in formulating public policy through debate in open forums. All other political parties were proscribed. Trade unions were incorporated into the ASU and strikes were forbidden. Qadhafi espoused his own political system—a combination of socialism and Islam, which he called the Third International Theory. Viewing himself as a revolutionary leader, he used oil funds during the 1970s and 1980s to promote his ideology outside Libya to hasten the end of Marxism and capitalism (CIA, *World Factbook*, 2002). The USA and Western Europe saw Libya as a sympathizer of international terrorism. The USA, in particular, viewed Libya's diplomatic and material support for what Tripoli called "liberation movements" as aid and ideological support for international terrorism. In general, after the early 1970s, relations between the two countries went from bad to worse. Qadhafi opposed US diplomatic initiatives and military presence in the Middle East. By the 1980s, Libya was a country embroiled in controversy. Consequently, the Security Council, under its Resolutions No. 748 of 1992 and No. 883 of 1993, imposed sanctions on Libya, which were partially lifted in 1999. It is reported that by 1997 the sanctions resulted in financial losses to Libya estimated at more than US$23 billion (Bait Elmal, 1997).

The context of resource management

As mentioned earlier, globalization of the world economy and marketplace has necessitated that HRM interventions in other contexts be investigated due to contextual differences. In Europe, for example, researchers have attributed failures of HRM prescriptions to the fact that they reflect US values and were just "grafted" into management systems instead of being allowed to take "root" (e.g. Guest, 1990; Sparrow and Hiltrop, 1994). In the case of countries that identify with the Arab world, studies have focused on the Middle East (e.g. Al-Shamali and Denton, 2000; Weir, 2000), ignoring North African countries such as Libya, Algeria, Western Sahara, Tunisia, and so forth.

Human resource management as a concept is said to have its origins in the USA, hence its transferability across nations is questionable (e.g. Jaeger, 1990; Adler, 1997; Harvey, 2002). Contextual implications on HRM practice in Libya could be of interest to practitioners and multinational organizations that want to invest in this economy. The understanding of current policy practice could help managers realign their practices to fit Libyan preferences. Organizations worldwide are faced with major challenges because of globalization that has not spared Arab businesses (Al-Shamali and Denton, 2000). Elgamal (2000) points out that Arab management faces an ever-increasing challenge to keep up with management in developed countries due to globalization. Researchers argue for context-based models of management in the Arab world because of the serious challenges posed by falling crude oil prices and the extension of their businesses into petrochemical industries (e.g. Elgamal, 2000; Weir, 2000). It is observed, for example, that Qadhafi's brand of politics has serious implications on employee management. His philosophy, that combines socialism and Islam, is unique and touches on every aspect of Libyans' lives. We briefly examine how this leader's philosophies and brand of politics have influenced Libya's society and economy.

Qadhafi's influence on Libyan society and economy

The remaking of Libyan society that Qadhafi envisioned and to which he devoted his energies after the early 1970s, began in 1973 with the so-called cultural or popular revolution (Wright, 1982). The revolution was designed to combat bureaucratic inefficiency, lack of public interest and participation in the sub-national governmental system, and problems with national political coordination. In an attempt to instil revolutionary fervor into his compatriots and to involve large numbers of them in political affairs, Qadhafi urged them to challenge traditional authority and to take over and run government organs themselves. The instrument for doing this was the "people's committees." People's committees were established in such widely divergent organizations as universities, private business firms, government bureaucracies, and the broadcast media, consequently having serious implications on the management of employees (Wright, 1982). In the scope of their administrative and regulatory tasks and the method of their members' selection, the people's committees embodied the concept of direct democracy that Qadhafi propounded in the first volume of *The Green Book*, which appeared in 1976. The same concept lay behind proposals to create a new political structure composed of "people's congresses." The centerpiece of the new system was the General People's Congress (GPC). All adults had the right and duty to participate in the deliberation of their local Basic People's Congress (BPC), whose decisions were passed to the GPC for consideration and implementation into national policy. Continuing to revamp Libya's political and administrative structures, Qadhafi introduced yet another element into the body politic. Beginning in 1977, "revolutionary commitees" were organized and assigned the task of "absolute revolutionary" supervision of the people's power.

Reviving the economy was parallel with the attempt to remould political and social institutions. Until the late 1970s, Libya's economy was mixed, with a large role for private enterprises except in the fields of oil production and distribution, banking, and insurance. According to Volume Two of Qadhafi's *Green Book*, however, which appeared in 1978, private retail trade, rent, and wages were forms of "exploitation" that should be abolished. Instead, workers' self-management committees and profit participation partnerships were to function in private and public enterprises. A property law was passed that forbade ownership of more than one private dwelling and Libyan workers took control of a large number of companies, turning them into state-run enterprises. State-owned "supermarkets" replaced retail and wholesale trading operations, where Libyans could purchase whatever they needed at low prices. This socialist orientation has implications for HRM policy practice in Libyan organizations, as discussed below.

Clearly, Libya's economy is socialist oriented, depending primarily upon revenues from the oil sector, which contributes practically all export earnings and about one-quarter of GDP. These oil revenues and a small population give Libya one of the highest per capita GDPs in Africa (GDP per capita is US$7,600, 2001 estimate). However, according to the year 2000 estimates, the country has an unemployment rate of 30 percent. Import restrictions and inefficient resource allocation have led to periodic shortages of basic goods and foodstuffs. Climatic conditions and poor soils severely limit agricultural output, and Libya imports about 75 percent of its food (CIA, *World Factbook*, 2002). The non-oil manufacturing and construction sectors, which account for about 20 percent of GDP, have expanded from processing mostly agricultural products to include the production of petrochemicals, iron, steel, and aluminum. Libya has an estimated labor force of 1.5 million (2000 estimate) (CIA, *World Factbook*, 2002).

The influence of culture and Islam on HRM

Culture is represented as a set of common beliefs, values and norms, theories of behavior, or mental programs that are shared by people living in a society (Hofstede, 1980; Harris and Moran, 1999). Since the 1960s, a great number of studies have been undertaken with a view to unravelling the influence of culture in impacting management practice (e.g. Haire *et al.*, 1966; Hofstede, 1980; Trompenaars, 1993). The success of the Pacific Rim countries made the issue even more central as awareness of culture's influence on HRM seemed to play a role in their success story.

Culture in the Arab world is closely linked to religion, as it relates to all aspects of life among Muslims. However, we are aware that Islamic beliefs and culture are quite diverse due to historical, economic, and social differences (e.g. Muna, 1980). Elgamal (2000) argues that key sources of Arab managerial conceptualization and practices are the Islamic religion, Arab culture, the Westernization effect, and the political, economic, and social systems. The emphasis on the effects of the Islamic religion and Arab culture is consistent with a body of research that underscores the importance of culture (e.g. Wright, 1981; Tayeb, 1996).

Studies have indicated that Arab countries exhibit higher levels of loyalty toward community (or collectivistic orientation), power distance, paternalism, femininity, uncertainty avoidance, fatalism, and context dependence (e.g. Hofstede, 1991; Harris and Moran, 1999). These cultural orientations manifest themselves in organizations in a number of ways. Individuals who, in these societies, maintain the tradition of extended family and joint family systems, feel a strong sense of loyalty to their families and communities. The extended family, clan, tribe, village, and Islam play a major role in community life and interpersonal relationships, which is a common practice in Africa. As a result, organizations are managed by fulfilling personal obligations toward in-group members rather than meeting organizational needs (Hayajenh *et al.*, 1994). In-group membership is often based on ethnicity, family, or religion. Hofstede (1980) reported that Arab countries rank highly in their emphasis on the importance of strong kinship and interpersonal networks. For example, family ties, sectarianism, and ideological affiliation, rather than academic qualifications, significantly affect managers' recruitment and promotion decisions. Work goals are accomplished by individuals and work teams primarily because of personalized relations with the supervisor, subordinates, and peers. The feature of high power distance stems from the rigid and hierarchical structure of social institutions. Hofstede (1980) argues that organizations in such societies would tend to have more levels of hierarchy, a higher proportion of supervisory personnel, and more centralized decision-making. Status and power would serve as motivators, and leaders would be revered or obeyed unquestioningly even if their instructions were deemed to be burdensome by subordinates.

The combined effect of high community loyalty and high power distance manifests itself in paternalism in managing the human resource. Paternalism characterizes the supervisor–subordinate relationship within the organization. Supervisors in positions of authority assume the role of a parent and consider it an obligation to provide support and protection to subordinates under their care. Subordinates, in turn, reciprocate such care, support, and protection by showing loyalty, deference, and compliance to the supervisors. Subordinates show loyalty and respect to their supervisors in the same way children do to their parents and students do to their teachers. People have been socialized to interact only with those within their age groups, and not to associate closely with their elders. Therefore, respect for age features prominently in the behavior of Libyan society and organizations. Abdul-Khalik (1984) posits that Arab managers often concentrate on seniority, rather than merit, in most of their decisions that affect employee relations. Moreover, most managerial practices in Libya result directly from the belief of in-group embeddedness and hierarchy. For example, the power of decision-making is largely in the hands of top management and subordinates prefer seeking guidance, direction, affection, and patronage from their superiors in all matters.

Libyans place much emphasis on masculinity, mediated by the requirement to have good working relationships with one's direct superior, and to work with people who cooperate well, to live in an area appropriate to one's self image, and to have employment security. This is evident from the fact that there are strong gender role distinctions and women's work is identifiable as lying within the family domain. By the 1980s, however, modifications in the traditional relationships between sexes were becoming evident, and important changes were appearing in the traditional role of women. The considerable number of girls in secondary school and the ability of young women to find modern sector jobs indicate the extent to which the Libyan community is changing. The high context dependency characteristic of Arab countries implies that people in these countries have a tendency to utilize salient contextual experiences to justify their behavior.

Current trends in HRM

The selection process

Libyan law defines selection as the process and procedures which are carried out by organizations for offering a job to a person who has passed all the legal requirements requested by an employer. This aspect of HRM has been subject to extensive research, most probably because it is the beginning of human resource entry into the organization. For a long time now, organizational psychologists have tried to find the means by which organizations can choose the best person who fits the job in question. Ferris *et al.* (1999) agree that a challenge is created by a focus on fit as a staffing criterion because it tends not to be well defined and it can be manipulated, managed, and shaped by the conscious efforts of applicants and employees. Several techniques have been developed or improved, i.e. the interview, psychological testing, application blank, and reference checks. In most cases, especially in Arab countries, the selection interview is the main technique used during this process. Guion and Gibson (1988) reported that, the world over, the interview is widely used in spite of repeated discoursing summaries of unreliability and questionable validity. In Libya, reliance is on personal contacts and getting people from the right social origins to fill major positions. Libya uses both internal and external sources to locate employees.

In Libyan organizations, this activity is mainly the responsibility of the HR department in liaison with the needy department or section. Before 1998, vacant positions were filled either internally or externally through a government body called the General Workforce Corporation (GWC). The GWC used to place advertisements nationally or internationally via the overseas branches of the companies in Europe, Canada, and the Far East. The notion of internal selection, whereby organizations consider their own employees, is not the sense in which the term is used here. Internal selection is normally aimed at recruiting domestic employees, especially from the Libyan labor market. It connotes national selection and not necessarily from the same company. Before the abolition of the GWC in 1998, the process followed was that the HR department of the affected organization provided each department's needs for new employees. The final decision was normally left to the concerned organization, though coordination was by the GWC. The human resource departments of most companies now carry out the selection responsibility. Also, external selection, as used here, refers to recruiting and selecting people internationally, especially when particular skills are not available within the Libyan labor market. Depending on the job specifications, the decision to select externally will be made by the company. Libyan industrial companies, like those in many other developing countries, are owned, managed and supervised by government institutions. However, Libya's case is unique in the sense that the concept of using "people's Committees," urged by Qadhafi, impacts the running of most organizations (Wright, 1982). Earlier on in this chapter, it was indicated that Qadhafi's brand of management required that workers' self-management committees and profit participation partnerships function in private and public enterprises. The government has substantial influence on most companies, which dictates that those who are well connected have the majority of the top jobs. As pointed out earlier, interpersonal relationships, family ties, sectarianism, and ideological affiliation are important factors in recruitment and promotion decisions. In most developing countries patronage is evident almost everywhere and group-oriented society politicians make it their duty to reward those who are loyal to the ruling elite. This fact influences selection decisions in most organizations in Libya.

It is pertinent to argue that societal values influence Libyan managers' approach to the selection process. For example, since Libyans are reported to exhibit high masculinity and adhere to Islamic ethos (e.g. Wright, 1982), women are not normally selected for high-level executive jobs. Since masculine cultures see work achievement as a major life goal, Libyans place more reliance on abstract criteria directly created in the workplace, such as procedures. Further, because Libya is a paternalistic society, selection might be made on the basis of patronage and associations. Such societies are more collectivist and those who are in high places may want to help those that belong to the same clan or ethnic group. Earlier, it was pointed out that supervisors in positions of authority assume the role of parent and consider it their obligation to provide support and protection to subordinates under their care. Consequently, subordinates reciprocate such care, support, and protection by showing loyalty, deference, and compliance to the supervisor. Since the power of decision-making is vested in the hands of top management, it is most likely that in Libya the same top brass makes selection decisions. In Libya, supervisors make a decision, which gains their superiors' approval. At the same time, they do not seek directly the boss's assistance, since this could imply a lack of deference. However, they do rely more upon formal rules, informal norms, and the guidance of peers. For most organizations Islam is a way of life, hence religion is a major consideration in selecting those who might fit into the organization's culture. Because Libya is a collectivist country, with rich social networks, most managers are aware of those potential personnel and where they can be found. Often the manager will consult with the boss and colleagues, who, being part of the same network, will have informed opinions about the prospective candidate. The purpose of such consultation will be to test indirectly whether there is consensus on the desirability of the prospective candidate prior to the formal selection process. Such groundwork provides a guarantee of continued smooth functioning of the team even after the induction of the new subordinate.

Performance appraisal

After selection there soon arises the need to evaluate or appraise the employee's work performance to satisfy the organization's effort. This is aimed at monitoring and improving effectiveness and to give the employee feedback about how well he or she is doing. According to U.S. management books and manuals, performance appraisal is an objective, rational, and accurate process. However, theory and research has shown that even executives engage in distorting and manipulating appraisals for self-serving and political reasons, consequently losing the intended objectivity (e.g. Longenecker *et al.*, 1990; Cleveland and Murphy, 1992). A common criticism is that this type of boss–employee relationship creates a kind of parent–child relationship; however, given the kind of interpersonal relations in Libyan culture, this is accepted and appreciated.

Performance appraisal problems in Libya are common to all enterprises in general, and industrial enterprises in particular. The process occurs as follows. The performance appraisal form is prepared in consultation with the concerned employee. The performance appraisal form is part of the appraisal system and should be completed at least three months before the employee's contract anniversary date. Each supervisor is responsible for ensuring that his or her subordinate understands the form. Therefore, performance appraisal is the responsibility of the supervisor in consultation with the HR department. The HR director carries out the final approval. This is normally carried out on a yearly basis. The aim is to identify areas of strength or weakness in his or her performance to improve performance and to identify training or development needs. This is in line with the Islamic values identified by Latifi (1997), where consultations at all levels of decision-making are encouraged. However, Muna (1980) reports that while consultation with subordinates occurs in Arab organizations, joint decision-making *per se* is rare. HRM scholars have also identified the importance of the social context of the performance evaluation processes (e.g. Judge and Ferris, 1993). Libyan organizations profess the Islamic faith, hence performance evaluations primarily focus on the total person and all are related to personal characteristics rather than on job performance. Informal control mechanisms are relied upon more. Performance appraisal information is mainly used for personnel decisions and employee feedback. The most frequently used sources of performance information are supervisory ratings and the personnel/HR department. Subordinate ratings are not common in Libya due to cultural factors. Also, peer rating is not common due to the favorable attitudes toward colleagues, which might not allow for reliable and objective information. Latifi (1997) reported that it is culturally acceptable for people in positions of power to treat subordinates kindly, as if their subordinates are their brothers and sisters. This contextual influence tends to render peer appraisals irrelevant. This could be due to the fact that people prefer not to report anything negative about their peers; if they did, it would affect their future within the organization—a reflection of what Cleveland and Murphy (1992) identified as self-serving reasons.

Reward systems

Pay, in the form of wages and salaries, and a wide range of legally required and agreed upon benefits represent the means by which employees are financially rewarded, for joining an organization, providing his or her services, and staying with the organization. Some of the legally required compensations are, for example, social security that will take care of an employee in retirement, whereas agreed compensation may take the form of medical cover and life insurance. Typically, the functions of a reward or compensation system include attraction of persons to seek and accept employment in the organization, retention of employees as members of the organization, and motivation of the behavior or performance desired.

In Libya, the reward system includes promotion, free medical care for employees and their families, housing allowance, payment for high performance, transportation allowance, private transportation for supervisors and executives, and long service awards for those who stay with an organization for five years and above (Agnaia, 1996). In pursuance of Islamic principles, some companies offer their employees interest-free loans for various needs (Wright, 1981). Rewarding employees by promotions at times does not prove to be a very popular way for motivating employees; for example, if the promotion, involves transferring the employee to another branch, away from family or home area.

In a study on Libya it was also found that young Libyans were demotivated because of top management styles (Agnaia, 1996). For instance, it was evident that management is characterized by centralized and pyramidal structures, authoritarian decision-making, ambiguity of authority and responsibility and paternalism. It is plausible to argue that those who were found to be demotivated were young, well educated and most probably exposed to Western education systems. Furthermore, Libya is characterized by instability, ambiguity, and uncertainty following hostility from countries like the U.S.A. due to Libya's foreign policies. Hence, employees feel threatened by such circumstances. Furthermore, companies' operations are extremely sensitive to legislative changes, particularly in areas of remuneration and management structures, which may limit an organization's ability to compensate employees freely.

Training and development

In order for an organization, and by extension the whole nation, to be more independent and self-sufficient in its human resource potential, there is need to train and develop their human resource. This is necessary because it will equip both managers and employees with the necessary abilities to carry out their work. Since Libya attained her independence in 1951, the acquisition of experience and skills in national economic management has not been a continuous or a progressive practice because there have been many discontinuities and lessons which they have had to learn. In the early 1970s, Libya had to compete with wealthy oil companies and other foreign firms for the limited supply of trained people (Farley, 1971). The drive for economic development beginning in this period was impressive. Current trends in organizations call for continuous upgrading of the skills of employees, be they supervisors or subordinates. As technology changes rapidly, aligning employees' skills with such changes is required. More complex equipment and processes boost the need for more highly-skilled workers. Training and development of the workforce is, in any case, seen as a key to having competitive advantage (e.g. Poole and Jenkins, 1996).

In Libya, the main objective of training and development is to meet the required quota of local employees. For example, to achieve the "Libyanization" levels planned for professional, industrial, and administrative jobs, requires that personnel who are lost through attrition be replaced, being technologically advanced, and upgrading employee skills in order for them to qualify for promotions. Libya has recently paid more attention to administration reform. Many management training and development institutions have been established, organizational structures of public sector companies have been reviewed, work procedures have been simplified and a lot of people have been sent abroad, especially to the U.K., in order to gain relevant knowledge and skills.

Training and development have been of great concern to the Libyan government in the pursuit to meet the above objectives. The first engineering college in the country was founded in 1961. The College of Higher Technical Studies was annexed to the Libyan University (now Al-Fateh University) in Tripoli and named the Faculty of Engineering. Also in 1970, the Institute of Petroleum Affairs was founded in the city of Tripoli, mainly to train and develop people with the skills needed by the petroleum industry. The government, in 1981, established the Bright Star University of Technology in the industrial city of Berga. Gannous *et al.* (1989) report that, earlier on in 1968, the National Institute of Public Administration was launched with the assistance of the United Nations, with the express aim of developing management staff in different sectors.

In addition, the petroleum sector sponsors training programs intended to develop company employees' competencies in particular skills.

In spite of the fact that Libya pursued its Libyanization policy with some zeal by legislating in 1955 that any company operating in the petroleum sector must have a good representation of Libyans, the Libyanization policy could not be realized due to lack of qualified people to take over important managerial positions (Ben-Omran and Kreshman, 1984). According to Agnaia (1996), Libyan management practices are not effectively carried out in order to meet required standards due to political and cultural factors. Further, state-owned companies have difficulty in identifying employees' training needs. This state of affairs has led most companies, especially in the private sector, to recruit from other countries to fill the shortfall. However, it is difficult for foreigners to take up jobs in the public sector given the selection requirements imposed by Libya. Elmahdawi (1995) refers to the criteria used to select an individual to join the public sector. The person must hold Libyan nationality, have a good reputation and be well mannered, meet all the conditions of employment, be medically fit for the job, and, if married, be married to a Libyan (with exemptions from the General People's Secretariat), must not have been convicted of any dishonorable acts, and be over 18 years of age.

The responsibility for training and development is now split between education, planning, and treasury (Agnaia, 1996). Consequently, organizations have major difficulties getting the information and finances they require. Moreover, too little effort is made to tie the syllabi to the needs of the economy. This is a problem in most developing economies, as the educational systems were designed or influenced by the former colonial powers. This system is not helpful to the challenges, growth, and opportunities desired for twenty-first century organizations in developing economies (Banutu-Gomez, 2002). The prevailing cultural attitude in these countries influences students to pursue degrees in the arts instead of the technical skills needed in industry. Such a direction in education has created an imbalance in the labor market. The shortage of appropriately trained staff continues to make the returns on investment in the industrial base woefully inadequate. Despite these problems, some managers resist the idea of attending training and development courses, because they see this as an admission of incompetence, with obvious unfavorable consequences for their careers and social status. Furthermore, the Libyan government has reduced the attractiveness of seeking training and development abroad, by cutting the allowance which trainees receive while out of the country, and limiting their local salary until they finish their program. Economic factors also hinder training and development efforts in Libya. Inflation is high and salaries are pegged to organizational performance following United Nations' restrictions on trade with the country. Consequently, cash-starved organizations find training and development an easy area in which to obtain savings. However, such restrictions were removed in 1999 and the economy has improved recording a GDP real growth rate of 3 percent (2001 estimates).

Conclusion

Human resource management practices as exhibited in Libya seem to be at the formative stages as is true in most developing countries, in spite of the country's riches from oil. The practice is heavily influenced by factors such as the socio-political context, religion, and family. These factors play a major role in shaping managerial practice. The socio-cultural structure in Libya has its origins in tribal and kinship relations that constitute the basic institutions, and which shape social values, norms, and behavior. Managers are more concerned with creating social relationships at the workplace than with the job itself. There is a clear indication that environmental factors have a great impact on HRM policy practice in Libya. Qadhafi's brand of politics, for example, engenders participation and involvement of employees in their organizations. Context can also influence the means by which managers perform their tasks and implement HR strategies in the organization, affecting their attitudes toward HR policy practices (Smith *et al.*, 1989). Ferris *et al.* (1999) also recognize that the potential for contextual constraints on the composition of HRM systems poses interesting questions for future research. Consequently, there is a need for researchers to directly investigate the extent to which such factors influence HRM policy practice by the contextual factors and their relationship to each other.

References

Abdul-Khalik, N. (1984) "The bureaucracy in Kuwait," *Journal of the Gulf and Arabian Peninsula Studies* 5 (38): 13–63.

Adler, N.J. (1997) *International Dimensions of Organizational Behavior*, 3rd edition, Cincinnati, OH: South-Western College Publishing.

Adler, N.J. and Boyacigiller, N. (1995) "Going beyond traditional HRM scholarship," in R.N. Kanungo and D. M. Saunders (eds.) *New approaches to employee management. Employee management in developing countries*, 3, Greenwich, CT: JAI Press.

Agnaia, A.A. (1996) "Assessment of management training needs and selection for training: The case of Libyan companies," *International Journal of Man*power 17 (3): 31–51.

Al-Shamali, A. and Denton, J. (2000) *Arab business: The globalisation imperative*, Kuwait: Arab Research Centre.

Bait Elmal, M.A. (1997) [Statement] World Bank Group Annual Meetings, Hong Kong, September.

Banutu-Gomez, M.B. (2002) "Leading and managing in developing countries: Challenges, growth and opportunities for the twenty-first century organizations," *Cross Cultural Management* 9 (4): 29–41.

Ben-Omran, A.M. and Kreshman, H.M. (1984) "The training needs of the Libyan energy sector," *OPEC Bulletin*, March.

Birks, J.S. and Sinclair, C.A. (1980) *Arab manpower: The crises of development*, London: Croom Helm.

Blundy, D. and Lycett, A. (1988) *Qadhafi and the Libyan revolution: The first full length biography*, London: Corgi Books.

Bruce, R.J. (1998) *Historical dictionary of Libya*, 3rd edition, African Historical Dictionaries, Boston, MA: Scarecrow Press.

CIA (2002) *World Factbook, Libya*. Online: http//:cia.gov/publications/factbook/geos/ly.html

Cleveland, J.N. and Murphy, K.R. (1992) "Analyzing employee appraisal as goal-directed behavior," in G.R. Ferris (ed.) *Research in personnel and human resource management*, Greenwich, CT: JAI Press.

Elgamal, M.A. (2000) "In search of an Arab model: Sources of Arab management practices, problems and development needs," in A. Al-Shamali and J. Denton (eds.) *Arab business: The globalisation imperative*, Kuwait: Arab Research Centre.

Elmahdawi, H.H. (1995) *Explanations of the public employment*, Tripoli: Al-Jamahiriya Publishing.

Farley, R. (1971), *Planning for development in Libya: The exceptional economy in the developing world,* New York: Praeger.

Ferris, G.R., Hochwarter, W.A., Buckley, M.R., Harrell-Cook, G., and Frink, D.D. (1999) "Human resource management: Some new directions," *Journal of Management* 25 (23): 385–415.

Gannous, S., Al-Touboli, B., and Shambish, A. (1989) *Economic, social and political transformations during twenty years (1969/89),* Tripoli: Libya.

Gishelli, E.E., Haire, M. and Porter, L. (1966) *Managerial thinking—An international study*, New York: John Wiley & Sons, Inc.

Guest, D.E. (1989) "Personnel management and HRM: Can you tell the difference?" *Personnel Management,* January, pp. 48–51.

Guest, D.E. (1990) "Human resource management and the American dream," *Journal of Management Studies* 27 (4): 377–397.

Guion, R.M. and Gibson, W.M. (1988) "Personnel selection and placement,"*Annual Review of Psychology* 39: 349–374.

Harris, P. R. and Moran, R.T. (1999) *Managing cultural differences: Leadership strategies for a new world of business*, 4th edition, Houston: Gulf Publishing.

Harvey, M. (2002) "Human resource management in Africa: Alice's adventures in wonderland," *International Journal of Human Resource Management* 13 (7): 1119–1145.

Hayajenh, A.F., Maghrabi, A.S., and Al-Dabbagh, T.H. (1994) "Research: Assessing the effect of nepotism on human resource management," *International Journal of Manpower* 15 (1): 60–67.

Hofstede, G. (1980) "Motivation, leadership and organization: Do American theories apply abroad?" *Organizational Dynamics* 9: 42–63.

Hofstede, G. (1991) *Cultures and organizations: Software of the mind*, London: McGraw-Hill.

Jaeger, A.M. (1990) "The applicability of western management techniques in developing countries: A cultural perspective," in A.M. Jaeger and R. Kanungo (eds.) *Management in developing countries*, London: Routledge.

Judge, T.A. and Ferris, G.R. (1993) "Social performance context of performance evaluation decisions," *Academy of Management Journal* 36: 80–105.

Krieger, J. (1993) *Political science encyclopaedias: The Oxford companion to politics of the world,* New York: Oxford University Press.

Latifi, F. (1997) "Management learning in national context," unpublished Ph.D. Thesis, Henley Management College.

Legge, K. (1989) "HRM: A critical analysis," in J. Storey (ed.) *New perspectives on human resource management,* London: Routledge.

Longenecker, C.O., Sims, H.P., Jr., and Gioia, D.A. (1990) "Behind the mask: The politics of employee appraisal," *Academy of Management Executive* 1: 183–193.

Muna, F. (1980) *The Arab executive*, London: Macmillan.

Peters, E.L. (1982) "Cultural and social diversity in Libya," in J.A. Allan (ed.) *Libya since independence: Economic and political development,* London: Croom Helm.

Pfeffer, J. (1994) *"Competitive advantage through people: Unleashing the power of the workforce,* Boston, MA: Harvard Business School Press.

Pieper, R. (1990) *Human resource management: An international comparison,* Berlin: Walter de Gruyter.

Poole, M. and Jenkins, G. (1996) "Competitiveness and human resource policies," *Journal of General Management* 22 (2): 1–9.

Roberts, K.H. and Boyacigiller, N.A. (1984) "Cross-national organisational research: The grasp of the blind men," *Research in Organisational Behaviour* 6: 423–475.

Smith, P.B., Misumi, J., Peterson, M., and Tayeb, M.H. (1989) "The cultural context of leadership action: A cross cultural analysis," in J. Davis, M. Easterby-Smith, S. Mann, and M. Tanton (eds.) *The challenge of Western management development: International alternative,* London: Routledge.

Sparrow, P. and Hiltrop, J.M. (1994) *European human resource management in transition,* London: Prentice Hall International.

Tayeb, M.H. (1996) *The management of a multicultural workforce*, Chichster: John Wiley.

Trompenaars, F. (1993) *Riding the waves of culture: Understanding cultural diversity in business,* London: Economist Books.

Weir, D. (2000) "Management in the Arab world: A fourth paradigm?" in A. Al-Shamali and J. Denton (eds.) *Arab business: The globalisation imperative*, Kuwait: Arab Research Centre.

Wright, J. (1982) *Libya: A modern history*, Baltimore, MD: Johns Hopkins University Press.

Wright, P. (1981) "Organizational behavior in Islamic firms," *Management International Review* 2 (2): 86–94.

Conclusions: toward a research agenda

YAW A. DEBRAH, FRANK M. HORWITZ,
KEN N. KAMOCHE, AND GERRY NKOMBO
MUUKA

This book has provided a broad overview of current human resources management developments and challenges in Africa. It has brought together in a systematic and coherent way, the major developments and current HRM issues on the continent. The individual chapters yield interesting insights into the changing nature of HRM, including the dynamics of employee relations in the workplace. In many respects, the issues discussed have illuminated our understanding of HRM practices in Africa. In particular, this book complements the efforts of a 2002 special issue of the *International Journal of Human Resource Management*, edited by Ken Kamoche (2002), in highlighting both the diversity and complexity of HRM issues in Africa. However, we should endeavor to eschew complacency and push further the frontiers of knowledge pertaining to HRM in that part of the world. The importance of this becomes apparent when one considers the dearth of HRM research focusing on Africa. A major objective of the book, and of this chapter, is to change this state of affairs. This chapter identifies and discusses some key themes arising from individual chapters in the book, and directs our attention towards a research agenda. Many interesting and important themes have emerged from individual chapters, making it possible for us to focus on key ones that we believe will not only generate interest in future research but may also have important implications for the management of human resources in Africa. The major themes are discussed below.

Emergent themes

The first major theme revolves around the HRM ramifications of structural adjustment programs (SAPs) in Africa. Except for Libya, and to some extent South Africa, all the countries represented in the book have in one way or the other implemented these World Bank- and IMF-inspired economic reform measures (market-led reforms) in an attempt to turn their economies around. Many of the countries that have liberalized their economies and privatized former state-owned enterprises (SOEs) as part of the

SAP have done so for a number of reasons, not limited to the need to: (a) reduce fiscal and administrative burdens resulting from the precarious state of public enterprises, (b) develop the private sector and broaden local ownership, as well as (c) increase productivity and efficiency in the management of organizations. Once these conditions prevail and there is positive and sustainable economic growth, the result is net employment growth in the longer run. Coupled with the influences of globalization, regionalization, and international competitive pressures, these forces are a good recipe for transforming personnel management into strategic HRM in Africa (Debrah and Budhwar, 2001).

The evidence of strategic HRM approaches in firms in Africa is largely limited to multinational companies and progressive African companies operating in global markets, and who themselves have become multinationals. Some of these, such as the Old Mutual and Investec (insurance and financial services), have listed off-shore. Other examples include AngloGold, SAB Miller (now one of the world's largest beer companies), de Beers, and Sappi (pulp, paper, and wood). In South Africa there is increasing focus on aligning HRM and organizational strategies. A number of local business schools run executive development programs on SHRM.

An important element of the SAPs, privatization of SOEs, has invariably led to job losses in all the countries with SAPs as new owners reduce employment to levels they consider both efficient and economic. The chapters on Zambia and Ethiopia, among others, provide clear evidence of how, in the pursuit of efficiency, privatization has led to massive job losses and deterioration of the conditions of service of workers. In view of this, trade union leaders and others have condemned the privatization programs, but proponents of privatization argue that rationalization of employment is a necessary condition for the survival of firms and will eventually lead to better pay and working conditions. Undoubtedly, these opposing views will be debated for some time to come. This is an important research arena for HRM scholars in and on Africa. Research on HRM implications of SAPs/privatization in Africa seems to lag behind similar studies done on China and East European nations, notably Poland and Hungary (see Redman and Keithley, 1998; Tung and Havlovic, 1996; Warner, 1995; 1996; 2000; Child 1994; Hassard *et al.*, 2002). In Africa, studies in this area all too often focus on trade unions' responses to SAPs/privatization (Tidjani, 1998).

There is an urgent need to go beyond this narrow confine and examine organizational HRM strategies and responses to privatization, globalization, and regionalization (Bezuidenhout, 2002). In so doing, it is necessary to conduct cross-national/comparative research both within Africa and with non-African emergent or developing economies. There is a need for empirical research on pertinent issues such as: (a) the changing nature of the psychological contract as the labor market becomes increasingly segmented between standard and non-standard employment patterns; (b) organizational justice; (c) trust, organizational and work commitment and workplace cooperation; (d) HRM practices and service delivery in changing markets; and (e) HRM strategies for attracting, motivating, and retaining talent. An examination of the relationships between these issues and employee work outcomes is necessary in view of the impact of international competitiveness on African organizations. As Aryee *et al.* (2002), Lo and Aryee, (forthcoming), and Lam *et al.* (2002) have pointed out, much of the interest in these concepts stems from organizational responses to the competitive pressures emanating from globalization and the changes in the employment relationship that these responses have precipitated.

The flight of knowledge workers from Africa or between African countries (the brain drain dilemma) is becoming critical as more African countries seek to attract, develop, and retain key skills to grow their economies and compete both domestically and globally. Research on these HRM strategies and their effectiveness is needed. An allied issue is the widespread move towards labor market flexibility and an increase in subcontracting and outsourcing as work is externalized. The informalization and casualization of the labor market is increasing even in countries with more regulated legal regimes such as South Africa. Numerical and temporal flexibility and even pay flexibility have a profound effect on employment security and the psychological contract. In a pioneering research on some aspects of these issues, Beugré (2002) has developed a conceptual framework for understanding organizational justice but it is necessary for African HRM researchers to conduct empirical research to test this framework.

Another theme that has emerged from the chapters is the issue of diversity management. Except perhaps for South Africa, evidence from the other chapters indicates the persistence of particularistic rather than universalistic practices in the management of human resources. This is particularly evident in Mauritius, where nepotism, favoritism, and ethnic biases are widespread in the labor market and are also widely practiced in both public and private sector organizations. Although the contributors to this book allude to anecdotal evidence about the declining influence of particularism and the increasing ascendancy of universalism, none argues against the view that the endurance of particularism is a problem in the practice of HRM in Africa. Particularism is based on ethnicity, gender, sexual orientation, and age differences and often manifests itself in favoritism in recruitment and selection, promotion, and pay decisions.

This favoritism may be a matter of public policy and legislative intervention or state decree in some countries, and in some cases to redress past racial or ethnic discrimination. Arguably, a positive manifestation of particularism is an emergent debate in some countries like South Africa about fostering a unique or special African organizational culture based on humanistic philosophies such as "*ubuntu*." Advocates of this approach argue that just as Japanese, American, or German firms may have organizational cultures which reflect particular values and practices in those societies, it is valid to endeavor to develop organizational cultures in Africa which reflect indigenous values. Detractors argue that the diffusion of Western business practices and their underlying tenets will more likely prevail, given the homogenizing influence of globalization and multinational firms. There is much scope for international cross-cultural research in Africa on HRM practices such as performance management, talent motivation and retention, and the extent to which the adoption of these practices reflects cross-cultural diffusion, convergence or the divergence of local uniqueness, or indeed a hybrid "crossvergence" (Horwitz *et al.*, 2002).

While Nyambegera (2002) has provided an excellent analysis of the ethnic dimension of the managing diversity discourse, the fact still remains that there is a dearth of empirical research on diversity management in Africa. As part of poverty alleviation programs many governments in Sub-Saharan Africa have implemented gender mainstreaming programs. These have implications for HRM and it may be worthwhile for researchers to conduct studies on these and other diversity management programs.

Allied to the theme of talent attraction and retention is the lament or decrying of the brain drain in Africa. While a brain drain is not new in Sub-Saharan Africa, the pace has accelerated in recent years with the deepening economic decline in many countries. The Kenyan chapter discusses the causes of the brain drain of professionals and skilled workers. These causes are congruent with evidence from the literature on factors behind the flocking of migrant workers from labor-sending to labor-receiving countries (APMJ, 1998; Athukorala, 1993). In Africa, the main labor-receiving countries are Botswana, Mauritius, and South Africa, though the latter also has an egress of professional and managerial skills to developed economies.

South Africa has had a history of migrant workers so it may be helpful to use the country as a case study to explore the reasons for migration of African professionals and skilled workers to the country. Equally, Mauritius can also be used as a case study on the cross-cultural management of foreign workers. In order to understand the factors or causes behind the brain drain, there is the need to develop a conceptual framework for empirical research on the phenomenon. On this issue, Bartram (1998) has suggested four approaches to studying international labor migration. These are: (a) neo-classical economic theory; (b) dual-labor market theory; (c) world systems theory; and (d) policy analysis relying on state theory. Debrah (2002) has used these approaches to examine labor migration dynamics within the Asia-Pacific region. These approaches are useful in explaining the movement of workers from labor-surplus (labor-sending) to labor shortage (labor-receiving)/skill deficient countries.

The neo-classical approach, for instance, maintains that international labor migration arises from supply and demand, or "push and pull" factors (Lee, 1966). According to this perspective, migrants are pushed out of underdeveloped countries by low wages, economic fluctuations, and political forces/crises such as wars and are pulled to other countries by the attraction of high wages, better job opportunities, and better social, economic, and political conditions. Similarly, Todaro (1969) has developed a model which is based on a concept of expected income. This is explained as a product of the wage differences and the probability of getting a job in the host country. Seen from this perspective, migration will occur when the expected income in the host country is greater that the existing/available income in the worker's native country, where employment is almost certain (Bartram, 1998). It is debatable as to the extent to which the implementation of both national and organizational HRM strategies in labor-sending countries in Africa can reduce the flow of workers to the labor-receiving countries. Only vigorous research can shed light on this debate.

The HIV/Aids pandemic is a global problem and has the potential to derail any gains in productivity in Sub-Saharan African organizations in the last two decades. Except for organizations in Botswana, Uganda, and South Africa, most organizations in Sub-Saharan Africa have not made serious attempts to tackle the spread of the disease. AIDS is devastating African economies and societies. It is estimated that over 28 million people in Africa are living with HIV and in some countries 30 percent of the adult population is infected with the virus (UNAIDS, 2002). HIV/AIDS is rapidly weakening economic stability in the already fragile markets of Sub-Saharan Africa. Current data indicate a 4 percent decline in the rate of economic growth due to the AIDS pandemic. Similarly, labor productivity has fallen by as much as 50 percent in countries that have been hardest hit by the pandemic. It is estimated that by 2020, over 25 percent of the workforce may be lost to AIDS in the most severely affected countries. In Zambia, for instance, it is estimated that nearly two-thirds of mortality of managers is attributable to AIDS. In Kenya, AIDS accounts for up to three out of four deaths in the police force (UNAIDS, 2002). In much of Sub-Saharan Africa the delivery of essential services is under threat as trained and skilled staff succumb to the disease.

The HIV/AIDS pandemic has many implications for the workplace. These include the costs of absenteeism, training, career and succession planning, and long-term sick leave. For instance, HIV/AIDS-related morbidity can force people to take early retirement or die prematurely, with serious implications for the loss of expertise, intellectual capital with an erosion of institutional culture, and adverse effects on medical scheme funding and company and state pensions. This also places added pressure on the critical need for human resource development as a vital priority of strategic HRM in African organizations, but may also raise the costs of training and development. The loss of these wage earners also often results in poverty for many families.

Hence, the response of organizations and workers to the HIV/AIDS pandemic in Africa is crucial in maintaining the success of organizations. Arguably, there is no organization in Sub-Saharan Africa that has not encountered HIV/AIDS. Hence, the need for organizations to develop and implement culturally sensitive, non-discriminatory workplace HIV/AIDS policies and programs cannot be overemphasized. This is happening in countries such as Botswana and South Africa, but has not been embraced by many organizations in other parts of Africa. Although the workplace is ideal for promoting HIV prevention to benefit workers, employers, and ultimately the business community, many workplaces are still not convinced or are ignorant of health education and promotion strategies to prevent new infections.

Few academic studies have concentrated on assessing workplace HIV/AIDS programs and business responses to the pandemic in Sub-Saharan Africa (see Baruch and Clancy, 2000). Most studies have focused mainly on South Africa, Tanzania, and Botswana and are usually carried out by trade unions and non-governmental organizations. Although we now know quite a lot about the dire consequences of HIV/AIDS in Africa in general, research is needed on its impact on the workplace. A recent study on HIV/AIDS prevention in the workplace in Ghana revealed that the majority of employers knew very little about it. Generally, employers considered HIV prevention to be the responsibility of individuals, their families, and the government (Ankomah and Debrah, 2001). Although a great majority of employers would consider the development and implementation of HIV/AIDS policies at the workplace, they were more supportive of policies on legal issues (e.g. compulsory pre-employment testing, unfair discrimination, and dismissal of HIV-positive employees) and not those relating to preventive programs (e.g. counseling, employee and family education, and supply of condoms at the workplace) (Ankomah and Debrah, 2001). Such views are interesting in light of the efforts of UNAIDS to use the workplace as a front for promoting non-discrimination towards people living with HIV/AIDS. In line with this perspective, the Council of Southern African Development Committee (SADC) has approved a regional code on HIV/AIDS and employment. The aim of the code is to guide employers, employees, and government towards the most economically sustainable and humane ways of responding to HIV/AIDS in the workplace. The code emphasizes the human rights challenges posed by HIV/AIDS in Southern Africa (UNAIDS, 2000). Undoubtedly, these issues will generate debate and hence the role of academic research in guiding HRM policies becomes crucial.

The challenges facing the management of people in Africa are clearly daunting. Almost all the countries in our book face a dualistic challenge of two imperatives. First, they require appropriate macro-economic policies and the political will to address poverty, high unemployment, and a serious lack of human resource development. Some do better in this regard than others. The redress of past unfair discrimination by colonial regimes and apartheid remains a key priority and "unfinished business" in some countries. Progress in fostering workplace equity and distributive and procedural justice have become imperatives in more African countries today than in the past. The second imperative is that of competitiveness in both domestic and global markets through high performance and productivity improvement. Africa does have world-class firms, but not enough. Human resource management and development will provide the key to unlocking Africa's human potential. That is why it is so important to research and develop best practice in this area. It is our belief that the dual imperatives of equity and competitiveness are indeed interdependent rather than dissonant, and that sound HRM can make the difference to the competitive advantage of African firms as has occurred in developed economies. We hope that this book has generated ideas and debates that will make a positive and enduring contribution to HRM research and practice in Africa, as well as to the search for solutions to the continent's multifaceted development challenges.

References

Ankomah, A.K. and Debrah, Y.A. (2001) "HIV/AIDS prevention in the workplace: Some evidence from Ghana," paper presented at the Inaugural Conference of the Postgraduate Institute of Health, University of Teeside, UK.

APMJ (1998) "Introduction: Migration in Asia in times of crisis," *Asian and Pacific Migration Journal* 7 (2–3): 137–44.

Aryee, S., Budhwar, P., and Zhen, Z.X. (2002) "Organizational justice, trust foci, and work outcomes: Test of a mediated social exchange model," *Journal of Organizational Behavior* 23: 267–285.

Athukorala, P. (1993) "International labour migration in the Asian Pacific region: Patterns, policies and economic implications," *Asian-Pacific Economic Literature* 7 (2): 28–57.

Bartram, D.V. (1998) "Foreign workers in Israel: History and theory," *International Migration Review* 32 (2): 303–25.

Baruch, Y. and Clancy, P. (2000) "Managing AIDS in Africa: HRM challenges in Tanzania," *International Journal of Human Resource Management* 11 (4): 789–809.

Beugré, C.D. (2002) "Understanding organizational justice and its impact on managing employees: An African perspective," *International Journal of Human Resource Management* 13 (7): 1091–1104.

Bezuidenhout, A. (2002) "'What we do' or 'Who we are?' Trade union responses to globalization and regionalization in South Africa," in Y.A. Debrah and I.G. Smith (eds.) *Globalization, employment and the workplace: Diverse impacts*, London: Routledge.

Child, J. (1994) *Management in China during the age of reform*, Cambridge: Cambridge University Press.

Debrah, Y.A. (2002) "Introduction: Migrant workers in Pacific Asia," *Asia Pacific Business Review* 8 (4).

Debrah, Y.A. and Budhwar, P.S. (2001) "International competitive pressures and the challenges for HRM in developing countries," in P.S. Budhwar and Y.A. Debrah (eds.) *Human Resource Management in Developing Countries*, London: Routledge.

Hassard, J., Morris, J., Sheehan, J., and Xiao, Y. (2002) "Globalization, economic institutions and workplace change: The economic reform process in China," in Y.A. Debrah and I.G. Smith (eds.) *Globalization, employment and the workplace: Diverse impacts*, London: Routledge, pp. 115–129

Horwitz, F.M., Kamoche, K., and Chew, I.K.H. (2002) "Looking East: Diffusing high performance work practices in the southern Afro-Asian context," *International Journal of Human Resource Management* 13 (7): 1019–1041.

Kamoche, K. (2002) "Introduction: Human resource management in Africa," *International Journal of Human Resource Management* 13 (7): 993–997.

Lam, S., Schaubroeck, J., and Aryee, S. (2002) "Relationship between organizational justice and employee work outcomes: A cross-national study," *Journal of Organizational Behavior* 23: 1–18.

Lee, E. (1966) "A theory of migration," *Demography* 3 (1): 47–57.

Lo, S. and Aryee, S. (forthcoming) "Psychological contract violations in a Chinese context: An integrative approach," *Journal of Management Studies*.

Nyambegera, S.M. (2002) "Ethnicity and human resource management practice in sub-Saharan Africa: The relevance of managing diversity discourse," *International Journal of Human Resource Management* 13 (7): 1077–1090

Redman, T. and Keithley, T. (1998) "Downsizing goes East? Employment re-structuring in post-socialist Poland," *International Journal of Human Resource Management* 9 (2): 274–295.

Tidjani, B. (1998) "African unions under structural adjustment programs," *Relations Industrielles (Industrial Relations)* 53 (2) 278–297.

Todaro, M. (1969) "A model of labor migration and urban unemployment in less developed countries," *American Economic Review* 59 (1): 138–48.

Tung, R. and Havlovic, S. (1996) "Human resource management in transition economies: The case of Poland and the Czech Republic," *International Journal of Human Resource Management* 7 (1): 1–20.

UNAIDS (2000) *A human rights approach to AIDS prevention at work*, Geneva: UNAIDS.

UNAIDS (2002) "UNAIDS releases new data highlighting the devastating impact of AIDS in Africa," press release, Geneva, 25 June.

Warner, M. (1995) *The management of human resources in Chinese industry*, London: Macmillan.

Warner, M. (1996) "Chinese enterprise reform, human resources and the 1994 Labour Law," *International Journal of Human Resource Management* 7 (7): 779–796.

Warner, M. (2000) *Changing workplace relations in the Chinese economy*, London: Macmillan.

Index